Body Talk and Cultural Identity in the African World

Body Talk and Cultural Identity in the African World

Edited by
Augustine Agwuele

SHEFFIELD UK   BRISTOL CT

Published by Equinox Publishing Ltd.

UK: Office 415, The Workstation, 15 Paternoster Row, Sheffield, South Yorkshire S1 2BX
USA: ISD, 70 Enterprise Drive, Bristol, CT 06010

www.equinoxpub.com

First published 2015

© Augustine Agwuele and contributors 2015

All rights reserved. No part of this publication may be reproduced or transmitted in any form or by any means, electronic or mechanical, including photocopying, recording or any information storage or retrieval system, without prior permission in writing from the publishers.

British Library Cataloguing-in-Publication Data

A catalogue record for this book is available from the British Library.

ISBN-13 978 1 78179 185 1 (hardback)
978 1 78179 186 8 (paperback)

Library of Congress Cataloging-in-Publication Data
Body talk and cultural identity in the African world/edited by Augustine Agwuele.
pages cm
Includes bibliographical references and index.
ISBN 978-1-78179-185-1 (hb) – ISBN 978-1-78179-186-8 (pb)
1. Gesture–Africa. 2. Body language–Africa. 3. Language and languages–Physiological aspects–Africa. 4. Identity (Psychology)–Africa. 5. Language and culture–Africa. 6. Anthropological linguistics–Africa. I. Agwuele, Augustine, editor.
P117.5.A4B64 2015
302.2'22–dc23
2015010616

Typeset by S.J.I. Services, New Delhi
Printed and bound by Lightning Source Inc. (La Vergne, TN), Lightning Source UK Ltd. (Milton Keynes), Lightning Source AU Pty. (Scoresby, Victoria)

Shadowy walk 1. By Augustine Agwuele, 2014.

Contents

Introduction: Nonverbal Communication in Some
African Societies and Institutions   1
Augustine Agwuele

Part One: Body Talk in the Arts and Literature

1. What Traditional Dances Tell Us about African Cultural
   Identity in Puerto Rico and Trinidad   17
   Ann Albuyeh

2. Fela's Clenched Fists: The Double "Black Power" Salute and
   Political Ideology   37
   Dotun Ayobade

3. Dressed-to-Kill: Don Mattera's *Sophiatown*   58
   Michael Sharp

4. Body Art, Body Decoration and Identity in Yorubaland   74
   Bukola Adeyemi Oyeniyi

5. Bodies in Motion: Gestures and Performance of Identity in Tess
   Onwueme's *Shakara*   94
   Maureen N. Eke

Part Two: Nonverbal Communication and Cultural Diversity

6. The Convergence of Language and Culture in Malawian
   Gestures: Handedness in Everyday Rituals   111
   Karen W. Sanders

7. Nonverbal Communication Codes among the Hamar:
   Structures and Functions   133
   Moges Yigezu

8. *So That We Might Find Ourselves:* Collective Identity in
   Yoruba Culture 147
   Abimbola A. Adelakun

9. Nonverbal Message: The Yoruba View of "Deviant"
   Male Hairstyles 162
   Augustine Agwuele

10. Embodying Holiness: Gender, Sex, Bodies and Patriarchal
    Imaginaries in a Neo-Pentecostal Church in Kenya 181
    Damaris Seleina Parsitau

    Index 202

Introduction: Nonverbal Communication in Some African Societies and Institutions

Augustine Agwuele[1]

The subject of this anthology is nonverbal communication signals, with contributing data from peoples of Africa and the African diaspora. The goals are to document popular gestures, explore their meanings and understand how they frame interactions. Analogous to Bonnie Raitt's "Something to Talk About" in the album *Luck of the Draw*, it is not uncommon for the claim to be made that two people are lovers just because they stand quite close, or their gazes tend to linger on each other, or the smiles on their faces in the presence of each other rarely wane. The people who surmise thus are no doubt reading into and perceiving from these instances something that the supposed lovers are perhaps not actually conveying.

The body is a site bearing multiple signs of cultural inscription. People's personal appearances, their postures, the movements of different parts of their bodies, how they make use of space, what they wear and how they wear it, the way they decorate or modify their bodies, their speech particularities and facial expressions form codes that send messages, whether intended or not, to observers. These messages differ across cultures. The various ways people use their bodies to "talk" may flag their unique personal style or their politics, in which case the body and its presentations become stances of the self. Different from this, forms of "body talk" may exhibit a society's or culture's standardized norms of valuation with respect to what conforms to or deviates from expectations. Without excluding statements of distinctions, the more collective concerns of body talk and body art may be in dialogue or conflict with the group, the community

---

1 Augustine Agwuele teaches in the Department of Anthropology, Texas State University, San Marcos. He is interested in experimental phonetics, language, culture and society, and the peoples and cultures of Africa. He studies closely the Yoruba people of Nigeria and in the African Diaspora, as well as the Amhara people of Ethiopia.

or "the system," and could elicit various interpretations and responses, or even garner severe consequences as shown in chapter 9 of this book.

At least since Birdwhistell's (1955, also 1970) quantification study, it is has been accepted that 65 per cent of interpersonal communication is nonverbal. Hall (1959) recognized 10 primary messages and determined that only one of them is verbal, thus furthering the preeminence of nonverbal over aural communication. Lindenfeld (1974) studied four people each speaking for eight minutes. Focusing on three areas of nonverbal communication – head, hand and foot movements – the study provided a numerical quantification of each area and underscored their dominance. While these and similar quantitative studies have helped cement in the popular and scholarly consciousness of recent times the dominance of the nonverbal aspect of communication, the interest in nonverbal signals is not new. About 400 years before the aforementioned works, for instance, young nobles as part of their education in rhetoric were told: "So gouerne thy gesture of body, foote and hande, Of countenaunce, eyne and mouth with fayre semblance, That who thee beholdeth, may see and understande, Thine inward behauour by outward countenance" (Barclay 1570 [1967]). In Letter LXXXII of 1749, Chesterfield, a dance master wrote: "Remember to take the best dancing-master at Berlin, more to teach you to sit, stand and walk gracefully ..." (see Huebler 2001: 208). By the early 19th century there were in circulation many letters of instruction on etiquette and manners considered appropriate for polite society, which underscore the place of nonverbal communication in interaction. The subject of these admonitions ranges from paralinguistic devices such as tone of voice, to appearance, facial expression, how to use a walking stick and wear a hat or gloves. Thus, for instance, young people were admonished: "Do not wear black or coloured gloves, lest your partner look sulky; even should you be in mourning, wear white gloves, not black ... ," while ladies were told to "Always wear your gloves in church or in a theatre" (Agogos 1834 [1946]: 23 and 33 respectively). This "outward countenance" was accorded great importance as it preceded and announced a person long before they were heard. In Act 1, Scene 3 of Shakespeare's *Hamlet*, Polonius recognized this fact, saying: "Costly thy habit as thy purse can buy, But not express'd in fancy; rich, not gaudy; For the apparel oft proclaims the man."

Although there are still in circulation many self-help books in the spirit of the ones cited above, modern scholarly interests on nonverbal signals reveal more serious, varied and purposeful research questions. There are works that identify and theoretically conceptualize nonverbal signals. For instance, the psychologists Ekman & Friesen (1969) systematized and categorized what they considered speech-accompanying signals into five types.

Following up on this, Johnson et al. (1975) provided a comprehensive method for identifying those gestures which remain meaningful without words (quotable gestures). Other works of influence in the development of modern conceptualization of nonverbal signals include Hall (1974) that developed proxemics, the study of perception and use of space; and Birdwhistell (1952) that focused on the study of body movements, facial expressions and gestures (kinesics). A mathematical notational system for the conceptualization of gestures was provided by Bouissac (1973). Further work on conceptualization done by McNeill (1992) suggests that verbal and nonverbal communication combine to reveal meaning that is not fully captured through one modality (i.e., speech or gesture). Different from McNeill is Kendon (1980) who considers gesture and speech as separate but interrelated aspects of the process of utterance; this view is analogous to that in Bolinger (1968) which sees verbal sound as embedded in gestures and consequently discusses the synchronization of both. A semiotic conceptualization of emblematic gestures is provided by Hanna (1996).

The nonverbal phenomenon has also received linguistic analyses such as that undertaken by Pike (1967). The work considers nonverbal communication not only an invaluable part of the theory of the mind, but a part of cultural behavior. Following in the footsteps of Pike, Arndt and Janney (1987) produced a "pragmatic natural grammar" through which they attempted to explain "what makes people understand each other." Discourse and conversation analysis related studies include van Dijk (1997a and b) and Kendon (2004) which provide a functional, semantic, pragmatic and grammatical analysis of gestures. The theoretical perspectives of these works have informed valuable documentation of nonverbal signals across cultures and help enrich our understanding of human use of language. For instance, Basso (1970) studied the circumstances that influence Native American Apaches in refraining from speech, where silence is taken as a culturally meaningful nonverbal communicative signal; Sherzer (1973) studied the phenomenon of lip pointing among the Kuna of Panama; Brookes (2004) documented and described quotable quotes in use among urban youth in South Africa and Orie (2009) provided a description of pointing gestures among the Yoruba of Nigeria.

Evolutionary perspectives on nonverbal communication have also implicated theorizing on the origin of human language. For instance, Bates and Dick (2002) and Corballis (2003) argue that human language, evolutionarily speaking, emanated from nonverbal systems of communication. Kendon (1988) provided an evolutionary perspective to the nonverbal repertoire. With respect to the development of language in childhood, Iverson and Goldin-Meadow (2005) studied children as they transitioned from the holophrastic to two-word stage and found that gesture is tightly related to their lexical and syntactical development. Aside from this perspective, scholars in the neuroscience of speech argue that spoken language and gesture form an integrated system that influences the production and perception of speech (Goldin-Meadow 2003; Beattie & Shovelton 1999; Willems & Hagoort 2007). The universality and perhaps innateness of nonverbal communication is suggested by Iverson and Goldin-Meadow (1998) when they show that blind people, like seeing people, make use of gestures even when communicating with other blind people.

The array of scholarly works, research questions, interdisciplinary approaches and perspectives on nonverbal communication have not escaped Holoka (1992: 237), who, while discussing the research opportunities in nonverbal communication in the classics, notes and refutes the supposition "that the field is in common parlance, well plowed." The field might very well be plowed in some areas, but in others – for instance, the African world – the systems of durable, transposable disposition acquired by human bodies in their social transactions and class-specific everyday lives (Bourdieu 1977; Streeck 1993) remain almost a virgin land inviting exploration. Thus, to further the understanding of the various manners in which the African world speaks without using words, including the rules which explain the manner in which their nonverbal repertoires convey information, and to explicate how perceivers decipher the codified information (cf. Ekman & Friesen 1969), this anthology casts a wide disciplinary and conceptual net. This approach is guided by the recognition of the complex and multidimensional web of meanings and action-laden demonstrations of "body talk" across various sociocultural institutions of the African world. The anthology *Body Talk* draws from the cited studies and relies on their theoretical background to study different aspects of the African world from a linguistics, anthropological, pragmatics, performative and semiotics perspective, and to demonstrate the cultural inventiveness of nonverbal signals.

The Scope and Approach of This Work

The scope of nonverbal communication is expansive. It has been suggested by Eisenberg & Smith (1970: 76) that the human body is capable of over 270,000 discrete gestures; this range of variation may be greater than the range of possible human speech sounds. In view of this expanse, and on the basis of the theoretical foundation discussed in the previous paragraph, each essay in this anthology includes a taxonomy of units of nonverbal signals, motivated by the question: What are some of the forms of "body talk" identifiable in the examined communities? Since all gestures are, according to Birdwhistell (1970), culturally patterned, each chapter includes the identification and description of the nonverbal signals, taking into consideration the perspective of native users in the context of their society, and the different belief systems that inform how they are variously deployed and perceived, in order to explicate the cultural institutions and phenomena of each society that the writer sampled. Thus, we see culture as fundamental, and the framework for all interactions within a group. In this book we use "body talk" to cover the following nonverbal communication strategies: dance (chapter 1), body posture and gestures (chapter 2), dress/clothing (chapter 3), body art and decoration (chapter 4), body movements – dancing, head-shaking, body rocking and facial gestures (chapter 5), handedness (chapter 6), signifying objects of bodily adornment (chapter 7), Aso-Ebi and family body marking (chapter 8), hairstyles (chapter 9) and female attire/appearance (chapter 10).

We adopt a holistic view to nonverbal signals, not minding theoretical distinctions that could be raised between verbal and nonverbal signals, either as speech or speech accompaniment. Thus "it [probably] makes no sense to speak of 'verbal communication' and 'nonverbal communication'" according to Kendon (1972). We find that it is obsolete and misleading to hold on to the classification of communication either as "verbal" or "nonverbal," as there is no doubt that we communicate with words and without them. In fact Kendon (1980) and McNeill (1992) provide strong evidence to suggest that verbal and nonverbal speech-forms are two surface expressions of a single underlying thought. For Birdwhistell (1970: 127) these two modalities are "alloforms," by which he means that they are structural variants of each other. The interrelationship of these modalities was further underscored when McQuown (1971: 19) concluded that "It is after all, only an historic accident … that linguists study data which can be heard, while the kinesicist studies data which can be seen. That the scientists have become specialized in this particular way does not indicate a fundamental separateness between the modalities in the stream of communication." The collected essays exploit these two modalities – in other words, the unitary mode of expressing language – to (1) document their diversity within the African world, (2) explore their usages across sociocultural institutions such as politics, religion, economics, identity and representation, and (3) to shed light on the psychological workings of language and their cultural ties with respect to perception as well as cultural dynamics, e.g., change. The basic issues guiding the discourse are: What information or messages do people communicate nonverbally when they interact; to what purpose are those messages; and how are they communicated? These questions are derived following Erving Goffman, as suggested by Kendon (1988: 19).

As noted by Ekman & Friesen (1969), some nonverbal behaviors provide specific information, others provide more diffuse information and some are intended to transmit messages. The collection of essays in this anthology provides specific information on specific cultures and cultural practices; we foreground culture because it is considered the organizing principle within which all the described observations derive their meanings. Thus, the anthology examines nonverbal communications from three perspectives: descriptive, interpretive/analytical and explicative/semantic. It documents, from a linguistic descriptive perspective, nonverbal signals as found among the Hamar of Ethiopia (chapter 7), the aTonga of Malawi, (chapter 6), the Yoruba of Nigeria (chapter 4) and the Tsotsis of South Africa (chapter 3). Since culture refers to the organization of behavior, emotion and other observed material manifestations of the society, linguistic, cultural and social theories or any other conceptual models require that their viability be tested with respect to the real situation in the society. The descriptive components of the essays aid the uncovering of the relations that the discussed nonverbal signals bear to the consequent behaviors observed within the different societies as well as the relationship of both to the material worlds of the societies. As part of the study of signs (Morris 1946), the icons studied elicit responses from the society; as such they are signifying concepts. Each gesture, movement or posture, including the indicative symbolic use of items, possesses properties by which it is recognized and through which its ultimate connotations and denotations are obtained. The stimulus value of each sign is of importance to the contributors to this book, as they document the communicative content of the nonverbal signals.

Transcending the descriptive and evidentiary goals of the anthology, the essays illustrate the various things we use nonverbal language to do. As a semiotic sign, there has to be a symbol that conveys meaning and there has to be that which is signified. These two sides of a coin include the questions: What are the signs? and What do they signify? Sanders explores this theme for the aTonga of Malawi (chapter 6); Sharp inquires into the intentionality of manner of dressing among the Tsotsis of Sophiatown in South Africa (chapter 3), while Oyeniyi (chapter 4) with Adelakun (chapter 8) and Yigezu (chapter 7) explicate the meanings of Yoruba and Hamar clothing, respectively. The second question of what the signs mean, relates in part to the issue of motivation and intentionality. Sometimes the intention of the user is at variance with the denotations and connotations of the sign projected onto it by the society, as shown by Agwuele in chapter 9. In addition to the connotative and denotative aspects of speech signals, the emotional overtones of nonverbal communicative signals are illustrated, for instance, by Parsitau (chapter 10) where she explores attire and personal appearance among the members of the Pentecostal movement in Kenya.

In examining meanings and usages of nonverbal signals, the anthology (1) considers the existence of a society that attributes intention and meanings to "things" it presumes the users employ to talk without words, and (2) assumes that there is active intention on the part of the user who deploys the signals strategically for various purposes. Thus following Jürgen Streeck's *Gesturecraft*, Ayobade (chapter 2) sees gesture not just as a sign-system or as body language but as "communicative *praxis* and *craft*" that comprises skills and techniques. Consequently, he shows how Fela's body generally, and his Afrobeat salute in particular, have served as the embodiment of his ideologies, and how these elements have helped retain the spirit of his politics since his death in 1997. Fela's salute reemerged during the 2012 Occupy Nigeria Movement as an embodied enactment of memory, both of the late musician but also of a collective experience of social distress. Similar to Ayobade, Sharp (chapter 3), based on a case study of the Tsotsi youth in Sophiatown, explores how clothing could be strategically deployed to agitate politically. The use of clothing is also shown to serve as a way to distinguish insiders from outsiders. Sharp reveals expressive meanings associated with the postures and stances that accompany the youths' "body talk." These action languages are loud requests to be heard; they amplify protest against societal convention in a unique way. Collectively, these studies explore the ways in which cultural items that tie to collective sensibilities are twisted by individuals or groups, and are used to cause offense so as to draw attention to certain socio-economic and political causes.

There is a pragmatic importance to appearance and use of items to signify position and status within the society; this is the case for the Hamar of Ethiopia. Object language (Reusch & Kees 1956) employed by the Hamar people involves intentional display of material items to achieve specific aims. For instance, Yigezu describes how the status of a Hamar individual is actively conveyed by the use of iconized and quotable nonverbal signals. For a different purpose and from a different perspective, Eke explores the "exploitation" of the body and manipulation of appearance by the characters in Tess Onwueme's play in order to obtain personal gains and advancement (chapter 5). Eke further shows how the main character of the play belies the expectations of the community, and changes her name to assume a new identity, claim individuality and escape to a new world and a new life that find expression through her "body talk." We live in societies that have cultivated ways of seeing and interpreting nonverbal communication; the frame of reference that different cultures employ could be rooted in tradition, i.e., religiously motivated as in the case of the Yoruba people, as shown by the designative significance of male hairstyles. It could be a case of received confession, as with the neo-Pentecostal movement of Kenya where forms of embodiment of holiness in relation to a conceptualization of gender and sexuality are pushed as a way to portray belongingness to the form of Pentecostalism that is practiced within this religious movement, in addition to being considered a physical, nonverbal mode of conveying a lifestyle of holiness. This interpretive approach informs chapter 10 which documents the various manners in which religious injunctions prescribe dress codes and appearance as means of materializing holiness. "Mens' minds are expressed in gestures" (Bacon 1605 [1902]: 120); for the psychologist Wundt (1921 [1973]: 55) gesture is an "expression of thought." By understanding the diversity surrounding nonverbal communication across the African world, we obtain an understanding of the people, the challenges they face and their ways of coping with these challenges.

The semantic, grammatical function of nonverbal signals cannot be readily understood without natural communicative data (Kendon 1972); in the spirit of this, *Body Talk* involves the collection and use of real-life, and extant, data. The data and the discourse surrounding them take their cues from life's persistent issues. On the one hand, the explored signals are derived from domestic, family and communal orientations, especially interpersonal relationships across sex, status and situatedness. For example Sanders' insightful descriptive exploration of the aTonga Malawian gestures documents previously unknown usages and shows how their conventional usage plays into the overall structure of the social configuration of the people. Males and females alike nurse a fear of the public embarrassment of being rejected verbally in front of others by someone for whom they express their love. The Malawian people get around this by using a nonverbal signal, a face-saving device of scratching the palm of their love interest during a handshake, to declare their intent. Conflicts and inequality, strangely enough, have also produced arrays of nonverbal signals, as exemplified by Ayobade for Fela, the activist musician who employed them in quest of political changes in Nigeria. Similarly, domestic and communal orientations too influence the interpretation of nonverbal signals, as documented in the case of the Yoruba people who view uncultivated hair (dreadlocks) with suspicion, attributing to this hairstyle the force of such dangers and evils as would be found in the wild, i.e., uncultivated nature.

Given that sociocultural change is inevitable, the third perspective of *Body Talk* pertains to nonverbal signals in relation to societal transformation. From the perspective of change or retention of cultural items, nonverbal signals, in some cases, become "memes" that are selected to mark the ancestorship of a people and their cultural ties. As a species whose biological and cultural survival depends on communication, the signals that are employed remain dynamic. There are several sources for the historiography of peoples of African descent; the approach of Albuyeh (chapter 1) in this regard is particularly interesting. Noting that the linguistic relics such as *bomba, bele* and *kalinda*, which are also dances in Puerto Rico and Trinidad, are by themselves not transparent enough with regard to what they reveal about African-Caribbean ethnic origin, she explores them using the ecology of language evolution as proposed by Mufwene (2001) and thus traces the provenance of Trinidadians and Puerto Ricans. This use of "body talk" for cultural forensics, in concert with other approaches, enhances the historiography of African peoples in the diaspora. According to Albuyeh, these dances "become a composite of individual expressions that jointly yield community solidarity; the music initiates a ritual between musical sound and dancing bodies, a ritual of belonging, of cultural citizenship."

Oyeniyi notes for Yoruba people that, despite the enormous cultural changes, bodily modifications, including clothing and decoration, are some of the means through which Yoruba people establish, sustain and reinforce their identities as individuals and as a group. Hence, body art and decoration do not only cover the body, they reveal it to indicate citizenship, gender, character, occupation, wealth, religion, position, power and status. In addition to this, Oyeniyi concludes: "On the whole, facial marking among the Yoruba is comparable only to a national passport, a kind of insignia, a badge of identity, or a uniform for all individuals of the same group, village or lineage and therefore differs from one community, group and sub-ethnic group to another."

A similar trope is found in chapter 8; here Adelakun explores the dynamics of cultures with reference to how the same motifs and cultural goals continue in spite of societal changes. In place of the mark of cultural identification that was previously imprinted onto the Yoruba skin, i.e., facial scarification, Yoruba people now bear the imprint of belongingness on their bodies in form of the Aso-Ebi (uniform) worn on celebratory occasions.

More forceful, persuasive and effective than oration, and more expressive than rhyme or song, the position of the self and the visual effect of imagery on the mind are more lasting than any eloquently composed arrays of speech sounds. In the parlance of the aged cliché, a picture says more than a thousand words. Nonverbal communication remains culturally and universally unassailable in expressivity and in the fascination it generates among scholars and non-scholars alike. The passionate emotions that nonverbal communication signals generate not only provide insights into the sensibilities of a culture, they also allow scholars to uncover those contrivances that propel individuals to violent actions, where there seems to be no obvious offense. That which comes to surface is that which culture has submerged subconsciously. Are *bomba*, *bele* and *kalinda* mere dance styles, or is each an expression of a "genetic" memory that tellurically links the Trinidadian and Puerto Rican in an essential way to their progenitors? Don't "we respond to gestures with an extreme alertness and, one might say, in accordance with an elaborate and secret code that is written nowhere, known by none, and understood by all?" (Sapir 1949: 137).

According to Birdwhistell (1970: 184) "the systematic body motion of the members of a community is considered a function of the social system to which the group belongs." Ward Goodenough noted that "much of ethnography is taken up with a description of the material setting in which a culture exists ... relatively little attention is devoted – systematically, at least – to isolating the concepts or forms in terms of which the member of a society deal with one another and the world around, and many of which are signified lexically in their language" (Goodenough 1964: 39). This anthology recognizes, following Csordas (1990), that the body is the existential ground of culture and self as well as the cognitive ground of culture (Johnson 1987). Informed by the three perspectives mentioned above (descriptive, analytic and explicative), the 10 chapters are thematically sorted into two parts. The chapters collectively sample different African cultures to document the nonverbal signals that are variously employed to achieve different societal goals. They explore the various ways in which people act and speak without words, in order to understand the different usages and roles, the coding of messages and the culture-specific patterns of meaning that are recovered from them within the context of their occurrences. Nonverbal signals are invaluable to the politics of visual perception, and to the quest for justice and democracy. They underscore the human need to establish and maintain status, they provide insights into the religious underpinning of morality and character, and they are important in retracing ethnicity and sustaining memory and continuity of identity in the diaspora. We find that people are the same everywhere, as they are worked upon by culture and in turn influence their own culture to sustain those values they consider fundamental and inalienable.

References

Agogos. (1834 [1946]). *Hints on Etiquette and the Usages of Society with a Glance at Bad Habits*. London: Turnstile Press.
Arndt, H., & R.W. Janney (1987). *Inter Grammar: Towards an Integrative Model of Verbal, Prosodic, and Kinesic Choices in Speech*. Berlin: Mouton de Gruyter. http://dx.doi.org/10.1515/9783110872910
Bacon, F. (1605 [1902]). *On the Dignity and Advancement of Learning*. Ed. John Dewey. New York.
Barclay, A. (1570 [1967]). *The Mirror of Good Manners Conteining the Foure Cardinal Vertues Compiled in Latin by Dominike Mancin*. New York: Franklin.
Basso, Keith I. (1970). "To give up on words": Silence in Western Apache culture. *Southwestern Journal of Anthropology*, 26(3), 213–30.
Bates, E., & F. Dick. (2002). Language, gesture, and the developing brain. *Developmental Psychobiology*, 40, 293–310.
Beattie, G., & H. Shovelton. (1999). Mapping the range of information contained in the iconic hand gestures that accompany spontaneous speech. *Journal of Language and Social Psychology*, 18(4), 438–62. http://dx.doi.org/10.1177/0261927X99018004005
Birdwhistell, R.L. (1952). *Introduction to Kinesics: An Annotation System for Analysis of Body Motion and Gesture*. Louisville, Kentucky: University of Louisville Press.
Birdwhistell, R.L. (1955). Background to kinesics etc. *A Review of General Semantics*, 13, 10–18.
Birdwhistell, R. (1970). *Kinesics in Context: Essays on body motion communication*. Philadelphia, PA: University of Pennsylvania Press.
Bolinger, D. (1968). *Aspects of Language*. New York: Harcourt, Brace & World.
Bouissac, P. (1973). *La mesure des gestes: prolegomenes a la semiotique gestuelle*. The Hague: Mouton.
Bourdieu, P. (1977). *Outline of a Theory of Practice*. Cambridge: Cambridge University Press. http://dx.doi.org/10.1017/CBO9780511812507.
Brookes, H. (2004). A repertoire of South African quotable gestures. *Journal of Linguistic Anthropology*, 14(2), 186–224. http://dx.doi.org/10.1525/jlin.2004.14.2.186
Corballis, M.C. (2003). *From Hand to Mouth: The Origins of Language*. Princeton, NJ: Princeton University Press.
Csordas, T.J. (1990). Embodiment as a paradigm for anthropology. *Ethos: Journal of the Society for Psychological Anthropology*, 18(1), 5–47.
Eisenberg, A.M. & Ralph Smith, Jr. (1970). *Nonverbal Communication*. Indianapolis, Indiana: Bobbs-Merrill.
Ekman, P., & W.V. Friesen. (1969). The repertoire of nonverbal behavior: Categories, origins, usage, and coding. *Semiotica*, 1(1), 49–98. http://dx.doi.org/10.1515/semi.1969.1.1.49
Goffman, E. (1971). *Behavior in Public*. New York: Harper and Row.

Goldin-Meadow, S. (2003). *Hearing Gesture: How Our Hands Help Us Think*. Cambridge, MA: Harvard University Press.

Goodenough, W.H. (1964). Cultural anthropology and linguistics. In D. Hymes (ed.), *Language in Culture and Society*. New York: Harper and Row.

Hall, E.T. (1959). *The Silent Language*. New York: Anchor Press.

Hall, E.T. (1974). *Handbook for Proxemic Research* (Studies in the Anthropology of Visual Communication, Special Publication). Washington: Society for the Anthropology of Visual Communication.

Hanna, B.E. (1996). Defining the emblem. *Semiotica*, 112 (3/4), 289–358.

Holoka, P. James. (1992). Non-verbal communications in the classics: Research opportunities. In Fernando Pyatos (ed.), *Non-verbal Communication*. Amsterdam: John Benjamins Publishing Co. http://dx.doi.org/10.1075/z.60.22hol.

Huebler, A. (2001). *Das Konzept Koerper in den Sprach-und Kommunikationswissenschaftern*. Tubingen, Basel: A. Francke Verlag.

Iverson, J.M., & S. Goldin-Meadow. (1998). Why people use gestures when they speak. *Nature*, 396, 228.

Iverson, J.M., & S. Goldin-Meadow. (2005). Gesture paves the way for language development. *Psychological Science*, 16(5), 367–71. http://dx.doi.org/10.1111/j.0956-7976.2005.01542.x

Johnson, H.G., P. Ekman & W.V. Friesen. (1975). Communicative body movements: American emblems. *Semiotica*, 15(4), 335–53. http://dx.doi.org/10.1515/semi.1975.15.4.335

Johnson, M. (1987). *The Body in the Mind: The Bodily Basis for Meaning, Imagination, and Reason*. Chicago: University of Chicago Press.

Kendon, A. (1972). Some relationship between body, motion and speech: An analysis of an example. In A. Siegman & B. Pope (eds.), *Studies in Dyadic Communication*. New York: Pergamon Press. http://dx.doi.org/10.1016/B978-0-08-015867-9.50013-7.

Kendon, A. (1980). Gesticulation and speech: Two aspects of the process of utterance. In Mary Ritchie Key (ed.), *The Relationship of Verbal and Nonverbal Communication*. The Hague: Mouton.

Kendon, A. (1988). Goffman's approach to face-to-face interaction. In P. Drew & A. Wootton (eds.), *Erving Goffman: Exploring the Interaction Order*. Boston: Northeastern University Press.

Kendon, A. (2004). *Gesture: Visible Action as Utterance*. Cambridge: Cambridge University Press. http://dx.doi.org/10.1017/CBO9780511807572.

Lindenfeld, J. (1974). Syntactic structure and kinesic phenomena in communicative events. *Semiotica*, 12(1), 61–73. http://dx.doi.org/10.1515/semi.1974.12.1.61

McNeill, D. (1992). *Hand and Mind: What Gestures Reveal about Thought*. Chicago: University of Chicago Press.

McQuown, N. (1971). *The Natural History of an Interview*. Chicago: University of Chicago Press.

Morris, C. (1946). *Signs, Language and Behavior*. Englewood Cliffs, New Jersey: Prentice Hall. http://dx.doi.org/10.1037/14607-000.

Mufwene, S.S. (2001). *The Ecology of Language Evolution*. Cambridge: Cambridge University Press. http://dx.doi.org/10.1017/CBO9780511612862

Orie, O. (2009). Pointing the Yoruba way. *Gesture*, 9(2), 237–61. http://dx.doi.org/10.1075/gest.9.2.04ori

Pike, K. (1967). *Language in Relation to a Unified Structure of Human Behavior*. The Hague: Mouton. http://dx.doi.org/10.1515/9783111657158

Reusch, J., & W. Kees. (1956). *Nonverbal Language: Notes on Visual Perception of Human Relations*. Berkeley: University of California Press.

Sapir, E. (1949). The unconscious patterning of behavior in society. In D. Mandelbaunm (ed.), *Selected Writings of Edward Sapir in Language, Culture and Personality*. Berkeley: University of California Press.

Sherzer, J. (1973). Verbal and nonverbal deixis: The pointed lip gesture among the San Blas Cuna. *Language in Society*, 2(1), 117–31. http://dx.doi.org/10.1017/S0047404500000087

Streeck, J. (1993). Gesture as communication: Its coordination with gaze and speech. *Communication Monographs*, 60(4), 275–99. http://dx.doi.org/10.1080/03637759309376314

van Dijk, T.A. (ed.). (1997a). *Discourse Studies: A Multidisciplinary Introduction* (2 vols.). London: Sage.

van Dijk, T.A. (1997b). The study of discourse. *Discourse as Structure and Process*, 1, 1–34.

Willems, R.M., & P. Hagoort. (2007). Neural evidence for the interplay between language, gesture, and action. *Brain and Language*, 101(3), 278–89. http://dx.doi.org/10.1016/j.bandl.2007.03.004

Wundt, W. (1921 [1973]). *Probleme der Volkerpsychologie* [Problems of cultural psychology] (2nd ed.). Stuttgart, Germany: Alfred Kroner.

Part One:
Body Talk in the Arts and Literature

Shadowy walk 2. By Augustine Agwuele, 2014.

1
What Traditional Dances Tell Us about African Cultural Identity in Puerto Rico and Trinidad

Ann Albuyeh[1]

> Because it is nonverbal, dance has often been perceived by Western observers as a relatively insignificant cultural medium, capable of communicating only abstract thought or emotion. In the African diaspora, however, bodily movement can be a form of prayer, or of protest... . In some cases, the brutal repression of verbal expressions ... has necessitated this other, more discreet form of communication. Meaningful motion is an important and continuous aspect of diasporic culture.
> – Browning (1999: 553)

1.1 Introduction

In "Dancin' on the shoulders of our ancestors" Aimee Glocke and Lawrence Jackson (2011: 2) criticize the lack of research into "African/Black dance," asserting that this is "one of the least developed areas in the discipline" of Black Studies. Studies of Afro-Caribbean dance can play a significant role in filling this gap by investigating the ways in which these dances express the identities of the performers in this important diasporic region.

That dance "speaks" to people living in the Caribbean is well documented. For example, in Puerto Rico, an African-derived dance form called the *bomba* shows up in popular surveys about Puerto Rican identity (e.g., Morris 1995), legislation regarding disbursement of commonwealth funds

---

1   Ann Albuyeh is Professor of English Linguistics at the University of Puerto Rico where she teaches in the Caribbean Studies doctoral program. She received her PhD from the University of Wisconsin-Madison. Her research in language and culture focuses on the Caribbean and Africa.

for island festivals (the Institute of Puerto Rican Culture),[2] and book titles such as Juan Flores' (2000) *From Bomba to Hip-Hop: Puerto Rican Culture and Latino Identity.*

In Trinidad, where carnival, calypso and steel pan bands have become famous representations of Trinidadian culture outside the region, dance forms are also important non-verbal expressions of identity. As in Puerto Rico, these dances are performed in a continuum concurrently illustrating tradition and innovation. From the stick-fighting dance called *kalinda*[3] to the dance competition called the *limbo*, to the newest hybrid Indo-Afro-Caribbean dance called *chutney*, Trinidadians' nonverbal expressions of cultural identity continue to evolve.

However, while many of these dances are perceived to communicate the African heritage of the people of the Caribbean, as discussed below, the sources of such dances are in dispute among scholars, the dancers themselves and the general public. For example, *bele*, found in Trinidad and various French islands, has been claimed to be "derived from the minuet, a court dance from Europe"[4] and contrastingly as "strongly reflect[ing] influences from African fertility dances."[5]

Adapting the linguistic model presented in Salikoko Mufwene's (2001) *The Ecology of Language Evolution*, I will propose that the contradictory claims made about the Puerto Rican and Trinidadian dances' provenance reflect an insufficient appreciation of the degree to which individual cultural features have been selected and creatively recombined. I will attempt to disentangle the ethnic influences in these Caribbean dances first by examining some of the limited data available regarding the sources of African slaves in Puerto Rico and Trinidad. Then I compare analyses and videos of current Afro-Caribbean dances to the characteristics of contemporary dance forms in West and Central Africa.[6]

---

2   Instituto de Cultura Puertorriqueña, http://www.icp.gobierno.pr/version-accesible-noticias-y-comunicados/81-gobernador-anuncia-inversion-de-sobre-5-millones-en-proyectos-culturales. Accessed August 14, 2015.
3   As will be noted below, there are many variations of these dances and the names they go by.
4   "Best Village celebrates 40 years with Bele festival," *Trinidad Express Newspaper*, April 16, 2013. http://www.trinidadexpress.com/featured-news/Best-Village-celebrates-50-years-with-Bele-festival-in-Siparia-203219931.html. Accessed October 14, 2013.
5   Bélé. https://en.wikipedia.org/wiki/B%C3%A9l%C3%A9. Accessed October 14, 2013.
6   See Albuyeh (2010) for historical references to Afro-Caribbean dances and discussion of the etymology of the dances' names.

1.2 Africans in Puerto Rico and Trinidad

Puerto Rico and Trinidad are small islands at opposite ends of the Caribbean chain; Puerto Rico is closer to the United States, and Trinidad is just off the coast of Venezuela. Although Puerto Rico became a territory of the United States in 1898, during the era of the transatlantic slave trade it was a colony of Spain. Trinidad was also a colony of Spain, but came under British rule in the late 18th century, and other Europeans, especially French planters, made it their home.[7] Since the late 19th century, the two islands of Trinidad and (the smaller) Tobago have been a political entity, gaining their independence from Britain in 1962.

Puerto Rico and Trinidad are not only far apart geographically, but also linguistically: Puerto Ricans speak Spanish with a minority of bilinguals in Spanish and English; Trinidadians primarily speak English, English-based creole and an older French-based creole. Culturally, Trinidad and Puerto Rico have significant differences.[8] In particular, there is the cultural impact of Trinidad's large Asian-descended population, and the unsurprising strength of US cultural influences in Puerto Rico. Although the two islands' strongest precolonial link, the cultural legacy of the Amerindian people who populated the Caribbean chain before the Europeans' arrival, was almost obliterated (Wilson 1997), a non-European link remains in the living cultural legacy of the thousands of Africans brought there.

As in the rest of the African diaspora, finding out who came to each place, and when, is daunting, and ultimately, we will never be able to recoup the full record. However, one of the more noteworthy attempts to do so exists in the slave voyages data continually updated on an interactive website hosted by Emory University in Atlanta, Georgia, with the support of international partners. As of the end of 2013, "Voyages, The Trans-Atlantic Slave Trade Database" http://www.slavevoyages.org/tast/index.faces) has information on more than 35,000 slave voyages, which transported more than 12 million Africans across the Atlantic Ocean and the Caribbean Sea.

With all the obvious disclaimers that need to be made (see below), this source, nonetheless, provides "harder" data than could be gleaned from the historical record existing before the database began to be collected. Among the areas where this is obvious is the provenance of Caribbean

---

7   Although e.g. Italian planters moved to Puerto Rico, their linguistic and cultural impact was insignificant compared to the French in Trinidad.

8   Culture is broadly defined here as the social heritage of a community: language, religion, cuisine, social conventions, music, dance, visual arts etc.

dance. For example, as will be discussed below, Puerto Rican *bomba* has been attributed to sources as different as the Ashanti (Asante) people from what is today Ghana and the Yoruba people from Nigeria.

As Table 1.1 illustrates, the Slave Voyages database would indicate that African slaves were brought to Puerto Rico earlier than to Trinidad. However, according to the available data, subsequent voyages brought almost twice as many slaves to Trinidad as to Puerto Rico.

The Slave Voyages database has information on a significant number of voyages in which Africans were brought on board directly from the continent. The Africans who were brought to Puerto Rico and Trinidad came from ports primarily along the west coast of Africa. The Slave Voyages database delineates the following areas: Senegambia and the Offshore Atlantic Islands, Sierra Leone, the Windward Coast, the Gold Coast, the Bight of Benin (*bight* meaning *bay*), the Bight of Biafra and the Gulf of Guinea Islands, and West Central Africa and the Island of St Helena. Map 1.1 shows the boundaries of modern African nations and the six slave trading regions listed above.[9]

Table 1.1 Number of slaves disembarked: Puerto Rico and Trinidad.

Years	Puerto Rico	Trinidad	Totals
1527–1550	122		122
1626–50	102		102
1651–75	259		259
1726–50	433		433
1751–75	7,610		7,610
1776–1800	210	7,548	7,758
1801–25	1,572	13,632	15,204
1826–38	1,353	201	1,554
Totals	11,661	21,381	33,042

Source: Voyages: The Trans-Atlantic Slave Trade Database, http://www.slavevoyages.org/tast/index.faces.

Note: The totals are derived from the sources for Tables 1.2 and 1.3. Numbers have been conservatively rounded upward. The database estimates that recorded voyages for all areas probably represent 80 per cent or less of the true total.

9   The modern countries from North to South are: Senegal, Guinea-Bissau, Guinea, Sierra Leone, Liberia, Côte D'Ivoire, Ghana, Togo, Benin, Nigeria, Cameroon, Equatorial Guinea, Gabon, Congo and Angola.

African Cultural Identity in Puerto Rico and Trinidad 21

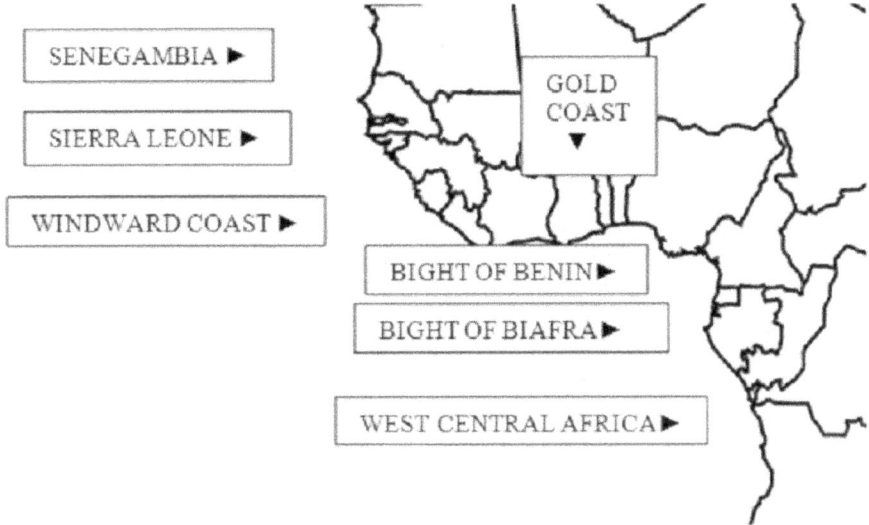

Map 1.1. Slave embarkation areas: West coast of Africa.
Map by Author. Source: http://www.slavevoyages.org/tast/index.faces.

That each of these regions contains many, possibly hundreds, of ethnic groups is illustrated by *Ethnologue: Languages of the World* (Lewis et al. 2013) which, for example, claims that 81 languages are currently spoken in Ghana, and 522 in Nigeria.[10] However, particularly along the river routes and fanning out from the coast, larger ethnic groups can at least be identified in many areas.

The Slave Voyages database currently has information on 63 slave voyages from Africa to Puerto Rico. Of this total, 37 voyages have provided embarkation data. Table 1.2 presents the number of Africans recorded as having disembarked in Puerto Rico from each of the database regions.[11]

10 Because languages exist in a continuum, counting languages vs dialects, for example, is difficult, and there is obviously cultural overlap, rendering one language-one culture an imperfect calculation; nonetheless *Ethnologue*'s estimates indicate the potential for great cultural diversity within the areas under discussion.

11 Slavevoyages.org allows researchers to create their own URL. My URL for the updated November 28, 2013 Puerto Rico search displaying different data arrays is: http://slavevoyages.org/tast/database/search.faces?yearFrom=1514&yearTo=1866&mjbyptimp=60000&mjslptimp=31200; for the updated Trinidad research my URL is: http://slavevoyages.org/tast/database/search.faces?yearFrom=1514&yearTo=1866&mjbyptimp=60000&mjslptimp=34500. Accessed November 28, 2013.

Table 1.2 Puerto Rico: Numbers of disembarking slaves from areas of West Africa.

Years	Senegambia and Offshore Atlantic	Sierra Leone	Windward Coast	Bight of Benin	Bight of Biafra and Gulf of Guinea Islands	West Central Africa and St Helena	Southeast Africa and Indian Ocean Islands	Other Africa	Totals
1527–50	122								122
1626–50						102			102
1651–75						259			259
1726–50						271		162	433
1751–75	43	404	482		3,621	2,666		394	7,610
1776–1800				210					210
1801–25	103	273			398	283	515		1,572
1826–38		556			797				1,353
Totals	268	1,233	482	210	4,816	3,581	515	556	11,661

Source: Voyages: The Trans-Atlantic Slave Trade Database, http://www.slavevoyages.org/tast/index.faces.

Note: Numbers are from the 37 voyages with data indicating where slaves were purchased, out of the total of 63 voyages in the database.

As Table 1.2 illustrates, the largest number of slaves embarked in the Bight of Biafra and Gulf of Guinea Islands, followed by West Central Africa and St Helena, and the majority of these Africans arrived in Puerto Rico between 1751 and 1775.

Of the 102 voyages to Trinidad in the database, there are embarkation data for 74 slave voyages, as presented in Table 1.3.

As illustrated in Table 1.3, the largest number of Africans embarked from the Bight of Biafra and Gulf of Guinea Islands. Fewer slaves, but nonetheless a significant number, were brought from West Central Africa and St Helena, and the Gold Coast.

Thus, the largest numbers of slaves on the voyages to both Puerto Rico and Trinidad are recorded as coming from the Bight of Biafra and West Central Africa. The major ethnic groups on the Slave Voyages maps in the Bight of Biafra area are the Igbo, Ibibio, Duala, Fang and Mpongwe. In West Central Africa the major ethnic group on the maps is the Vili (also called Loango), one of many Koongo-speaking subgroups which include the Yombe, Kakongo, Nsundi, Bembe and Kenge, among others (Voyages: The Trans-Atlantic Slave Trade Database; Warner-Lewis 2003: 15). Sierra Leone and the Gold Coast are the third most important embarkation areas for Puerto Rico and Trinidad, respectively. Major ethnic groups in Sierra Leone featured in the Slave Voyages maps are the Biafada, Baga, Susu, Temne, Mende and Fulani people, while in in the Gold Coast region these are the Baule, Asante and Fante people.

A number of cautions should be sounded here. These data are suggestive, but not, of course, conclusive. For example, some of the Africans living on the coast worked in the slave trade in places such as Cape Coast Castle, Ghana (St. Clair 2007), and captives from more inland areas were often brought down river to the embarkation points, and this makes assessing the ethnic make-up of the slave population on the voyages more difficult. Moreover, it is known that slave ships often sailed along the African coast picking up slaves at more than one embarkation point, and Trinidadian linguist Maureen Warner-Lewis (2003) also points out that slave ships sometimes hid the real source of the slaves when they were violating another European country's monopoly. Africans were also carried from Europe to the Caribbean and from one Caribbean country to another. And the later groups of Africans who came to various colonies as indentured laborers are, of course, not represented here. Nonetheless, noting these cautions, it would seem that the embarkation totals are large enough (documenting over 30,000 slaves transported) to be able to suggest important sources of African cultural influence on the islands of Puerto Rico and Trinidad.

Table 3. Trinidad: Numbers of disembarking slaves from areas of West Africa.

Years	Senegambia and Offshore Atlantic	Sierra Leone	Windward Coast	Gold Coast	Bight of Benin	Bight of Biafra And Gulf of Guinea Islands	West Central Africa and St Helena	Other Africa	Totals
1779–1800			256	597	360	5,273	1,062		7,548
1801–25	683	983	396	1,231	310	7,354	2,483	192	13,632
1826–33						201			201
Totals	683	983	652	1,828	670	12,828	3,545	192	21,381

Source: Voyages: The Trans-Atlantic Slave Trade Database, http://www.slavevoyages.org/tast/index.faces.

Note: Numbers are from the 74 voyages with data including where slaves were purchased, out of the total of 102 voyages in the database.

1.3 Dance in a Creole Continuum

Just as creole language scholars have sometimes conceived of these languages on a continuum with "deep creoles or pidgins" called "basilects" at one end, "mesolects" in the middle, and European standard languages or "acrolects" at the other end, Caribbean dance scholars such as Ivonne Daniel (2011) have placed dances in the Caribbean on a dance continuum. Daniel's dance continuum begins with African forms, with creole forms in the middle, and European forms at the other end. Her African forms reflect an "African Style of Movement" characterized by: flexed posture, all body parts in isolation, divided torso, and serial, solo and couple dancing in front of drums. Her "European Style of Movement" is characterized by: erect posture, emphasized extremities, undivided torso and partnered ballroom dancing (Daniel 2011: 46). For example, the flexed posture, i.e., a forward tilted back with flexed knees (or a "grounded" stance), that Daniel (2011: 68) refers to, reflects what Marian Aguiar (1999) and Kariamu Welsh (2010) characterize as the earth-centeredness of African dancing, illustrated in Figure 1.1, showing dancers in Kumasi, Ghana.[12]

Figure 1.1. Dancers in Kumasi, Ghana. Photo by Author, Summer 1996.

12   I would also note that these African and Afro-Caribbean dance characteristics were stressed by the instructors of the dance workshops I participated

Aguiar (1999: 558) states that "One of the most remarkable aspects of African dance is its use of the movements of daily life. By raising ordinary gestures to the level of art, these dances show the grace and rhythm of daily activities." The Senegalese dancers in Figure 1.2 exhibit a flexed posture, but also appear to be performing gestures related to farming.[13]

In *Yoruba Dance: The Semiotics of Movement and Body Attitude in a Nigerian Culture*, Ọmọ́fọlábọ̀ Àjàyí (1998: 1) focuses on Yoruba dance, but her introductory statement applies to dance throughout West Africa:

> At significant events, such as end-of-year rituals and festivities, rites of passage, political ceremonies, and professional activities, dance not only serves as a popular convivial accompaniment but also serves to illustrate the meaning and underline the symbolism of these occasions ... the dynamic form of dance functions to visually and kinesthetically enhance and complement the aesthetic as well as the symbolic impact of other art forms, whether verbal or non-verbal, bringing out their full significance and meaning.

Àjàyí further reflects on the capacity of dance to transcend linguistic boundaries, and this has certainly also been the case in the Caribbean. The

Figure 1.2. Senegalese dancers and musicians. Photo by Author, 1997.

---

in, which focused on Ewe dancing, held at the University of Ghana, Legon in 1996, and *bomba* dancing at the University of Puerto Rico, Río Piedras in 2007, respectively.

13   I took this photo in the Senegalese resort of Saly Portudal. Unfortunately the performance did not involve explaining the dances to the audience, and I have so far been unable to corroborate my impression.

wide dissemination of types of Afro-Caribbean dances transcends the linguistic differences referred to earlier which are in large part a legacy of the region's colonial past.

Among the most "African" of these dances is the Puerto Rican *bomba* which Daniel places toward the African end of her continuum. One of the most salient characteristics of *bomba* is the interaction which can be found between musicians, vocalists, dancers and audience. Aguiar (1999: 557) has pointed out that much African music is characterized by this rhythmic dialogue. In West Africa this dialogue typically involves the dancers and the musicians.

The emphasis of these dances on rhythm causes the percussion instruments to predominate. In classic Puerto Rican *bomba*, which consists of only percussion instruments, the dancers, in the words of Jorge Arce (1999), "sustain a rhythmical dance conversation" with the improvising drummer. In Puerto Rican *bomba*, the musicians play low-pitched drums called *buleador*, and a high-pitched drum called *primo* that holds the tempo and simultaneously improvises over the strong rhythmic pattern of the other drums. The dancer signals the *primo* drummer through abrupt, sometimes repeated, movements which the drummer spontaneously follows (Figure 1.3).[14]

Figure 1.3. Female Puerto Rican *bomba* dancer. Photo by Author, March 2014.

14 My thanks to dance professor and Caribbean Studies doctoral candidate Awilda Sterling-Duprey and founder and lead singer and percussionist of the

Figure 1.4. *Bomba* and *bele* dancers in classic postures and traditional costumes. Illustration by Author, 2013.

The lifting of the skirts of the female dancers is understood to be a European influence, and the classic *bomba* costume consisting of head ties combined with ruffled long-skirted dresses shows elements of both African and European provenance. Similar costumes and skirt waving characterize *bele* as it is danced in Trinidad. Figure 1.4 above illustrates a Puerto Rican *bomba* dancer on the left and a Trinidadian *bele* dancer on the right.

Like *bomba*, in *bele* the dancers sometimes exhibit a flexed posture, but also perform some of the dance standing erect. Relating the development of *bele* to the European quadrille, Daniel places *bele* closer to Europe on her dance continuum. That Africans and those of African descent were under pressure to abandon dances of the drum has been well documented, and Daniel claims that this was one of the motivations for their adaptation of a European dance form. However, she singles out the "Queen's solo"[15] in one

---

    group *Viento de Agua*, Tito Matos, for both insight into the varieties of *bomba* found in Puerto Rico and an invaluable *bomba* workshop. Not all *bomba* is interactive. Not only is there recorded music, but some folkloric groups choreograph their performances, even when they have live musicians. In addition, some *bomba* features non-percussive instruments such as guitars or horns.

15 See for example, Youtube video of the Trinidad and Tobago Sanfest showing Trinidadian *bele* with a "queen" dancer. https://www.youtube.com/watch?v=wz_3f_5VnpI. Accessed September 24, 2012.

form of Trinidadian *bele* as "no longer a 'mincing' European imitation, but a challenge" (Daniel 2011: 73).

> [The *bele* Queen] wore skirts that referenced European fashion and camouflaged African understandings; overskirts above multiple petticoats outwardly imitated European conventions, but when [the skirts] opened they alluded to escaping enslavement, "flying away to Africa." (Daniel 2011: 72)

If the skirt waving of *bele* can look very European, this is not as true of the skirt waving in *bomba*. Certainly, the shaking or waving of the hem of a costume is not limited to Europe, as the Ashanti male dancer from Kumasi, Ghana in Figure 1.5 illustrates.

Figure 1.5. Ashanti dancer. Photo by Author, Summer 1996.

1.4 Creolization in Language and in Culture

"Creole" can refer to the results of language contact (such as the Trinidadian creole languages mentioned above), but also to the results of cultural contact in the Caribbean. Some scholars object to using linguistic models to analyze culture. For example, Richard Cullen Rath (2000: 99) states, "Students of cultural creolization have treated it as analogous to linguistic creolization. This analogy is mistaken." However, I think that, as with the creole continuum alluded to above, there are useful linguistic analogies to be made.

Linguists have been adapting models from the natural sciences since they began producing "family trees" for languages in the 19th century. A useful more recent adaptation can be found in Salikoko Mufwene's (2001) *The Ecology of Language Evolution.* Figure 1.6 presents my adaptation of a model he produced to attempt to graphically illustrate the selection and recombination of linguistic features which occur in language contact situations and result in the development of creole languages.

In the figure, the input languages in contact provide features (syntactic, phonological and lexical elements), visualized here in a kind of arena of competition where some features win out and others do not, resulting in unique output languages, the creoles. Moreover, as I indicate in this graphic, innovation occurs in this arena as well, resulting in new forms not present in the source languages.

It seems to me that the contradictory claims made about the provenance of both Afro-Caribbean dances and their names are not only due to the difficulties entailed in tracing the sources of the region's African cultural

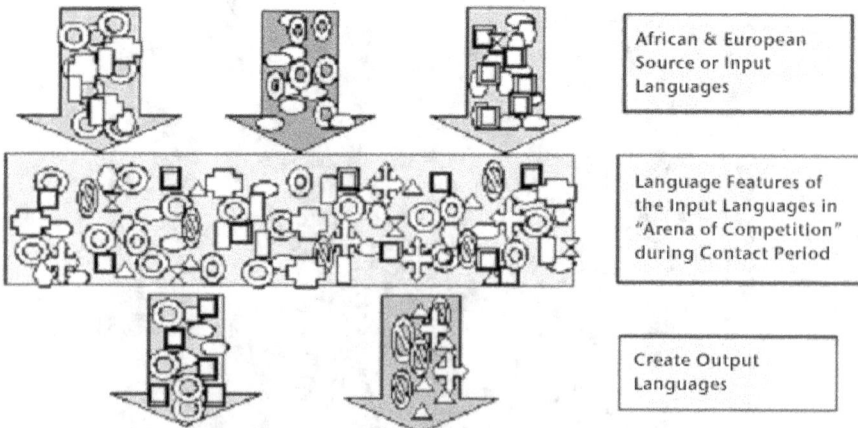

Figure 1.6. Author's adaptation and modification of diagram in Mufwene (2001: 4–6).

heritage, but are also a product of an insufficient appreciation of the degree to which individual cultural features have been selected and recombined, a la Mufwene's characterization. Moreover, dance lends itself to this analysis because it involves a combination of elements such as posture, orientation, movement type, body parts emphasized and so forth, which can be selected from various sources, recombined and added to through innovation.

Like all forms of dance, contemporary Puerto Rican *bomba* comes in many varieties. However, there are a number of characteristic postures and movements. Female *bomba* dancers wave their skirts with arms at their sides, unlike *bele* dancers whose arms are stretched high over the head as depicted in Figure 1.4 above. Also, what appears to be the European component where the dancers sashay in, waving their skirts in an upright posture, is briefer in *bomba* than *bele*. The *bomba* dancers dance longer and interact with the drum sooner.

As indicated in Table 1.2, the largest number of Africans in the Slave Voyages database for Puerto Rico embarked in the Bight of Benin area, which suggests strong cultural influences from ethnic groups such as the Igbo might be in evidence on the island. Although they wave scarves instead of their skirts, some Igbo women's dancing in videos of both southeastern Nigeria and performances in other countries resembles the gentle swaying movement of female *bomba* dancers, especially during the beginning of the dance. (See sample video list in Appendix.)

However, the intense subsequent movements of the women dancing *bomba* may reflect the influence of the second most important area in the table, West Central Africa. In fact, the hip movements and "bottom shimmying" of both female and male dancers look more like contemporary videos of Congolese and Gabon Ikoku dancing. The male *bomba* dancer in Figure 1.7 below illustrates bottom shimmying with the body flexed and the bottom pointed toward the drum. Moreover, some of the male dancers' footwork, with quick crosses of feet and quick turns, is similar to that of male Caribbean dances described in Warner-Lewis (2003: 234–5) which she attributes to West Central African influence.

Although shoulder movements are seen in West African dances (for example, Warner-Lewis refers to descriptions of a "shoulder dance" among the Nsundi) the shoulder snapping seen in some *bomba* dancing is very distinctive. Although the Slave Voyages database for neither Puerto Rico nor Trinidad shows many Africans embarking in the Bight of Benin area, in fact, this dance move resembles the shoulder movement in contemporary Yoruba *bata* dancing. Despite the data from slave voyages, Warner-Lewis' (1996) book, *Trinidad Yoruba: From Mother Tongue to Memory*, documents a strong Yoruba cultural component in Trinidadian society. It may

32 Body Talk and Cultural Identity in the African World

Figure 1.7. Male Puerto Rican *bomba* dancer. Photo by Author, March 2014.

be that many Yoruba destined for Trinidad were embarked in the Bight of Biafra, and/or Yoruba may have been significantly present in Africans brought to Trinidad from other parts of the Caribbean.

However, evidence for a Yoruba presence is lacking in Puerto Rico, although, for example, due to the spiritual beliefs of Santería, all Puerto Ricans seem to be aware of the Yoruba language. Toyin Falola and Matt Childs (2004) argue in *The Yoruba Diaspora in the Atlantic World*, that the Yoruba had a disproportionate influence on diasporic culture, and this, in fact, motivated their producing this book. Falola and Childs quote David Eltis, who began the transatlantic slave trade database which grew into the current Slave Voyages database cited here. "Eltis [2000: 253] remarked that although the Yoruba did not constitute a majority of the forced African captives shipped across the Atlantic, they have 'had an impact out of all proportion to [their] relative demographic weight' on diasporic culture in the Americas" (Falola and Childes 2004: xi).

1.5 Conclusion

Academics have too often neglected research which attempts to learn more about the specific cultural legacy of the transatlantic slave trade.

Richard Cullen Rath (2000: 104–5), for example, objects to studies such as that by Robert Farris Thompson (1990) which point to the source of US baton-twirling as being northern Kongolese. "Here then is a well-documented Africanism," Rath states, "but then the question becomes 'So what?'" Rath argues:

> By shifting the focus of inquiry to the path between underlying structures and concrete cultural expressions, it becomes possible to discern how Africans from diverse regional backgrounds came to understand each other in ways that were broadly "African" rather than "Coromantee," "Mende," or "Angolan." (Rath 2000: 112)

Michael A. Gomez (1999: 111) has criticized this point of view:

> Leading authorities on slavery in North America produce with impunity tome after tome, with little regard for the fact that their subjects came out of specific social and political contexts, that they had collective identities, and that they participated in recognizable cultures.

One way to fill the void is by listening to what Afro-Caribbean dance forms can tell us. Throughout the African diaspora, dance is an important expression of the elements which have combined and evolved and are part of a diasporic identity which is unique. In Puerto Rico and Trinidad, dances vary along Daniel's continuum reflecting their relative "Africanness." Moreover, these dances can speak to us of community identity. In a review of Angel Quintero-Rivera's 2009 book *Músicas Mulatas*, Daniel (2012: 199) applauds his perspective that "The dance becomes a composite of individual expressions that jointly yield community solidarity; the music initiates a ritual between musical sound and dancing bodies, a ritual of belonging, of cultural citizenship." Yet, for "black identity," whose survival was considered decades ago by Fernando Ortíz (1953), to reveal all that it communicates in the nonverbal dances of the Caribbean, it is important to go beyond Quintero-Rivera's conception of the composite, beyond even Daniel's dance continuum, as exemplary as both are. As Alma Concepción (2007: 4) states, "dance holds a central position in the construction and practice of complex, mixed histories and identities." Afro-Caribbean dances, where head-ties mix with European petticoats, in which culturally salient hip movements and shoulder snaps direct the polyrhythmic drumming, have yet more to say to us about the cultural heritage of this important diasporic region.

References

Aguiar, M. (1999). Dance in Sub-Saharan Africa. In K.A. Appiah & H.L. Gates, Jr. (eds.), *Africana* (pp. 555–8). New York: Basic Civitas Books.

Àjàyí, Ọmọ́fọlábọ̀. (1998). *Yoruba Dance: The Semiotics of Movement and Body Attitude in a Nigerian Culture*. Trenton, NJ: Africa World Press.

Albuyeh, A. (2010). Tracing African language and culture in Trinidad and Puerto Rico. In Nicholas Faraclas, Ronald Severing, Christa Weijer, Elisabeth Echteld & Marsha Hinds-Layne (eds.), *Anansi's Defiant Webs: Contact, Continuity, Convergence and Complexity in the Languages, Literatures, and Cultures of the Greater Caribbean* (pp. 79–92). Curaçao: University of the Netherlands Antilles Press, the Fundashon pa Planifikashon di Idioma and the Fundashon pa Planifikashon di Idioma and Universidat di Kòrsou (University of Curaçao).

Arce, Jorge. (1999). Plena and Bomba. In K.A. Appiah & H.L. Gates, Jr. (eds.), *Africana* (p. 1531). New York: Basic Civitas Books.

Browning, B. (1999). Dance in Latin America and the Caribbean. In K.A. Appiah & H.L. Gates, Jr. (eds.), *Africana* (pp. 553–5). New York: Basic Civitas Books.

Concepción, Alma. (2007). Dance and belonging: Transformations of rituals in Puerto Rican music and dance forms. *Journal for the Anthropological Study of Human Movement*, 14(4), http://jashm.press.illinois.edu/14.4/conception.html.

Daniel, Y. (2011). *Caribbean and Atlantic Diaspora Dance: Igniting Citizenship*. Urbana: University of Illinois Press.

Daniel, Y. (2012). Cuerpo y cultura: Las músicas "mulatas" y la subversion delbaile. *Caribbean Studies* (Rio Piedras, San Juan, PR), 40(1), 197–204. http://dx.doi.org/10.1353/crb.2012.0009

Eltis, D. (2000). *Rise of African Slavery in the Americas*. Cambridge: Cambridge University Press.

Falola, T., & M.D. Childs (eds.). (2004). *The Yoruba Diaspora in the Atlantic World*. Bloomington: Indiana University Press.

Flores, J. (2000). *From Bomba to Hip-Hop: Puerto Rican Culture and Latino Identity*. New York: Columbia University Press.

Glocke, A., & L.M. Jackson. (2011). Dancin' on the shoulders of our ancestors: An introduction. *Journal of Pan African Studies*, 4(6), 1–6.

Gomez, M.A. (1999). African identity and slavery in the Americas. *Radical History Review*, 1999(75), 111–20. http://dx.doi.org/10.1215/01636545-1999-75-111

Lewis, M. Paul, Gary F. Simons & Charles D. Fenning (eds.). (2013). *Ethnologue: Languages of the World* (17th edition). Dallas, TX: SIL International. Online version: http://www.ethnologue.com.

Morris, N. (1995). *Puerto Rico: Culture, Politics and Identity*. Westport, CT: Praeger Publishers.

Mufwene, S.S. (2001). *The Ecology of Language Evolution*. Cambridge: Cambridge University Press. http://dx.doi.org/10.1017/CBO9780511612862.

Ortíz, F. (1953). La Bombaen Puerto Rico. *Asomante*, 9(2), 8–12.

Quintero-Rivera, Ángel, G. (2009). *Cuerpo y cultura: Las músicas "mulatas" y la subversion delbaile*. Madrid: Iberoamericana/Frankfurt am Main: Vervuert.

Rath, R.C. (2000). Drums and power: ways of creolizing music in coastal South Carolina and Georgia, 1730–1790. In S. Reinhardt & D. Buisseret (eds.), *Creolization in the Americas: Cultural Adaptations to the New World* (pp. 99–130). Arlington: A&M Press.

slavevoyages.org allows researchers to create their own URL. My URL for the updated November 28, 2013 Puerto Rico research displaying different data arrays is: http://slavevoyages.org/tast/database/search.faces?yearFrom=1514&yearTo=1866&mjbyptimp=60000&mjslptimp=31200; for the updated Trinidad research my URL is: http://slavevoyages.org/tast/database/search.faces?yearFrom=1514&yearTo=1866&mjbyptimp=60000&mjslptimp=34500. Accessed November 28, 2013.

St. Clair, W. (2007). *The Door of No Return: The History of Cape Coast Castle and the Atlantic Slave Trade*. New York: Bluebridge Publishing.

Thompson, R.F. (1990). Kongo influences on African-American artistic culture. In J.E. Holloway (ed.), *Africanisms in American Culture* (pp. 148–84). Bloomington: Indiana University Press.

Warner-Lewis, M. (1996). *Trinidad Yoruba: From Mother Tongue to Memory*. Tuscaloosa: University of Alabama Press.

Warner-Lewis, M. (2003). *Central Africa in the Caribbean: Transcending Time, Transforming Cultures*. Barbados: University of the West Indies Press.

Welsh, Asante Kariamu (ed.). (1996). *African Dance: An Artistic, Historical and Philosophical Inquiry*. Trenton, NJ: Africa World Press.

Welsh, Kariamu. (2010). *African Dance*. 2nd ed. New York: Chelsea House.

Wilson, S. (ed.). (1997). *The Indigenous People of the Caribbean*. Gainesville: University of Florida Press.

Appendix

Ayan'jo Dance Bata. https://www.youtube.com/watch?v=ma-wH3fUDJA. Accessed May 7, 2013.

Bata Dancers Appeasing Sango. https://www.youtube.com/watch?v=WZpuFKfteH0. Accessed November 15, 2013.

Bata from West of Nigeria performed by National troupe of Nigeria in NY USA. https://www.youtube.com/watch?v=FVdYc8VMGu8. Accessed November 15, 2013.

BOMBA!!!! Grupo Yuba. https://www.youtube.com/watch?v=K4OFgIKkLDk. Accessed June 3, 2010.

Bomba de Puerto Rico: Encuentro de Tamboresen Juncos 2011. https://www.youtube.com/watch?v=yeK0bO9HB0g. Accessed November 6, 2013.

Congo-Danse Traditionnelle "Région du Pool" BOKO. https://www.youtube.com/watch?v=PdH1EnctEpo. Accessed November 1, 2013.

Congolese drum dancing workshop. https://www.youtube.com/watch?v=K4L6vrl1xIM. Accessed June 15, 2010.

Ikoku dance, Gabon. https://www.youtube.com/watch?v=jd_bfKZfFAI. Accessed June 15, 2010.

Puerto Rico Percusionistas, bomba con loshermanos Ayala Loiza PR. https://www.youtube.com/watch?v=VbNKeM-Wb1A. Accessed November 6, 2013.

Trinidad and Tobago Sanfest showing Trinidadian *bele* with a "queen" dancer. https://www.youtube.com/watch?v=wz_3f_5VnpI. Accessed September 24, 2012.

Women Celebrate the Opening of Their Village Health Clinic. https://www.youtube.com/watch?v=ML9qDSK_V8s. Accessed January 5, 2012.

2
Fela's Clenched Fists: The Double "Black Power" Salute and Political Ideology

Dotun Ayobade[1]

2.1 Introduction

To the extent that bodies are capable of encoding cultural phenomena and transporting them across time and space, Fela Kuti's body constitutes one of Nigeria's greatest cultural exports of the 20th century. This claim about Fela's body complicates a dominant understanding of his creative output in terms of his musical productivity. The body, as I invoke it here, situates Fela's music within the realm of the corporeal, so that it is not understood as a mere appendage to his music, but rather as a critical extension of its very meaning.

As one of Africa's most influential musicians and activists, Fela Anikulapo-Kuti is credited with creating Afrobeat, a music style that fuses jazz, funk, Nigerian highlife and traditional African polyrhythms. Fela's Afrobeat preoccupied itself with advancing anti-neocolonial, -imperialist and -oppression ideologies. Through Afrobeat, Fela pursued ideas that challenged the constellation of forces that perpetuated the systemic subjugation of Nigeria and undermined the lives of Nigerians. This meant, therefore, that the music attacked multinational institutions (the IMF, World Bank etc.) as well as key actors in the Nigerian military establishment. Afrobeat has earned global repute not only for its unique style, but also for the radical politics that undergirded it.

1   Dotun Ayobade is a PhD candidate in the Performance at Public Practice (PPP) program of the Department of Theatre and Dance at The University of Texas at Austin. Ayobade's research broadly investigates the intersections between gender, performance and colonialism in Nigeria. His dissertation explores the works and politics of Fela Kuti's Queens.

Given Fela's preeminence in the development of Afrobeat, it is often difficult to distinguish the man from the music. In certain circles, Fela is held as the symbolic manifestation of Afrobeat itself. It is not uncommon to find Afrobeat groups celebrating Fela even when they mostly compose their own original Afrobeat songs. This act of fastening artist to art can be attributed largely to Fela's role in the creation of the style and in the articulation of its politics. It is also true, however, that Fela perpetuated himself as "Afrobeat" through a practice that involved a constant negotiation between his ideology, his performance style and the location of his physical body in an ontological sense. In other words, as Afrobeat gained traction as a distinct style of music in the 1970s, and as its radical ideologies began gaining public attention, Fela's body – lanky, pliant and sinewy – played a significant role in advancing its course. Whether by thrusting himself right at the center of every major political controversy or generating controversy for himself, Fela situated his body within the very discursive environment of his music.

Most existing literature on Fela and Afrobeat has traditionally leaned into the spectacular – such as the genius of Fela's music; his marrying 27 women in one day; his endless face-offs with the Nigerian government; or with his insurgent ideologies in general. And, judging by the nature of the musician's political choices, the focus on the spectacular is justified. However, it has meant that scant attention has been paid to the role that Fela's body played in communicating aspects of his political ideology. It has also meant that meager consideration has been given to the implications of Fela's embedding his body within his music and politics in the ways that he did. While it might appear counterintuitive to discursively detach Fela from the realm of the spectacular (and, in a sense, from the musical) and locate him rather within something as banal as the *gestural*, I will contend that this detachment yields important insights about the political uses of the performing body in contesting varying outlooks of coloniality. Indeed, it is incredibly difficult, even as I proceed with writing this essay, to sustain this discursive fastening of Fela to the gestural. Much of this difficulty stems from the fact that Fela's art and politics thrived on an adept engagement with spectacle, the most important of which, in my estimation, was his success as a public intellectual that educated and entertained the Nigerian public through music.

On a certain level, this essay makes a case for appreciating the subtle connections between the spectacular and the gestural. I examine the salience of the gestural in perpetuating the spectacular not just in a particular moment of performance, but also in subsequent iterations of that performance. By gesture I refer specifically to Fela's double "Black Power" salute: the statuesque pose that entails holding up both fists firm in the air with arms aligned with the erect body so that the upward pull of the fists extends the body's height, highlights its frame and holds the performer's body (and, presumably, the performer) in tension.[2] In enacting the salute, the head is held erect, with the enactor's gaze directed forwards at the receptors (audience or fellow-protesters, as the case might be). This gesture, which I refer to henceforth as the Afrobeat salute, has endured as an important symbol in the overall distinctiveness of Fela's Afrobeat.

The paucity of intellectual engagement with the Afrobeat salute and the purposes it has served provides the impetus for this essay. It is striking that even as Fela circulates globally,[3] this most visible of his signatures has eluded scholarly interest altogether. In an attempt to bridge this intellectual gap this essay discusses the ways in which Fela's body generally, and his Afrobeat salute in particular, have served as containers for his ideologies and how these elements have helped retain the spirit of his politics since his death in August 1997. I conclude this essay by analyzing one of the ways that Fela's Afrobeat salute reemerged during the 2012 Occupy Nigeria Movement as an embodied enactment of memory, both of the late musician and of a collective experience of social distress.

2.2 Gesture and the Reading of History

Imagining the ways that the performing body encodes history and character through gesture requires an understanding of the breadth of meanings accruable to any one gesture within a cultural moment. It also entails deconstructing the established market-driven hierarchies of creative products in relation to the performing body. Such market-driven hierarchies require that the body be partly or wholly absented from its creative

---

2 By tension, I refer to muscular tension, in the sense that holding both fists in the air tenses the triceps and shoulder muscles, as well as the abductor pollicis muscles of the fists and around the fingers.
3 We have experienced a resurgence of Fela's work in recent years, particularly since the 2009 Broadway performance *Fela!* by African American choreographer, Bill T. Jones. Even more recent is Red Hot's 2013 tribute album to Fela, *Red Hot + Fela*. These are aside from the proliferation of Afrobeat bands in Africa, North America, Europe and Asia.

products, so much so that value becomes placed on artifacts (music, albums, books etc.), which by virtue of their reproducibility and marketability potentially generate profit. In defying this capitalist logic, the body as an ontological category becomes necessarily undervalued in the marketplace of history.[4] At the level of discourse, the body is detached from its own history in ways that violently conscript traces of its existence to the logics of commodification.

In the event of its incorporation into these discourses on value, the body is mobilized for the larger need to capitalize on its products and productivity. We, thus, characteristically attach value to a body based on the measured productivity, or achievements, of its bearer. To a certain degree, this question of value accounts for the paucity of interest in the body in and of itself at the level of discourse. In addition, the fact of its corruptibility, its inevitable death and decay, subordinates the body to its products, which accrue value for much longer. In some cases, this accumulation in value of *bodily* products might occur over an eternity. Therefore, insofar as a non-living body can be preserved, embalmed and interesting to its preservers, or deemed of value to, say, anthropologists or morticians, to such a degree will that body endure in the realm of discourse as a *thing* unto itself. Even in this scenario, its "productivity" yet governs the terms upon which the body is re-membered. Following this thinking, it becomes interesting to contemplate how gestures simultaneously relate to and complicate this idea of the body's "productivity."

Understood as an expression intrinsic to, and not necessarily as a product of, the body's epistemological character, gesture enacts communication between actors in a social environment in the same way that it codifies aspects of cultural memory. The productive power of gesture, and indeed of the performing body in this marketplace of memory, suggests that it might

---

4   I use the word market here in a Marxist sense to suggest the flow of capital, especially economic capital. I, however, also use market to suggest the other ways in which capital might be generated, accumulated and exchanged. Pierre Bourdieu offers an extensive treatment of this idea of capital in "The forms of capital," where he argues that "capital can present itself [...] as economic capital, which is immediately and directly convertible into money and may be institutionalized in the forms of property rights; as cultural capital, which is convertible, on certain conditions, into economic capital and may be institutionalized in the forms of educational qualifications; and as social capital, made up of social obligations ('connections'), which is convertible, in certain conditions, into economic capital and may be institutionalized in the form of a title of nobility" (Bourdieu 1986).

contain alternative logics around which certain histories might be comprehended. Unpacking such alternative logics ranks high in the concerns of performance scholars and, in a different sense, for scholars of gesture studies. Diana Taylor's *The Archive and the Repertoire*, for example, effectively re-centers the body as a category of epistemic significance and memory preservation for some (particularly non-Western) cultures. Through what she terms the *repertoire* – embodied praxis such as movement, gestures, singing, dance and so on – alternative modes of cultural memory are enacted and sanctioned. Different from archival forms of knowledge that remain relatively stable over long periods of time, "the actions that are the repertoire do not remain the same. The repertoire both keeps and transforms choreographies of meaning" (Taylor 2003: 20). Cultural meanings are therefore constantly in flux, being simultaneously preserved and altered by performing bodies interacting in space and time. In my estimation, even in gestures that present limited possibilities for variation in performance, Taylor's notion of repertoire still applies to the idea that such gestures can accrue unto themselves a multiplicity of cultural meanings, particularly when enacted in different spatiotemporal contexts. Importantly, these "choreographies of meaning" invite a dynamic understanding of the ways in which a gesture might signify differently not only across time and space, but also inside of a given cultural frame. In the same way that Taylor's theorization of embodied memory implies a retrospective orientation toward cultural production – that is, culture as expressed at a period in the past, and into which performance yields insights – her work might also prove useful in understanding the ways that cultures and individuals as cultural actors both imagine and insert themselves into a future world through a corpus of gestural enactments. In other words, performance simultaneously reveals cultural history as well as sanctions incipient imaginations of subjecthood. And, this occurs both at the level of individual human bodies and at the level of cultural collectivities.

Inserting oneself into a future world through gesture entails understanding the cosmology of meanings obtainable in one's social world, alongside the range of gestures available to communicate the meaning(s) that one intends. It might equally entail "crafting" *new* gestures that speak to *new* social realities or experiences, or repurposing existing gestural vocabularies to communicate *new* ideas. In thinking about gesture as a "craft" or as "crafting" I draw on Jürgen Streeck's *Gesturecraft* where he understands gesture not merely as a sign-system or as body language but as "communicative *praxis* and *craft*" that comprises skills and techniques:

> We can assume that [gesture] is acquired through observation, imitation, and practice, as well as variation and invention by individual human bodies, who develop gestural *signature* or style in the process. Gesture is a *personal* set of skills, and it synthesizes practical, communicative, and cognitive functions: being able to index the surroundings or to depict a world by motions of the hands are also ways of knowing these worlds and of structuring them in meaningful ways so that others can reckon with them. (Streeck 2009: 203)

Streeck's understanding of gesture as *craft* or *praxis* underscores gesture not as an embodied practice that is prescribed or taught, but as one that is acquired through the everyday *praxis* of observation, practice, enactment and, importantly, reflection. Of necessity, the principle of repetition inherent in "praxis" produces variation in these gestural enactments. Streeck's imagination presupposes gesture in all its complexities – as "body language," in relation to psychic processes and as communicative apparatus – so that seemingly *simple* gestural enactments like the Afrobeat salute that invites minimal variation and requires virtually no practice, might be dismissed as "craft-less," i.e., requiring little or no craft. To this end, I will offer that Streeck's concept of *craft* should be understood for *simple* gestures (gestures that do not require complex movements to execute) as inhered in the labor of "structuring them in meaningful ways so that others can reckon with them" (Streeck 2009: 203). In addition, the complexity of the simple gesture might rest not only in the physiological processes that entail its execution, but also in the aggregation of ideas that it is capable of communicating – what it reveals about history, genealogy, society and formulations of power.

Perhaps most importantly, the potency of the simple gesture might be most fully appreciated in accounting for the agency invested in ascribing meaning to such a gesture at the level of a cultural collective. For Fela, this notion of *craft* can be found in the pedagogical aspects of his performance wherein he had to share political ideology with his skeptical audience. Tejumola Olaniyan aptly captures the tensions that attended Fela's use of performance as pedagogy: "A chief cynic himself, Fela never expected to convince the audience without a struggle. So he kept an array of rhetorical strategies to aid his task" (Olaniyan 2004: 213). Verbal cues, political rhetoric, quips, were among these strategies through which Fela immersed his audiences into the world of his politics. On a different level, the Afrobeat salute emerged as one of such embodied "rhetorical" strategies through which Fela acculturated his audiences into his leftist ideologies.

2.3 Tracing Origins/Tracing Spaces

I proceed here to map the genealogy of the Afrobeat salute by tracing some existing narratives around the history of the genre. I approach this endeavor totally cognizant of the epistemological disparities between the gestural and the textual as modes of preserving and/or knowing the past (Taylor 2003: 18–21). My intention here is, in fact, to highlight the limits of the narrative in order to make space for a different understanding, or mapping, of Afrobeat history – which does not end with the death and decay of Fela's body, but extends to a multitude of bodies through the apparatus of performance.

The beginnings of Afrobeat can be traced either to when Fela named it (Moore 2009),[5] or to the formative days of his politics when he encountered the Black Power Movement (BPM) in the United States in 1969.[6] Depending on the commentator, Afrobeat might even be historicized by examining the development of its form vis-à-vis musical influences, or by sketching, however tentatively, the evolution of its ideologies. Though the discrepancies between these diverse narrative charts might appear subtle, they reveal on a deeper level the nature of the narrator's investment in Fela's politics. For commentators who tend to think about Afrobeat more as a comprehensive political ideology than merely a musical style, the BPM and the mid-1970s might emerge as originary. The reference point goes further back (as far as the early 1960s) for commentators who are invested in the musicality of Afrobeat and its formal evolution.

Regardless of the narrative choices, these histories bear testament to the impact of a transatlantic exchange between the musician and the BPM, which was gathering momentum in the late 1960s. Even when concerned

---

5   Although Moore does not explicitly cite this naming as an origin, it is significant that he sets it before Fela's US encounter with the Black Power Movement, which suggests the author's intention to show Fela's self-refashioning before his famed travel.

6   Subtle contentions exist about the origin of Afrobeat. While the Black Power Movement (BPM) narrative endures among most scholars, others have suggested that Fela's radicalization was not a direct consequence of the BPM, but of his subsequent encounter with the Nigerian government upon his return in 1970. Olaniyan (2004) suggests that "Fela had indeed been groping for a new and revitalizing musical form and ideology well before the 1969 trip [to the United States]" (p. 41), and further that Fela's encounter with BPM did not immediately translate into the radicalism that Afrobeat would espouse later in the 1970s (p. 77).

with Afrobeat's musical history, one eventually encounters characters like James Brown, John Coltrane and Miles Davis along the way. Nonetheless, my investment here is in a more explicit connection between Afrobeat and the BPM. A cursory reading of the BPM and Fela's Afrobeat will yield productive insights into their shared anti-establishment, and pro-black ideological resonances. However, since ideology is in itself often fluid and contested, tracing the fine lines of ideological continuities from the BPM to Afrobeat will prove counterproductive. I propose that analyzing the movements at the level of their symbols might yield more fruitful, historiographical insights. It is in this sense that the body and the gestural emerge as important signifiers.

The clenched fist endures as the most symbolic parallel between Afrobeat and the BPM. This symbol maps, albeit tentatively, ideological continuities between these movements. Attempting to trace ideological continuities in this way is only thinkable given the concentration of Black Power activities in California in the late 1960s, at the time of Fela's visit. From the movement's logo, to organized protests, to casual salutations on the streets, the Black Power salute saturated almost every communication channel of the BPM. It is impossible to overstate the significance of the Black Power fist in advancing the BPM's agenda. The gesture marked who was in with the movement and who was not. In a most plebian sense, it represented racial solidarity. So much so, that the role of the body – the black body in the case of the BPM – in concentrating and transmitting political ideology becomes of crucial importance in historicizing the movement. By the end of the 1960s, the clenched fist was the embodied symbol of the BPM and became the image of solidarity even for non-black groups in the United States. Joseph Peniel highlights the adoption of the salute by members of the Asian American Civil Rights movement ("Yellow Power"), to show solidarity with a common Asian identity and with the BPM (Peniel 2006: 212). This suggests that the enactment of the BPM salute by Asian American bodies complicated (in a positive sense) the racial undertones of the protests at that historical moment. Beyond employing political rhetoric, black bodies during the BPM era represented and communicated the political urgency of the times in ways that sought to challenge hegemonic whiteness, as well as express aspects of the lived realities of blackness. With the help of the broadcast media, the protesting black body functioned as one of the more potent tools available to Black Power activists. And given that the state's reaction to the protests involved disciplining protesting bodies through surveillance, incarceration and/or punishment, the *living* black body during the BPM may be understood as always defiant if only for its ability to materialize the movement's ideologies by enacting the Black Power salute.

Along this line of thinking, it becomes safe to assert that a certain quality of omnipresence is inhered in the body's ability to transcend itself by transporting ideology through time and space, and between bodies. At the level of the body, therefore, blacks could claim for themselves a level of political autonomy. So potent is this notion of autonomy that its effects can neither be contained nor anticipated. When, for example, during the 1968 Mexico Olympic Games Tommy Smith and John Carlos enacted the Black Power salute on the gold and bronze medal stands in the full glare of the world, their bodies claimed for themselves a level of political autonomy, which was amplified by the power of broadcast and imaging technologies (Cogan & Kelso 2009). Some of the reactions of the Olympic Committee and the larger United States public highlight the shock and displeasure that the gesture elicited. Letters in the archive around the Carlos and Smith controversy, as well as opinions in the print media, range from praise of their heroic act – a sentiment that endures till date – to bitter criticisms that described the podium salute as a "blatant political manoeuvre," "Hitler-type salute," or "public display of petulance" (Henderson 2010: 80–1). This moment of "political manoeuvre" achieved the effect of "troubling" the most sacrosanct space of sporting excellence – the Olympic podium – with the plebian concerns of US racial politics. Henderson underscores the complexity of racial, political exigencies that the gesture captured: "The symbolic gesture encapsulated so many facets of the racial struggle in the United States in the late 1960s that it was open to a myriad of interpretations. Many of these interpretations, in fact, mixed competing or contradictory messages of the civil rights agenda" (ibid.). In many ways, therefore, the podium salute became both image and canvas: it simultaneously read as a visible extension of the Black Power struggle and became an image upon which larger Civil Rights claims could be impressed.[7] In this sense, the relationship between a gesture and the ideologies it purports

---

7   In "Fists of freedom," Dave Zirin examines the broad context for the protest as well as the variety of Civil Rights causes that the athletes hoped to project with the salute. According to Zirin, the athletes wanted "South Africa and Rhodesia banned from the games for their apartheid politics. They wanted more black coaches. They wanted International Olympic Committee President Avery Brundage held accountable for his open and virulent racism. They wanted Muhammed Ali … to have his title restored." The broad range of concerns attached to the salute is indicative of how a gesture can support a dominant racial ideology, but also be fluidly linked to specific political concerns.

to represent could be complex and, at times, tenuous. Yet, the power of gesture to communicate political ideology cannot be underestimated, as is evidenced in the public's reactions to Smith and Carlos's salute at the 1968 Olympic Games.

This idea of the body transcending itself in time and space might be understood as *corporeal transgression*. In this notion of transgression is implied the body's capacity to encode, concentrate and circulate political ideologies through performance within specific socio-political, historical and geographic contexts, in ways that trouble formulations of power. This idea of corporeal transgression also gestures toward the ways that the body explodes simple or singular narratives to which any one gesture could be arbitrarily fastened. In other words, since there is no one fixed meaning ascribable to any single gesture, and since meaning is itself not essentially self-evident in gesture, the onus of ascribing meaning to a gesture or imbuing it with meaning falls therefore upon the collective for whom the gesture must invite certain interpretations instead of others. To this end, performance studies scholar Richard Schechner contends that "There is no meaning inherent in objects or events treated as settled or finished 'things.' Meaning – and the bodies and objects and relations of which meaning is a function – is always unstable, shifting as circumstances and historical process shift" (Schechner 2000: 4).

The recent documentary *The Black Power Mixtape 1967–1975* reveals a variety of contexts within which the Black Power salute was enacted during the course of the Civil Rights movement. One particularly striking moment in the film is a video recording immediately following the 1971 Attica Prison Revolution in Buffalo, New York. The footage features inmates brandishing their fists in the Black Power salute at the roving cameras. Despite the state's "disciplining" of the prisoners' bodies through confinement and regimen, the prisoners yet exerted a level of autonomy over their bodies and the meanings that they would communicate – resolution instead of retreat. Enacting the salute in that historical moment leaves little margin for misrepresenting the political ethos that the gesture appealed to. Compared to the "free" blacks on the streets of the United States, the salute by these prisoners registers a slightly nuanced idea of defiance. Similarly, it bore a different meaning when made by the body of Fela, a struggling Nigerian musician and a postcolonial subject who observed the revolution from the sidelines.

Figure 2.1. Fela performing at a concert. Photo: Femi Osunla.

2.4 The Black Power Fist and Afrobeat

Fela's 10-month visit to California meant that he had caught the fire of the Black Power Movement. While he assimilated the general political spirit at the time, his romance with Sandra Izsadore, an activist and herself a member of the Black Panther Party, has been credited as the immediate catalyst for his revolutionary ideas. Their romance is well documented in print as well as in performance (for example, in *Fela!*, the Broadway musical based on the life of the musician). Sandra gracefully shared some of the details of their encounter:

> I had just completed [*The Autobiography of Malcolm X*] and I gave it to him to read.... There were so many things I shared with Fela: novels, poetry, politics, history, music. Poems by Nikki Giovanni, The Last Poets (you know, "Niggers Are Afraid of Revolution"), Angela Davis, Martin Luther King, Stokeley Carmichael, Jesse Jackson, Nina Simone's "Four Women," Miles Davis.... It was something that happened over a period of time. It was constant talking every night, every day, over a period of six months. Politics. Love. Love and Politics. Just the two of us. (Moore 2009: 95–6)

The corpus of texts, artifacts and stories that Sandra exposed Fela to constitute a fair representation of black revolutionary tradition in the 20th-century United States. The blend of politics, romance and pedagogy between the lovers would help cement the productivity of their encounter. In countless interviews, Fela has referred to this relationship as one of the defining moments in his development as an artist and a revolutionary.

In addition to catching the Black Power fire, Fela also incorporated the symbolic Black Power fist in his budding performance style. It would become a principal mode of nonverbal communication between himself and his audience, as well as with fans and collaborators. And even though Fela offered almost no insights into the significance of the salute, the gesture's conspicuity in Afrobeat readily betrays its significance. It is interesting to contemplate whether Fela's relative silence on the gesture – in relation to its hypervisibility – might be understood as him taking as self-evident the significance of the salute.

Upon return to Nigeria in 1970, Fela introduced the salute to his audience there in hopes of spreading the fire. To his utter dismay, he did not receive the desired "Black Power" feedback since his audience was untrained at reading its meaning. Furthermore, they did not share the urgency of the revolutionary racial politics that imbued the gesture with its potency in the United States. Idowu Mabinuori recounts that Fela's "first appearance at the 'Afro-Spot' was a pointer to the difficulty of the task ahead of him. He greeted the audience with the Black Power salute, but there was no response from the crowd – because at the time, they did not know what a Black Power salute stood for" (Mabinuori 1997: 36). The gulf between the audience's initial reactions to Fela's salute at the time and their subsequent acceptance of the gesture as part of the Afrobeat experience is indicative of the *craft* that attended the task of aggregating intelligible meaning to the salute for his Nigerian audience. It follows, therefore, that as his music gained more acceptance in the early 1970s, Fela's audience, who were mostly underclass citizens of Lagos state, came to accept the salute as part of the Afrobeat experience.

The phenomenon of offer and reciprocation that attended this gestural exchange can be best explained within the framework of ritual. Theatre scholar, Stephen Di Benedetto, offers a productive way of understanding the osmotic process through which Fela's salute might have gained a hold on the bodies of his audience. Di Benedetto suggests that by "manipulating" an audience's expectations or repeating specific themes and motifs, artists actively shape social behavior (Di Benedetto 2012: 102). This hypothetical process of offer and reciprocation (or manipulation as Di Benedetto frames it) of the Black Power salute in Fela's Afrobeat can equally be inferred in

Fela's Clenched Fists **49**

Olaniyan's description of the composition of Fela's primary audience – the suburban underclass – and their reaction to his early Afrobeat:

> These were (and still are) the people whose faces and actions never make the news except as lawbreakers; they are never the subject of great works of art except as caricatures. Fela took their daily social lives and artistically – musically – monumentalized it in their very own language. They recognized themselves in the music and embraced it wholeheartedly. (Olaniyan 2004: 59)

Fela's commitment to the underclass experience and their appreciation of his efforts meant that Afrobeat achieved a kind of followership that was

Figure 2.2. Album cover for Fela Kuti's *Expensive Shit*, 1975.

uncommon to other Nigerian musical forms at the time. Afrobeat's form and distinctive ideological slant meant that ingraining the idea of the Black Power salute in the audience's consciousness would simply be a matter of time and repetition.

Randall Grass also highlights Fela's active role in familiarizing his audience with the salute by performing it for the press and in pictures on his album covers (Grass 1986: 133). Fela's 1975 *Expensive Shit* album, following his release from prison, bears a cover picture of him enacting the Black Power salute along with about 20 of *his* women; everyone topless. This image could be read as both communal defiance and a challenge to the unrelenting government.

Although tracing the distinct evolution of the Afrobeat salute proves difficult, we know that by the early 1980s, when Fela's notoriety had entered into the realm of legend, the gesture had become a formal feature of Afrobeat. At this time, it had become "indigenous" to the outlook of Afrobeat and had found a degree of consonance with Fela's ideologies. However, to suggest that the Afrobeat salute in the Afrika Shrine (Fela's nightclub) bore a one-to-one relationship to its Black Power cousin in the United States would be dubious, to say the least. For one, unlike the "original" Black Power salute that involved one fist, Fela had modified the gesture to include the second fist. This upgrade had some historiographical and semiotic implications. Historiographically, the second fist has helped reify narratives of Fela as "inventor" and "originator" not just of Afrobeat, but also of "Black" revolutionary thinking in contemporary West Africa. The inclusion of the second fist becomes one example of Fela's "inventiveness." In addition, such a narrative potentially undercuts the symbolic affinities between the Black Power movement and Fela's Afrobeat. I will contend, however, that the most significant implication of the double fists was that it became possible to simultaneously insert Fela into and yet abstract him from subsequent enactments of the salute. Artistic works such as paintings and murals could invoke Fela simply by presenting the outline of *a* body with both fists held up. In this system of signs, the Afrobeat salute becomes a script that momentarily conjures Fela into being.

The transition of the Black Power salute from the streets of Los Angeles, California, to Fela's notorious Afrika Shrine illustrates the body's ability to not only *transgress* the geographies of space through gestures, but also to amplify political meaning in the process of transgression. Recounting her first visit to Nigeria since meeting Fela in California, Sandra Izsadore hinted at the body's power to encode and transfer "racial" meaning across space transatlantically. She recalled: "I was just ready to absorb all of the Black I could get and bring it back to America to spread. And if you could have seen the Black I took back and how it manifested there in my friends…" (Moore 2009: 96). Although Sandra refers primarily to her experience of Nigeria, her description confers legibility to the body as a container of racialized consciousness. In this vein, Richard Schechner advises that we "pay closer attention to behaviors, to actions enacted, and of course to the complex social, political, ideological, and historical contexts not merely surrounding behavior, but profoundly interacting with it" (Schechner 2000: 4).

Significantly, the body remains a crucial component to the articulation of Fela's ideologies. Outside the Shrine, the Afrobeat salute continued to hint at a connection between US blackness and Nigeria's postcolonial condition. In the Shrine, it played an important political and aesthetic role in heightening the political significance of the performative present. The Afrobeat salute ritually concluded every session-long performance of hypnotic dance, call and response music, inflammatory political commentary and haywire rhythms. The salute brought it all together: it marked the closing of the performance. It became the denouement of Fela's scathing satire. It recalled everyone to the potency of the performative present. It functioned to reconcile popular entertainment with political ideology in communion with the bodies present. Fela has himself declared, "Afrobeat is an occasion for politics because that is the occasion we are in now, people suffering" (Collins 2009: 135). Thus, the salute reminded the audience that Afrobeat existed in the realm of the counter-discursive. The gesture served as a stark reminder that the body is a site of struggle whereon oppression, characteristically imagined as being *outside* of the Afrika Shrine, stifles the corporate desire for citizenship among the Nigerian underclass.

Additionally, when Fela enacted the double-fisted Afrobeat salute, the upward stretch that ensued left an exaggeratedly lanky outline of the musician's body, which fed off the Nigerian social imagination of the "thin" body. In a culture where body mass has a curious bearing on class and well-being, looking lean conjures specific class associations. In this thinking, the "lean" body is readily associated with suffering, lack, and deprivation. Therefore, in dialogue with a predominantly underclass audience for whom lived experience remained crucial to knowledge claims, Fela's meager frame, accentuated by repeated enactments of the salute, helped validate his body's communication of the revolutionary ideologies of his Afrobeat music. To put it differently, Fela's body as an ontological category helped reinforce whatever claims he would make about ideologies steeped in concerns around race and class.

2.5 "Music Written in Blood"

By 1981, the year of Fela's Paris performance that is documented in *Fela in Concert*, an hour-long video, the salute had become a significant part of his performances. At the beginning of the concert, Fela came on stage and sauntered playfully downstage to salute his Paris audience. He then proceeded to salute people on the left and right sections of the auditorium. The informality with which he enacted the salute, wearing a smirk on his face, suggested that he intended the salute merely to acknowledge the audience. This stands in stark contrast to his 1984 Glastonbury Concert in England documented in *Fela Live* (2000), where most members of his Egypt 80 band jointly partook in the salute, in a more ritualized manner. By 1984, the salute was already popular even with his European audiences with some of them frantically enacting the salute as Fela arrived onstage. The Afrobeat salute had filtered through the presence of Fela to European bodies, who by now were already familiar with Fela's radical ideology. This offers an interesting notion of political solidarity: in this instance, the body *transgresses* race in its ability to broadcast meaning.

Before he began his 1984 concert, Fela reminded his audience of the danger of his cause: "All of you cannot really imagine the horrors I have to go through to get on this stage this evening (he smiles)."[8] Fela's opening caveat served as a reminder to both himself and the audience that the ideologies that underlay his music yielded backlashes – and these were often literal lashes to the body that entailed corporeal pain. Such moments in the life and politics of the musician could present useful evidence for the painful harmony between his ideology and his "saluting" body. Michael Veal and David Niles provide a particularly insightful review of the 1981 Paris concert, paying particular attention to the visible impact that Fela's anti-establishment politics had on his body and those of his musical collaborators onstage:

> In spite of the enthusiastic reception, the concert was not one of Fela's strongest. His well-documented personal difficulties, including a murderous military attack on his compound, the death of his mother (a well-known anti-colonialist and women's rights activist), and the defection of his Afrika 70 band variously took their toll on his health, concentration, and musical output. (Veal and Niles 1999: 197)

---

8   *Fela Live: Fela Anikulapo-Kuti and the Egypt 80 Band* (2000).

As Fela's troubles with the Nigerian military government left visible marks on his body, the musician's ideas left the indelible impression of an "undying" patriot in the minds of his followers. In other words, his body's capacity to endure pain and punishment in brutality and imprisonment had some bearing on the public's reception of his radical ideas. In an attempt to explain the intersections between embodiment, pain and affect in Fela's art, journalist Chris May described Afrobeat as "Music written in blood," a description that drives home the corporeal repercussions of Fela's ideologies. His double fists became at once a symbol of solidarity among his core collaborators – his wives, band members and crew – as well as the members of the larger Afrobeat community. To date, the gesture remains tangible evidence of the cult followership of Fela's ideology. By virtue of embodiment in the performance moment, the audience becomes implicated on a certain level in Fela's politics and is recruited as a partaker in Afrobeat's ideologies.

2.6 Repurposing the Gesture: The Occupy Nigeria Movement

Despite Fela's demise in August 1997, the concerns of his works remain germane to contemporary Nigerian politics. Much of this has been attributed to not only the musician's bitter critique of corruption and coloniality, but also to his uncanny ability to articulate complex social and political processes by means of folksy language and popular idioms. The bitter lyrics of his multiple albums remain the primary medium through which Fela lives in the public imagination. Even as Fela has enjoyed global recognition, the Afrobeat salute endures as the more subtle medium though which his radical ideas are preserved. In this final section, I examine a recent political event – the Occupy Nigeria Movement – in which the Afrobeat salute functioned in the service of reanimating Fela's ideologies.

On the January 1, 2012, the Federal Government of Nigeria announced the removal of subsidies on the nation's oil. This meant a 120 per cent rise in the price of fuel, from N65 to about N140 per liter. Although the government had conducted a town hall meeting to solicit the support of stakeholders in the oil sector and members of the public, the eventual removal of oil subsidies was no less a shock to the people. One drastic consequence of this policy would be an exponential rise in the cost of living that would particularly hit medium- to low-income-earning Nigerians. The President's announcement of the policy change on New Year's Day (supposedly a day of celebration), compounded by the general economic hardship, gave birth to the Occupy Nigeria Movement, the biggest political revolution in Nigeria's history.

Drawing immediate inspiration from the ongoing Arab Spring and the global Occupy movements, Nigerians took their protests to the streets under the umbrella of Occupy Nigeria. The protests took place in all six geopolitical zones of Nigeria, but manifested in their most spectacular forms in Lagos, the commercial capital of Nigeria and Fela's principal *playing* field. The protests in Lagos took the format of a rally at the state-sponsored Gani Fawehinmi Freedom Park.[9] Even though the rally was centralized at the park, protests were being held simultaneously in different areas of the state. Significantly, though, once the movement kicked off, Afrobeat emerged as the unofficial theme music of the protests. For the most part, Fela maintained a prominent presence in the protests, even posthumously. Not were his songs booming from loudspeakers, he manifested in the bodies of the protesters through a variety of embodied practices ranging from outright impersonation to symbolic association by enacting the Afrobeat salute. In one video, we saw a young man appear in underpants (one of Fela's signature costumes) and facial painting in what was an obvious attempt at invoking the late musician's presence. For full effect, this protester occasionally brandished the salute to a teeming crowd of admirers.

I contend that in invoking Fela through the double-fisted salute, protesters were not merely expressing identification with the musician's ideologies, but they were also mobilizing Fela to historicize their claims to being oppressed by the Nigerian ruling class. In another video recording of the protests[10] – recorded by an independent videographer – protesters are seen dancing and chanting in procession to Fela's 1978 classic, "Shuffering and Shmiling." In "Shuffering and Shmiling," Fela highlights the cyclical hardships that ordinary Nigerians suffer in the wake of a failed polity, as well as the complicity of religious leaders in perpetuating the subjugation

9   Gani Fawehinmi was a famed Nigerian human rights lawyer and activist, who dedicated his practice to fighting for justice for the underprivileged Nigerian populace. This park was commissioned in his memory by the Lagos State government, with the laudable intention of creating a space where citizens could express their civic right to conduct public protests. However, I think that the government neither anticipated nor welcomed the scale and intensity of the Occupy Nigeria movement.
10 See "Occupy Nigeria: Day 4 protest in Lagos," youtube.

of the masses, in order to maintain a hegemony of the elites. In the Occupy Nigeria protests, "Shuffering and Shmiling" took on a slightly nuanced and haunting character. First, the time lag between the song's original release in 1978 and the 2012 protests exposed the pathology of institutionalized corruption, even as it simultaneously provided impetus for the mass action. Second, in enacting the Afrobeat salute along with the song, protesters became for a brief moment living bodies of the late Afrobeat musician. The gesture reanimated Fela's ideologies, refracted them through the protesting bodies and amplified the urgency of the protests. Dance scholar Susan Leigh Foster suggests that when political subjects "fathom injustice, organize to protest, craft a tactic, and engage in action, [their] bodies read what is happening and articulate their imaginative rebuttal. In so doing, they demonstrate to themselves and all those watching that something can be done" (Foster 2003: 412). Nigerians' willful reanimation of Fela through gesture was one of the ways that this "imaginary rebuttal" manifested during the movement. Knowing the history of Fela's spats with the government, the protesters mobilized the music and gesture to stage a spectacle that troubled the national conscience. On a certain level, the gesture by multiple bodies "exhumed" Fela and, though unspoken, allowed the protesters make political claims not only about oil price but also about a collective ability to invoke the dead in the service of the living at a time of national crisis. Conversely, this invocation underscores some of the ways that gesture, in this case the Afrobeat salute, can inscribe a future world as well as transport political meanings in nuanced ways.

2.7 Conclusion

In this chapter, I have traced a tentative genealogy of the Afrobeat salute from the Black Power movement up to Fela's assimilation of the gesture into his music and politics. With this narrative, I make the case that the Afrobeat salute has played a crucial role in cementing Fela's ideologies in the Nigerian public imaginary, carrying forward elements of the racial politics of its Black Power extraction. I have discussed the nuanced ways in which the salute embedded Fela's ideologies within the landscape of the 2012 Occupy Nigeria movement, as well as in the larger terrain of contemporary Nigerian politics. Since the salute persists as one of the currencies of participation for Afrobeat, we can expect that it will remain an important medium for memorializing Fela as well as constitute a primary entrée through which newcomers can identify with his ideologies. By implication, living bodies enacting the gesture, whether in Fela's Afrika Shrine or on the streets protesting a rise in oil price, constitute active agents not just in remembering the late musician, but also in grafting his ideologies in contemporary social realities. In a complex process of gesture crafting, transfer and identification, the Afrobeat salute helped forge Fela's identity, reify his politics and sustain his political ideologies.

References

The Black Power Mixtape 1967–1975 (2011). Directed by Göran Olsson. DVD.
Bourdieu, P. (1986). The forms of capital. In G. John (ed.), *Handbook of Theory and Research for Sociology of Education*. Richardson, New York: Greenwood.
Cogan, B., & T. Kelso. (2009). 1968 Olympics and Black Power Salute. *Encyclopedia of Politics, the Media, and Popular Culture*. Santa Barbara, CA: Greenwood Press. Gale Virtual Reference Library website, accessed October 20, 2012.
Collins, J. (2009). *Fela: Kalakuta Notes*. Amsterdam: KIT Publishers.
Di Benedetto, S. (2012). Sensual engagements: Understanding theories of the senses and their potential application within theatre practice. In M. Alrutz, J. Listengarten & M. Van Duyn Wood (eds.), *Playing with Theory in Theatre Practice*. New York: Palgrave Macmillan.
Fela in Concert. Directed by David Niles (1981). VHS videotape, 57 minutes, 1991. New York: Lagoon Productions.
Fela Live: Fela Anikulapo-Kuti and the Egypt 80 Band. (2000). DVD. United States: Yazoo.
Foster, S.L. (2003). Choreographies of protest. *Theatre Journal*, 55(3), Dance (Oct.), 395–412.
Grass, R.F. (1986). Fela Anikulapo-Kuti: The art of an Afrobeat rebel. *Drama Review: TDR*, 30(1), 131–48. http://dx.doi.org/10.2307/1145717
Henderson, S. (2010). "Nasty demonstrations by negroes": The place of the Smith–Carlos podium salute in the Civil Rights movement. *Bulletin of Latin American Research*, 29, 78–92. http://dx.doi.org/10.1111/j.1470-9856.2009.00339.x
Mabinuori, I. (1997). *Why Blackman Carry Shit*. Paris: Florent-Massot.
May, C. (1977). Music written in blood: Fela Anikulapo-Kuti, the Afro-Rock giant they cannot silence. *Black Music*, May 1977, 22–5.
Moore, C. (2009). *Fela: This Bitch of a Life*. Chicago: Lawrence Hill Books.
Occupy Nigeria: Day 4 protest in Lagos, Tina Armstrong-Ogbonna, http://www.youtube.com/watch?v=owK-eXcdYIk, accessed August 12, 2012.
Olaniyan, T. (2004). *Arrest the Music: Fela and His Rebel Art and Politics*. Ibadan: Bookcraft.
Peniel, J. (2006). *The Black Power Movement: Rethinking the Civil Rights-Black Power Era*. Abingdon, Oxon: Routledge.

Schechner, R. (2000). Post post-structuralism. *Drama Review*, 44(3), 4–7. http://dx.doi.org/10.1162/10542040051058573

Streeck, J. (2009). *Gesturecraft: The Manu-facture of Meaning*. Amsterdam, Philadelphia: John Benjamins Publishing Company. http://dx.doi.org/10.1075/gs.2

Taylor, D. (2003). *The Archive and the Repertoire: Performing Cultural Memory in the Americas*. Durham, NC: Duke University Press. http://dx.doi.org/10.1215/9780822385318

Veal, M., & D. Niles (1999). Fela in concert. *Ethnomusicology*, 43(1), 197. http://dx.doi.org/10.2307/852710

Zirin, Dave. (2008). Fists of freedom. *The Progressive* 72(9), 16. Biography Reference Bank (H.W. Wilson) website, Web. 27, accessed September 27, 2012.

3
Dressed-to-Kill: Don Mattera's *Sophiatown*

Michael Sharp[1]

> I speak through my clothes. – Umberto Eco, 1973

3.1 Introduction

The sartorial rebellions of the Teddy Boys and the Mods and Rockers of working-class Britain and the glam look of the Punks and the Goths of London's housing estates represent to many an aesthetic of nihilism which defines a style of nonverbal behavior. The unspoken lingo of secondhand Edwardian jackets and Brylcreem, of razor-sharp suits and Vespas, of bovver boots and "liberty spikes," of piercings and bondage gear, point toward a poetics of swagger where menace struts with fashion to shock the perceived complacency of authority. The "implicitly coherent," while "explicitly bewildering, systems" of dress, Hebdige (1979: 103) suggests in his assessment of Claude Levi-Strauss' *The Savage Mind*, perfectly equipped these aggressive fashionistas to contemplate and respond to the world about them. If one applies Levi-Strauss' manipulation of the French word bricoleur – something analogous to a jack-of-all-trades, then counter-cultural groups like the Teddy Boys make use of "the tools, objects, and knowledge they have readily available to find a solution to a problem" (ibid.). In the

---

1 Michael Sharp is Professor of English & Caribbean Studies at the University of Puerto Rico. Educated in Britain and the United States, he received his PhD from the University of Wisconsin-Madison. He has been a Faculty Associate of the International School of Theory in the Humanities at the University of Santiago de Compostela in Spain and has taught at Harvard University as well as at Binghamton, Wisconsin, and in Scotland, Greece and Portugal. His research centers on literature written in English in Africa and the Caribbean, and his poetry has been published on both sides of the Atlantic.

case of the Tsotsi gangs of South Africa, the idea of bricolage gains credence in Don Mattera's play *Sophiatown: Coming of Age in South Africa* (first performed at The Market Theatre in Johannesburg in 1986) as gang members used their made-to-measure presence to not only dominate their turf but also to "re-dress" their racial disadvantage under apartheid into political action.

3.2 Clothing and Visual Language

Observation of nonverbal communication and behavior began in earnest with Charles Darwin's *The Expression of the Emotions in Man and Animals* (1872). Arguing that he was "superior to the common run of men in noticing things which easily escape attention" and "observing them carefully" (Ekman 1998: unpaginated), Darwin recognized that all mammals express emotion through facial expressions. While he had tentatively touched on such instinctive behavior in *On the Origin of Species by Natural Selection* (1859), Darwin was confident enough, after the publication of *Descent of Man* (1871), to write unequivocally that such emotions as suffering and weeping, anxiety and grief, hatred and anger, disdain and contempt were common to both animal and man. Darwin's observations gave rise to research in the 20th century on the categories, consequences and languages of nonverbal communication and resulted, most importantly, in B.F. Skinner's work on observable behavior and Ray Birdwhistell's studies in kinesics or body motion.

Apropos the importance of clothing, Fred Davis prefaces his discussion in *Fashion, Culture, and Identity* (1992) with a quotation from Oscar Wilde's *The Picture of Dorian Gray* (1890): "It is only shallow people who do not judge by appearances. The true mystery of the world is the visible, not the invisible." Asking the question "Do Clothes Speak?" Davis wonders if the notion that clothes have their own visual language is "nothing more than a cliché" (Davis 1992: 2). If it is a truism, however, then the off-the-rack choice of the Teddy Boy from south London attempting to buy status by outdoing the tailored extravagances of the Edwardian toff is speaking in bespoke tongues in order to be valued in a society which had disdained him for his accent, his skills and his background. Similarly, the Skinhead in his "Never Mind the Bollocks" T-shirt and Doc Martens clashes viciously with a Britain that marginalizes him without understanding or forgiveness for his societal indiscretions. If clothing is an outward interpretation of a counter-culture's signs, then its visible language speaks, as Roland Barthes

Figure 3.1. Sophiatown Tsotsi. Drawing by Ann Albuyeh from a poster advertising a performance of *Sophiatown*.

suggests in *The Fashion System* (1967), the invisible dread of those seemingly unable to throw off the uniform that society forces them to wear. As well as the embedded signs of nonverbal communication in Don Mattera's memoir *Sophiatown* – posture, stance, gesture, threat – the importance of clothes to the Tsotsi gangs was paramount.

Despite news coverage of Britain's subculture of Teddy Boys (also nicknamed British Cosh Boys) screened in the cinemas of greater Johannesburg in the 1950s and the potential influence of their adaptation of Edwardian styles, it was the gangster clothing presented in the American movies of the 1940s and '50s which spoke to Tsotsi youth. The spiv suits of American gangsters could enhance the dangerous posture of the Tsotsi wide-boy more than "Slim Jim" ties and suede brothel-creepers of the Teddy Boys.

While Teddy Boy behavior often included racial attacks on West Indian communities in Britain or ripping up the seats of local cinemas, Tsotsi notoriety centered on internecine fights for street-corner dominance in the Johannesburg townships, which eventually turned – in the case of Mattera and his gang, the Vultures – to confronting the condition of South Africa under apartheid, addressing old scores not in the name of township territory but in the name of liberation of the country.

3.3   Literature of the Underbelly

There is a paucity of literature relating to firsthand accounts of gang violence in the townships surrounding Johannesburg in the late 1940s and '50s. This may simply be explained by the restrictions placed on non-whites in South Africa after the National Party was elected in 1948. Since Clive Glaser's ground-breaking study in 2000, of the Tsotsi gangs in the Witwatersrand between 1935 and 1976, there has been a small body of literature in books whose subject is peripheral to the phenomenon of the Tsotsis. Don Mattera's *Sophiatown* (1987) is the first autobiographical account of the life of a Tsotsi gang-leader in the years following the implementation of racial segregation and the concomitant policies which controlled all aspects of the lives of South Africa's whites, blacks and coloreds.

While it may seem presumptuous to suggest that the life of a criminal, detailed by Mattera in his memoir, could be "turned" around both socially and politically, one need only think of Jean Genet, dandy, dramatist, poet, novelist, thief and "thug of genius" (De Beauvoir 1969: 594) who turned from delinquency and a life on the lam to become the author of such celebrated books as *Our Lady of the Flowers* and *The Thief's Journal* and a political activist who championed the Palestinians and the Black Panthers. Genet's flamboyant life of crime parallels Mattera's, as both men from disadvantaged beginnings were able to survive, as if by some Darwinian fluke, to become writers of significance in the 20th century because of their resolve to escape the determining environments they faced.

In *The Making of the English Working Class*, E.P. Thompson urges historians to write the histories of not only Great Men and Great Places but also of the "blind alleys, the lost causes and the losers" and rescue them from "the enormous condescension of posterity" (Thompson 1968: 13). The "blind alleys" of Johannesburg's Sophiatown in the 1950s are described by the short-story writer Can Temba in "Through Shakespeare's Africa" as counter-cultural cul-de-sacs of "action … passion [and] lasciviousness" (Temba 2006: 131). In suggesting the cut-throat violence of a Jacobean drama, Temba's remark was fuelled by Anthony Sampson's observation that "Sophiatown had all the exuberant youth of Shakespeare's London. It was the same upstart slum with people coming from a primitive country life to the tawdry sophistication of the city's fringes. Death and the police state were round the corner: and there was the imminent stage direction: *Exeunt with bodies ...*" (Sampson 1956: 80). The fraternity of black writers who wrote for *Drum*, Africa's most courageous magazine of the 1950s, took it upon themselves to "penetrate behind the high wall of apartheid" while not blurring "the stark realities of the African situation" (Sampson 1956: 11). In what was "almost an obsession with crime, gangsters, thugs, and Tsotsis" (Nichol 1991: 42), many of the young hoods of Sophiatown, their fashionable togs, their body talk, and their studied identities were rescued by *Drum* from "the enormous condescension of posterity." The South African poet Don Mattera was one of those Tsotsi gangsters whose art and individuality were forged on the cruel anvil of Sophiatown's forbidding streets.

3.4 Boss of the Vultures

In *Sophiatown*, Mattera writes that he was brought up "locked in a fraternal embrace of filth and felony," in a slum "inhabited by an estimated 200,000 people of different ethnic backgrounds who lived tightly-knit, mixing cultures, traditions and superstitions in a manner perhaps unique in Southern Africa" (Mattera 1987: 49). For Mattera, Sophiatown was a place of "subtle exploitations" where "a five penny loaf would be sliced into twelve or fifteen pieces and sold at a penny a piece," where a "single lavatory, and one tap were shared by 150 to 200 residents," where "people and dogs relieved themselves against the same walls and put their mouths under the same taps," where "beneath the same tree" they had "their brief sexual encounters" (Mattera 1987: 50).

Angry streets determined the way that Mattera was to live as he moseyed out of necessity into larceny, intimidation, violence, murder and imprisonment as a gangster *don* of terror who understood that to survive Sophiatown's "Bullet Corner" and "Murder Street" (Sampson 1956: 112) was to cheat the deterministic laws of the slum. As Karl Marx noted in *A Contribution to the Critique of Political Economy* (1859), the environment makes the man, and Mattera's memoir is a telling commentary on both the accumulation of brief riches and the thinking and the support which hastened his escape from the "blind alleys" and "lost causes" of his violent youth. In 1951, when he formed the Vultures as protection against the township bullies,[2] "the white world," as Jack Kerouac remembered in his own memoir *On the Road* (1957), had not offered Mattera "enough ecstasy … not enough life, joy, kicks, darkness, music, not enough night" (Kerouac 1957: 161).

A second-generation "bi-racial" man from a broken home, Mattera was the leader of a gang of Tsotsis who took their name from Henry Watt's *Where Vultures Fly* (1951), a British film about ivory poaching in East Africa. Sampson notes that the Vultures were part of what was called "the Chaka complex" named after the Zulu king who "massacred defeated tribes and ruled his regiments with iron discipline." During the Second World War, Hitler – "a kind of hero to the *tsotsis*" – reminded people of Chaka, not least because the "all white" South African Armed Forces were involved in the hostilities in Europe (Sampson 1956: 111). As boss of the Vultures, it was a "risky business refusing him [Mattera] anything" (Mattera 1987: 3): sex, favors outstanding, offers of protection, clothes, money – all the benefits of being a Tsotsi don.

3.5 Dressing to Kill

The everyday reality for nearly all the black readers of *Drum*, Sampson wrote, depended on "keeping on the right side of gangsters." The townships in the vicinity of Johannesburg, a city with one of the highest murder rates in the world in 1950, were "largely ruled by criminals who had 'the big money, the big cars, the best girls.'" If they were offended, Sampson mused, "they will beat you up. If you bring a case against them, they will beat up the witnesses. If you cause them any trouble they will kill you. At the inquest, the witnesses will be absent" (Sampson 1956: 96).

One of the first crime articles that *Drum* published was on the Tsotsis. Describing them as "young small-time criminals who often have respectable jobs during the day" and who supplemented their earnings with "handbag snatching, shoplifting, housebreaking or robbery by assault," Sampson, wary of what he was getting into, had to hire a young saxophonist called Spike to "pose for a picture" for the magazine. When Spike appeared at the *Drum* offices in downtown Johannesburg, he was wearing "*Tsotsi* rig,

---

2   Mike Nichol records that Mattera told him that "Older guys used to pick on us. They would send us to town to fetch cigarette butts with lipstick on, white women's lipstick. They would spit in the sand and tell us to complete the errand before the spit was dry" (1991: 59).

with very narrow 'sixteen-bottom' trousers, a long floppy coat, a bright scarf tucked into it, and a slouch hat." Taken in by Spike's acting ability, his home-grown cool, Sampson records his staff writer, Henry Nxumalo, retorted: "He wasn't acting. You don't think he could live as well as that if he wasn't a *Tsotsi*?" (Sampson 1956: 98).

According to Glaser, "the term *Tsotsi* entered township vocabulary around 1943–1944" and "the word referred to a style of narrow-bottomed trousers that became popular among urban African youth in the early 1940's" (Glaser 2000: 50). To be in fashion, street hoods from Sophiatown had to wear drain-pipe *tsotsis*, perhaps a corruption of the African-American *zoot-suit*. This fashion, Glaser writes, became popular after the influential 1943 musicals *Cabin in the Sky* directed by Vincente Minnelli and *Stormy Weather* directed by Andrew L. Stone, both with African-American casts, were screened in the Johannesburg townships between 1945 and 1950. A Tsotsi rig-out initially distinguished its black lumpen male as urban and "with-it," but the semi-Faustian plot of *Cabin in the Sky*, for example, seemed to encourage township youth toward a hedonistic, do-nothing life.[3] Eventually, Glaser writes, "*Tsotsi* became synonymous with *skelm* or 'villain' or 'trickster,' and referred generally to someone who is disrespectful towards elders, laws, and employment" (Glaser 2000: 51). Dick Hebdige's description of Teddy Boys captures the "swaggering machismo – that quaint combination of chauvinism ... and sudden violence" (Hebdige 1979: 83) that emphasized what the novelist Angela Carter called an "iconography of hopelessness" (quoted in Hebdige 1979: 150) that articulates the body language of the dressed-to-kill street-corner dandy in Sophiatown.

As the Tsotsi phenomenon proliferated in the Johannesburg area, criminal gangs "constituted the *core* of the subculture" (Glaser 2000: 53). Young males who wore tight trousers, drank alcohol, smoked *dagga* (cannabis), and spoke Tsotsitaal[4] which gave them ostensibly a secret lingo in which they could converse with each other without fear of being generally understood. Thus rigged out, the Tsotsi wannabe could sashay his way around the "hood" and eventually be received into membership of a gang as if he were joining a church or a Masonic temple.

---

3   In the movie, however, Little Joe's pact with Lucifer Junior is sentimentally dissolved as a dream, and he and Petunia begin a happy, storybook life together – something hardly in keeping with the hand-to-mouth existence of the average street heavy.
4   Tsotsitaal has been described as an Afrikaans-based creole which originated in the diggers' camps of the goldfields of the Transvaal in the 1880s.

By 1950, Glaser discerns three different types of gangs: "'big shot' gangs, 'small-time' criminal gangs, and noncriminal street-corner networks" (Glaser 2000: 54). There were, he writes, "only three 'real' gangs during the 1950s: the Americans, the Spoilers, and the Msomis" (Glaser 2000: 56). While the "Big Three" were well known on the Reef, he concedes that others, including Mattera's Vultures in Sophiatown, could also be placed in the "big time" category with the Black Caps, the Jakes Gang and the Berliners. Sampson notes that the Americans took their name from the American clothes, "straw hats, elegant cardigans, brown and white shoes and narrow blue trousers called 'Bogarts'" because Humphrey Bogart liked blue pinstripe suits (Sampson 1956: 106) and, as Raymond Chandler once said, the actor could look "tough without his gun" (Chandler 1997: 217). In addition "they drove Buicks, and girls clustered around them" (Sampson 1956: 106). In ex-*Drum* editor Sylvester Stein's *Who Killed Mr. Drum* (1999), an investigation into the killing of the investigative reporter Henry Nxumalo ("Mr. Drum"), the chapters are interspersed with original advertisements run by *Drum* to tickle the well-cut fancy of any upwardly mobile Tsotsi: fancy band and multi-flex felt Baronet Hats from the House of Dorian, All Spice Browns from the shoe-maker John Drake, Pandora Permanent Hair Strate, Dr. Pagel's Pills for "smashing strength and glowing health," Lewis' "Two Action MASTER PILLS," Ever Ready Batteries because "Streets **ARE** safe when you can see" (Stein 1999: unpaginated). Not every gang could boast such good taste. Sampson writes, for example, that the Russians gang from the slums of Newclare, near Sophiatown, were Basutos and came from the independent Basutoland. While they often wore Baronet hats and gabardine trousers, they wore "large blankets draped around them, defiant in their very design" (Sampson 1956: 110).

In addition to the Americans' home-grown expensive clothing, often stolen from the white community and offloaded "back-door,"[5] Rob Nixon writes that Kort Boy, a Bogart aficionado and founder member of the Americans, credited MGM "for his initial schooling in knife-work." In an interview, Kort Boy (George Mbalweni) says that his gang "used to wear American clothes, like Palm Beach, Palm Dale, Magregor Shirts, Magregor trousers, Florsheim shoes, Stetson hats" but that he "used to specialize in straw hats like Frank Sinatra" (Nixon 1994: 32). Dismissing

---

5   Sampson writes: "'Back-door' was one of the more expensive by-products of apartheid. The sharp division of black and white made all black crimes safer – blacks were unlikely to betray their own race, and whites dare not penetrate the black locations. Theft and prevention in an apartheid world build up into a vicious circle" (1956: 109).

Kort Boy as "a five-foot nothing knife-man," Mattera nevertheless pays homage to the Americans under his leadership, as a gang of "bright boys – daring thieves, and ruthlessly violent men" (Mattera 1987: 102) for whom "nothing was holy," whose "symbol was nothingness, a vacuum, a void" (Grosz 2012: 172).[6]

3.6 Hollywood Style

Almost everything that Mattera and his fellow thugs wore was fashioned after American styles. Watching Hollywood movies at Sophiatown's two iconic "bioscopes," the Odin Cinema and the Picture Palace, and aping such tough guy actors as "George Raft, John Garfield, and John Wayne" became de rigeur for the up-and-coming Tsotsi. Mattera writes:

> Some fashion shops actually overpriced their clothes on the recommendation of the Americans gang who wanted – and were prepared to pay for – the exclusive privilege of wearing USA imports such as Florsheim, Nunn Bush, and Jarman shoes. What they probably did not realize at the time was that the shops would bequeath the high-price legacy into the sixties, seventies, and eighties. "Made in the USA" became the sole criterion and any rubbish that carried the USA label was desirable for that alone. And Sophiatown had many shops and tailors – invariably Jewish or Indian owned – that raked in huge profits on the "Made in the USA" craze. Even the traditional herbalists used brightly painted signs to advertise their USA aphrodisiacs, blood mixtures and lucky charms. And if you rejected the American fad, you would quickly be dubbed *moegoe* or greenhorn. (Mattera 1987: 75)

Glaser singles out one movie that achieved a kind of cult-status among the controlling gangs of Sophiatown: William Keighley's semi-documentary thriller *The Street With No Name* (1948) which announces at the beginning of the film that gangsterism was on the up-and-up. The movie starred Richard Widmark, "arguably the quintessential *noir* protagonist," (Silver 2010: 285–6) as a misogynistic fight-promoter called Alec Stiles whose elegant wardrobe of fedora, bow-tie, and double-breasted suit, was designed by Academy Award winners Kay Nelson and Charles LaMaire. With the added affectation of a Benzedrine inhaler and an apple, the hard-nosed toffs of Sophiatown could not have been given a worse role

---

6 Quoted in Cateforis (2012).

model. As a consequence, Sampson quotes Temba who remarked "the sales of Benzedrine rocketed" and "everybody munched apples" and "wore those raincoats" (Sampson 1956: 102). Widmark's reprise of the maniacal cackle of the sadistic hood Tommy Udo as he pushed wheelchair-bound Mrs Rizzo (Mildred Dunnock) down the stairs to her death in Henry Hathaway's *The Kiss of Death* (1947), gave the actor, whose other bad guy roles included such film noir features as Jean Negulesco's *Road House* (1947), Elia Kazan's *Panic in the Streets* (1950), and Joseph L. Mankiewicz's *No Way Out* (1950), a fanatical following in the township fleapits around the Golden City, as Johannesburg is nicknamed. Because of his lack of height, Mark Stevens, Widmark's co-star as Gene Cordell in *The Street With No Name*, also appealed, despite his being an FBI undercover agent, to thugs like Kort Boy whom Mattera dismisses as "kort" (short) of stature.

Keighley's movie was popular in South Africa throughout the 1950s and under the influence of Widmark's other roles as the degenerate thief Ray Biddle in *No Way Out* or the murderous Jefty in *Road House*, Mattera boasts:

> One night I led the Vultures against the Styles gang at their haunt on the corner of Edward Road and Gold Street. It was a fierce, toe-to encounter with no quarter given on either side. Knives penetrated into dark flesh. Axes, swords, tomahawks crudely manufactured at home or newly-purchased from the hardware stores – crushed into bone and skull. Uncle Willie's army bayonet cracked with its jagged edge into Mkhuba's head. He turned around to stare at me in disbelief and terror as his blood spurted into my face and onto my clothes. He screamed. He ran. It was the end of the Styles gang. (Mattera 1987: 61)

Nixon notes that the authorities in Pretoria did their utmost to "limit black exposure to films that might be interpreted as subverting white authority" and, quoting Glaser, writes that letters to the editor of the *Johannesburg Star*, for example, often accused Hollywood and its glitzy body-language of dragging the city's youth into a "mutually damaging, degenerate embrace" (Nixon 1994: 34). By way of assurance, William Carr, a well known war veteran and head of Johannesburg's Non-European Affairs Department, suggested that in such films as *The Street With No Name* thugs like Alec Stiles got their come-uppance and that the law triumphed over criminals.

3.7 Men Are Like Leaves

"The roots of violence in South Africa are deep," Bernard Magubane writes in his Introduction to Mattera's *Sophiatown*. Developing an argument from Frantz Fanon in which "the native is declared impervious to ethics," (Fanon 2004: 6) he writes that in order "to 'pacify' the colonized peoples and to compel them to accept the new alien order, the white minority often finds it necessary to wage constant war against them." Magubane notes that by disingenuously branding the black majority as the evil *Other*, "the defiler of white civilization," the besmircher of Boergeois über-kultur, Mattera bombards the apartheid ideology as if it were Dresden (Magubane 1987: xviii). For example, before the final razing of Sophiatown in 1962, Mattera asks *baas* Potgieter: "*Meneer* when are you people going to break down our houses." Enraged by the phrase "you people," Potgieter replies:

> "*Kleinbooi*" he said with sudden tenderness, "'*Baas*' Pottie doesn't go around smashing people's houses – that's for Speedy Demolishers; it's their job although the Government pays them. *On wilnieonsvuilmaaknie; die hulle Wek...* . So don't you 'you people' me, understand! Otherwise *Baas* Pottie can become very nasty, you hear?" Saying "you people" to a rival gang was one thing, saying it to a group of "die-hard Afrikaner nationalists" in camouflage kit, Mattera reflects, "you could end up lying on your back." (Quoted by Magubane 1987: viii–xix)

At the height of their notoriety in Sophiatown, the Vultures fit Fugard's description of "the tsotsi-type, the no-good loafers of the street corners and shebeens, the ones you avoided at night, the scum who killed for pennies or tickeys or no reason at all and who never did a day's work in their wicked lives" (Fugard 2009: 214). As to why young people might pursue a way of life simply for kicks, Antonio Gramsci asks:

> Is it preferable to "think" without having critical awareness ... to "participate" in a conception of the world "imposed" mechanically by external environment ... or is it preferable to work out one's own conception of the world consciously and critically, and so out of this work of one's own brain to choose one's own sphere of activity, to participate actively in making the history of the world, and not simply to accept passively and without care the imprint of one's own personality from outside? (Gramsci 1971: 58)

Whereas Marx noted that "Men make their own history, they do not make it just as they please, they do not make it under circumstances chosen by themselves, but under circumstances directly encountered, given, and transmitted from the past," (Elster 1986: 277)[7] it may be that the dilemma the Tsotsi gangs found themselves in, as Gramsci suggests, is akin to "the ambivalent triumph of the oppressed" (Angela Carter quoted in Thomson & Gutman 1995: xiii) even though they may have thought through their place in the world with which they had a legitimate quarrel. If crime is a desperate quasi-political act, then the outcome, in this instance, was beyond the control of Mattera who sought to subvert the social order, one which was already beset from the outside by "cops on horses, the sietkommando" with their "long lances and .303 rifles" (Nichol 1991: 57). Nevertheless, the skirmishes of Mattera and his gang of "primitive rebels" (Hobsbawm 1959: unpaginated) with apartheid's law, were in the end more profound than just street-corner bluster, more than just "semiotic guerilla warfare" (Umberto Eco quoted in Ross and Sibley 2004: 167) prosecuted by an oppressed society's pre-political losers in fashionable togs in the "dark alleys" of White Man's Land.

Just as space and movement in Sophiatown were socially arranged, if power suits and the menacing swagger were for local esteem and for some kind of authenticity in the blackened apartheid world, then the Vultures' perceived dysfunctional behavior within the local ecosystems of the impoverished townships could justifiably be an adolescent resistance-in-the-making through ritual. One in which criminals are in the process of being "turned" politically, as Fanon suggests, and, given the obscenity of racial segregation, work themselves out in other social works, other practices which will be beneficial rather than detrimental to a society trying to break out from the racial lock-down of apartheid.

There were "many foul chapters," Mattera writes, of "bloodletting, turbulence, misunderstanding and being misunderstood," which, while leading eventually to his incarceration, ended in his being acquitted of murder in 1956 (Mattera 1987: 133). While he barely survived the nine stabbings and three bullets wounds as "a street-fighter and a thug for whom violence and obstinacy were the golden rule in the game of self-preservation" (Mattera 1987: 61), the Darwinian nature of gang-life ensured that many of Mattera's fittest henchmen would not survive the tooth-and-claw challenges of other hoods or the security forces. For example, Victor is "butchered in broad daylight in the presence of a clergyman who had pleaded for his life to be spared," Maasanto's "rotting corpse is found in a ditch, badly hacked."

7   From "The 18th Brumaire of Louis Bonaparte" quoted in Elster (1986).

Churchill is "crushed to death against the wall of his Meadowlands home." Big Man Jacob Senne is "cut to pieces in a football stadium." Raaphalene and his kid brother Deadline are "gunned down" (Mattera 1987: 61). Of the pitiless determinism enacted on the brutal streets of Sophiatown, Mattera broods poetically:

> Men are like leaves. Now fresh and green with the strength and vigor of youth. Voluptuous leaves adorn and clothe the tree of life that others may find the support and conflict of shade.
> Shade from the blistering heat of passion and anger and human cruelty. Men are like leaves: now the beauty and the zeal; now the change and decay and the slow dive to the waiting earth where all is equal. Then the burial. The oblivion. Men are like leaves… . (Mattera 1987: 59)

3.8 Recuperation and Self-transformation

Growing "tired of bloodshed," the "stinking, lice-infested, urine-dripping" police cells, and, having made the decision that "genuine rehabilitation would be possible if [he] changed friends" (Mattera 1987: 126–7), Mattera records that "the first seeds" of his "political awareness were sown" during the defiant "WE WON'T MOVE" campaign against the government's order to vacate homes in Sophiatown under the Native Resettlement Act of 1954. This was his "first introduction into a new world, where men and women spoke their minds and openly challenged the police and the government in Pretoria." Taking his "scars and wounds" with him, Mattera discovered the thinking world of "youth clubs, libraries, and education centers … lectures, debating societies and public meetings" which took the place of gang hide-outs and sinister streets. After most of the Vultures have been dispersed by the forced removals that scattered them into the far-corners of Meadowlands and Diepkloof, Mattera dusts off his old clothes and writes that "constitutions, preambles and manifestos – strange words to ears accustomed to police whistles and gunshots, war cries and gang calls – replaced guns and knives" (Mattera 1987: 127). Like Genet's "rescue" by Jean Cocteau and Jean-Paul Sartre from a life-sentence after 10 convictions, the infectious humanity of Father Huddleston, the "dauntless one" of the Community of the Resurrection who was in the 1950s recognized as "the leading white opponent of apartheid" (Goodhew 2004: 94), and Robert Resha, a prominent member of the armed wing of African

National Congress (ANC),[8] guided Mattera and other disheartened young men toward a new wardrobe of recovery and recuperation and helped them enunciate a "grammar of protest" (Goodhew 2004: 93) by encouraging them to temper their social frustrations, their body-language, by redirecting them into political activity after the Sharpeville Massacre in 1960.

In *The Wretched of the Earth*, Fanon writes that "the shanty town is the consecration of the colonized's biological decision to invade the enemy citadel at all costs, and if it need be, by the most underground channels." For him, "the *lumpen proletariat* – the *Tsotsi* gangs, in this case – constitutes a serious threat to the 'security' of the town [the State] and signifies the irreversible rot and gangrene eating into the heart of colonial domination" (Fanon 2004: 81). Like "the pimps, the hooligans, the unemployed, and the petty criminals" who "give the liberation struggle all they have got" and "devote themselves to the cause like valiant workers," so Mattera and one or two of his friends, déshabillé, as it were, by the pacifism of Huddleston or the liberation rhetoric of Resha, were, in the poet Dennis Brutus' words, proof-positive that "the criminals, the Tsotsis, the riff-raff, the people compelled to live their lives outside the law because no opportunity exist[ed] for them inside the law, or simply because they lost their documents and there is no way of reestablishing their identity" could bring about a viable rebellion against the State (Denis Brutus quoted in Lindfors 2011: 108). These are the people who, Marx, and later Fanon, predict, will find "their way back to the nation thanks to their decisive, militant action" (Fanon 2004: 82).

"Fanonian violence," wrote Jean-Paul Sartre, "is part of a struggle for psycho-affective survival and a search for agency in the midst of the agony of oppression" (Fanon 2004: xxxvi). Sartre's famous misreading of Fanon's guarded belief in non-violence makes Mattera's sea-change more meaningful as he abandoned gangster clothes, the Tsotsi strut, and the flick-knife to become a prominent community activist and a poet, with Breyten Breytenbach and Dennis Brutus, of the liberation movement in South Africa. Becoming active in Steve Biko's Black Consciousness Movement in the early 1970s, Mattera's new life was devoted to the eradication of suffering from peoples' lives. "In another day, in another time," he predicted, "we would emerge to reclaim our dignity and our land" and "it was only a

---

8   Mattera writes that two of his friends, "Mrs. Mokgosi and her daughter Patricia, both staunch members of the African National Congress, had often asked me to join the movement. I had refused on many occasions but protected them and other women from being molested when they marched through the streets of Sophiatown, Western and Newclare" (1987: 125).

matter of time and Sophiatown would be reborn" as a place "where [racial] laws and guns cannot reach nor jackboots trample" (Mattera 1987: 151). Once "demented, restless, searching for answers, making equations," the "Slumville" (Mattera 1987: 10) of Mattera's precarious life was reborn from apartheid's Triomf into freedom's Sophiatown.

Just as "the newspapers are tattered" when they reach Jean Genet's cell in *Our Lady of the Flowers* and the "finest pages" – of male pin ups – "have been looted of their finest flowers," (Genet 1943: 63) they are, Hebdige writes, "so much graffiti," adding that as graffiti, they make thought-provoking reading drawing attention to themselves as "an expression both of impotence and a kind of power – the power to dis-figure" (Hebdige 1979: 3), to undress that which has been cloaked to give new prominence. Like Genet, Mattera had, in Edmund White's words, "remarkable powers of self-transformation" and "neither his family history nor his environment readily explains his ascent to the top." White continues that few would expect a "social deviate" to provide "an example to others." Yet while the world became alien and lost to both *don* Mattera and "Saint Genet"[9] they became through resilience "apostle[s] of the wretched of the earth," (White 1993: xv, xvii) dressed in new clothes and giving themselves thanklessly to homeless nations and disenfranchised folk.

References

Barthes, R. (1967 [1990]). *The Fashion System*. Trans. Matthew Ward and Richard Howard. Berkeley: University of California Press.
Cateforis, T. (ed.). (2012). *The Rock History Reader* (2nd ed.). London: Routledge.
Chandler, R. (1997). *Raymond Chandler Speaking*. Ed. D. Gardiner & K.S. Walker. Berkeley: University of California Press.
Davis, F. (1992). *Fashion, Culture, and Identity*. Chicago: University of Chicago Press.
De Beauvoir, S. (1969). *La Force d l'âge*. Paris: Éditions Gallimard.
Ekman, P. (ed.). (1998). *The Expression of the Emotions in Man and Animal*. Oxford: Oxford University Press.
Elster, J. (ed.). (1986). *Karl Marx: A Reader*. Cambridge: Cambridge University Press. http://dx.doi.org/10.1017/CBO9780511809668
Fanon, F. (2004). *The Wretched of the Earth*. New York: Grove Press.
Fugard, A. (2009). *Tsotsi*. Edinburgh: Cannongate.

---

9 Sartre's nickname for Genet.

Genet, J. (1943 [1963]). *Our Lady of the Flowers*. Trans. Bernard Frechtman. New York: Grove Press.
Glaser, C. (2000). *Bo-Tsotsi: The Youth Gangs of Soweto 1935–1976*. Oxford: James Curry.
Goodhew, D. (2004). *Respectability and Resistance: A History of Sophiatown*. Westport, CT: Praeger.
Gramsci, A. (1971). *Selections from the Prison Notebooks of Antonio Gramschi*. Ed. and trans. Geoffrey Smith and Quintin Hoare. London: Lawrence and Wishart.
Grosz, Stephen. (2012). *The Examined Life: How We Lose and Find Ourselves*. London: Chatto & Windus.
Hebdige, D. (1979). *Subculture: The Means of Style*. London: Routledge.
Hobsbawm, E.J. (1959 [1965]). *Primitive Rebels: Studies in Archaic Forms of Social Movement in the 19th and 20th Centuries*. New York: W.W. Norton.
Kerouac, J. (1957 [2007]). *Road Novels 1957–1960*. New York: Library of America.
Lindfors, B. (ed.). (2011). *The Dennis Brutus Tapes*. Woodbridge, Suffolk: James Currey.
Magubane, B. (1987). Introduction to *Sophiatown: Coming of Age in South Africa*. Boston: Beacon Press.
Mattera, Don. (1987). *Sophiatown: Coming of Age in South Africa*. Boston: Beacon Press.
Nichol, M. (1991). *A Good-Looking Corpse*. London: Secker & Warburg.
Nixon, R. (1994). *Homelands, Harlem, and Hollywood: South Africa Culture and the World Beyond*. New York: Routledge.
Ross, C. & R. Sibley (eds.). (2004). *Illuminating Eco: On the Boundaries of Interpretation*. Warwick, UK: Ashgate Publishing Ltd.
Sampson, A. (1956). *Drum: A Venture into the New Africa*. London: Collins.
Silver, A. (ed.). (2010). *Film Noir: The Encyclopedia*. New York: Overlook Duckworth.
Stein, S. (1999). *Who Killed Mr. Drum*. Bellville, South Africa: Mayibuye Books.
Temba, C. (2006). *Requiem for Sophiatown*. Johannesburg: Penguin.
Thompson, E.P. (1968). *The Making of the English Working Class* (rev. ed.). London: Victor Gollancz.
Thomson, E., & D. Gutman (eds.). (1995). *The Bowie Companion*. London: Sidgwick & Jackson.
White, E. (1993). *Genet: A Biography*. New York: Knopf.

4
Body Art, Body Decoration and Identity in Yorubaland

Bukola Adeyemi Oyeniyi[1]

4.1 Introduction

Dress, broadly conceived, is an assemblage of modifications and/or supplements to the human body (Roach-Higgins & Eicher 1995: 7). In this view, dress includes, but is not limited to, coiffed hair, colored skin, pierced ears and scented breath, besides an equally long list of garments, jewelry, accessories and other items worn on the body.

Drawing on the biological theory of dress, dress-use is premised on the need of the human body for protection from the vagaries of nature so as to sustain efficient and effective functionality of body processes, as well as protection from unauthorized (visual) intrusion. Symbolic interaction theory however places emphasis on micro-scale social interaction and holds that people act toward things based on the meaning those things have for them and that these meanings are derived from social interaction and modified through interpretation. Hence, while the biological theory sees dress as interfacing with both the micro and macro environment, the symbolic interaction theory sees dress as a communicator of shared values, meanings and social categories.

Identity, as a sociological and psychological concept, describes a process by which an individual or a group develops a distinct personality or characteristics through which the individual or group is known and/or recognized. It could also be defined as the means through which social subjects

1   Bukola Adeyemi Oyeniyi is an Assistant Professor of History at the Missouri State University. He has published extensively on African history. His recent essay on terrorism, "One Voice, Multiple Tongues: Dialoguing with Boko Haram," appeared in *Democracy and Security Journal*, 10(1), 2014. His current researches focus on conflict memories, intellectual history and development of the Nigerian state.

construct relationships of taxonomic sameness and difference. Understood in this way, identities then become multi-scalar and are constantly undergoing negotiations with tension between similarity and alterity (Meskell 2002; Young 1995). Individual or group identity includes a sense of continuity, a sense of uniqueness or difference from others, and a sense of affiliation. Identity therefore defines the person or a group as well as differentiates them from other individuals and groups.

Identity, whether of an individual or a group, is inexorably tied to self-concept or self-identity. Self-concept, which is the sum total of an individual's (or a group's) knowledge and understanding of his/her/itself, comprises physical, psychological and social attributes. These attributes can be influenced, on the one hand, by the individual's or group's attitudes, habits, beliefs and ideas; and, on the other, by its bio-social environment. It can be argued that dress – most fundamentally body art and decoration – interfaces with identity at the level of self-concept.

In this study, I extend the conceptualization of dress to include body art and decoration and examine how these contribute to identity construction among the Yoruba people of Nigeria. As this Yoruba folksong, among many others, shows, the Yoruba regard dress as a sine qua non to living itself:

> *'Adaba ti ko l'apa; kini yo fi fo?*
> *Olomoge ti ko l'aso;*
> *Kini yo fi lo'gba?*
> A wingless dove; with what will it fly?
> A lady without dress;
> How will she survive the season?

In addition to folksongs and everyday sayings, other Yoruba cultural practices such as praise names or poems describing a family or clan (*oriki*), chants and traditional customs demonstrate the importance of dress in constructing and establishing individual and group identity among Yoruba people. For instance, the Opomulero family's eponymous poem goes:

> *Keke ta didun;*
> *Aso l'edidi eniyan,*
> *Bi kosi Aso, Bi kosi egbigba Ileke;*
> *Oniruru Idi la bari.*
> The spindle spurns beauty;
> Cloth beautifies the human body,
> If not for cloths, If not for the big beads;
> We will see varying sizes of buttocks.

From these and other Yoruba cultural practices underscoring the place of dress, it can be argued that dress, for Yoruba people, includes not just cloth and clothing traditions, but all bodily adornments including tattooing and facial marking, jewelry and hairdressing, including barbing (Adeoye 2005: 179–218). And anybody, whether male or female, young or old, who lacks dress or dresses improperly is considered to be "naked," therefore incapable of surviving.

Without prejudice to the various positions espoused by the folksong and eponymous poem above, Yoruba people also say: "*Aso Nla, koni Eniyan Nla*," i.e., a well-dressed person is not necessarily a well-placed or highly remarkable person. Yet, Yoruba people reverenced the king in the following words: "*Kabiyesi, Alase Ekeji Orisa, Ki Ade pel'Ori, ki Bata pel'Ese*" (Kabiyesi, the Commander and the Vice-Regent of the Gods; May the crown and the royal shoes stay long on the king's head and feet). In this particular instance, the king's personality is fused with his dress; a king's crown and shoes are symbols of authority and units of identity. Other witty Yoruba sayings go: "*Ibere osi, bi oloro lo ri; ti nwo aso Ile r'oko*" (The commencement of poverty is usually like wealth, which compels a poor man to wear his best cloth [dress] to the farm) and "*Aifi eni p'eni, aif'eniyan p'eniyan, lo mu ara oko san Bante wo'lu*" (It is sheer discourteousness that makes a peasant dress poorly when going into the town). While the folksong and poem emphasize the place of dress in establishing and constructing individual identity, the adages serve as caveats that the image or impression dress presents may differ markedly from the reality of the individual's circumstances. From these, it can be asserted that Yoruba people understand the distinction between identity and dress.

Although different in their conceptualizations of dress, biological and symbolic interaction theories share the view that dress performs roles other than merely covering the human body. As the biological theory notes, while dress's overt function may be to cover the body, it can also alter body processes. A good example in this regard would be the removal and replacement of a bad tooth with a denture. This procedure, which may help reduce pain and odor, could, all the same, disfigure the face and cause embarrassment and discomfort. Plastic surgery, like a denture, may help in fixing ailing or defective body parts, but could also lead to serious complications, as the example of Michael Jackson's nose jobs suggests.

Essentially, biological theory conceptualizes dress as an interface between the microphysical and macrophysical environment. At the microphysical level, dress interacts directly with the body – for instance, woolen socks, which insulate the feet from cold. Dress, in this way, protects the human body and helps or alters the body processes. However, items such as gloves or spectacles also increase human capabilities to perform tasks. Dress, in this way, functions as an interface between the body and the macrophysical environment.

Symbolic interaction theory holds that dress, as a form of nonverbal communication, helps in establishing, maintaining and altering identity. In any communication encounter, Stone (1962: 57) argues, dress is seen and analyzed before speech. Given this, dress is just as important in the establishment and maintenance of the self as is speech. Dress provides a powerful lever for the formulation of a conception of the self since it is communicated through nonverbal symbols or codes such as gestures, grooming, clothing and location; while speech is a mainly verbal symbol. Nonverbal and verbal symbols, according to symbolic interaction theory, are both important to identity formation and establishment.

Having said this, dress has a certain priority over speech in establishing the identity either of an individual or of a group. From this viewpoint, it can be argued that as individuals and groups acquire identities through social interaction in various social, physical and biological settings, dress announces social positions such as age, sex, religion, political affiliation, school etc. And just as dress announces identity, identity can, in turn, announce dress.

In view of these layered meanings, our attempt here is to understand what dress signifies to Yoruba people and, in relation to identity, whether dress establishes and reinforces identity or conceals it. We also study how body art and decoration influence and/or contribute to identity construction.

The next section of this chapter provides a brief history of dress among Yoruba people, with a special emphasis on body art and decoration. This is followed by a section that discusses the role of body art and decoration in identity construction with special reference to the facial marks used by Yoruba people. The concluding section summarizes the basic findings of the study while, at the same time, applying the basic insights of both the biological and symbolic interaction theories to the discourse on body art and decoration and their place in identity construction.

4.2 The Provenance of Dress in Yorubaland

Yoruba is a generic word that describes a people, a land, a culture and a language. As a people, the Yoruba live predominantly in southwestern Nigeria. Though they share the same language or variants of the same language, customs and traditions, the Yoruba comprise people of different precolonial nation-states or political groupings. They range across several groups of the Ijebu, Oyo, Ondo, Ilorin and Kabba divisions. Others are found in "the kingdom of Ketu, Sabe, Idaisa, ... the people of Atakpame, the Yanturuku and the Oku-oku in the Republic of Togo ..." (Akinjogbin 2009: 9). Traditional accounts have also mentioned the Edo people as also a stock of Yoruba, especially Egharevba's (1960) accounts (but see Ereduawa 2004). Also included in the list of Yoruba are Kaba, Bunu, Owe, Igala and Nupe. In fact, Saburi Biobaku argued that it was from Nupe that the Yoruba spread to the southwestern parts of Nigeria (Akinjogbin 2009: 10). Other peoples included as Yoruba are the Ebira (Igbira), Egun, Ewe, Aja or Arada (all in the Republic of Benin), and the Gaa, Krobo and Adangbe (all in Ghana).

Whether narrowly or broadly defined, it is difficult to trace the origin of dress among these different (Yoruba) peoples. Although Akinwumi (2006) is concerned with tracing "the introduction of certain Arab-styled men's robes and trousers, and the development of characteristic dress items associated with certain political and religious leaders," he however claims that dress use among Yoruba people could be linked to the mythological figure of Esu. Akinwumi's views are essentially derived from the *Odu Ifa Obara Meji* and *Okanran Meji*. According to these two Ifa texts, the use of "women's bosom coverings" among Yoruba people could be traced to the dawn of time when God (Eledumare) created humans naked and sent them to the earth. On their journey, they met Esu, who challenged them to offer him a sacrifice in return for a cloth to cover their bosom (Akinwumi 2006: 50). It must however be noted that Akinwumi's use of the Ifa corpus, rather than helping to solve the problem of origin of dress, raises a number of fundamental historiographical questions. For instance, in the same Ifa corpus, we have accounts of Sango, one of the kings that ruled Old Oyo many years after Orunmila, the famed composer of the Ifa corpus. Orunmila could not have known about Sango, so parts of the corpus may not be as old as believed.

Perhaps the most dependable work that attempts a discussion on the origin of cotton textile production in West Africa remains Collen Kriger's (2006). Depending on reports from early Muslim and European traders, Kriger claims that the earliest clothes in sub-Saharan Africa were made from nonwoven bark-cloths, goats' wool, raffia and cotton (2006: 102). As noted below, the period when Africans began to use bark-cloths may never be determined; however, the earliest Arab/Muslim invaders of the 12th and 13th centuries mentioned the use of clothes in sub-Saharan Africa (Kriger 2006). Furthermore, early accounts of slave raids in Africa confirm that, from Senegal to Angola, the use of "either bark-cloth or a sarong-like body wrap ... called kijipa was rampant" (ibid.).

A rather bold but plausible claim made by this writer (Oyeniyi 2010) is that while the precise date of first clothes-use in Yorubaland may never be known, using excavated ancient art works and rock paintings, one may assert that clothes were being worn among Yoruba people between 500 and 900 CE. Buttressing this claim is the fact that most ancient art works from Yorubaland depict one form of dress or the other; the majority of these works have been radiocarbon dated to between 500 and 900 CE. The problem however is that with new archeological findings the dates keep shifting, though the theory remains tenable.

From recent oral interviews across Yorubaland,[2] it is surmised that the use of *kijipa* began among the Ila-Orangun people, also known as Akoko, in the Igbomina province. It was believed that cloths and the art of cloth production were exported from this area to other parts of Yorubaland, both by inhabitants of the area and traders from other parts. Among the Oyo people, this earliest Yoruba cloth is known as "Akoko cloth" (Johnson 1920). The Egba and Ijebu call it *Egbedi Aso Ila* (Ila cloth),[3] while among the Igbomina, from where the cloth emanated, it is called *kijipa*.[4]

Just as it is difficult to trace the provenance of cloth among the Yoruba, it is equally difficult to trace the origin of body art and decoration, most especially facial markings and scarifications. Oral, archival and written records gave two accounts of the origin of facial markings and scarifications among Yoruba people. In the first, when Oduduwa and his band departed from the East, he was advised by Ifa to give all his children facial marks purely for identification purposes. Ifa was reported to have warned Oduduwa that he would face serious problems on his way, which would disperse many of his followers. So, marking their faces in a particular way would make it easier to recognize them.

The second account, which revolves around Sango, a king in Old Oyo, claims that facial marking started with Sango. As part of his preparations for a war, Sango consulted Ifa, who asked him to honor his late mother with a sacrifice, lest he be defeated in the planned campaign. Sango, who had

2   More than 50 people were interviewed across Yorubaland and the consensus was that *kijipa* was the first Yoruba cloth. However, there is a divergent view on where it originated. For eight people, it was an Ijesha cloth, while others maintained that it was from Ila-Orangun. It is important to note that Ila-Orangun, until after the settlement of the 19th-century Yoruba civil wars, was an Ijesha enclave, which was ceded to the Ibadan warriors. Given the above, I reckon that the divergence is unnecessary.
3   Interview with Baba Fatimoh, Sagamu, June 12, 2010.
4   Interview with Oba Lamidi Adeyemi Olayiwola, Oyo, April 12, 2010.

forgotten his mother's name, ordered one of the palace officers, accompanied by a slave, to go to Tapa, Nupeland, and find out her name.

Well-received and lavishly entertained at Nupe, the palace officer was so heavily drunk that he forgot the purpose of his journey. However, the slave who accompanied him memorized Sango's mother's name. In other to punish this slip, Sango ordered that the palace officer be tied to a stake and all manner of marks be made on his face. As the marks were made, the palace officer writhed in pain. Sango was surprised to see this and asked that similar marks be made on his own shoulder. After the third mark, he recoiled in great pain and ordered them to stop; however, when the wound healed, the scar turned out beautiful, and so Sango ordered similar marks to be made on the faces of his children. It is claimed that facial marking became a tradition in Oyo from then on.

However, a number of folk songs and *oriki* or praise names exist among Ife people that are diametrically opposed to the traditions above. In spite of this, there is incontrovertible evidence, especially in early Ife art, that supports the claim that facial marking was present from ancient times in Ile-Ife. It could be that while Oduduwa may have at some point stopped marking the faces of his children, his chiefs and towns' people continued the practice, as most excavated figures from Ile-Ife have facial marks and scarification patterns.

In his classification of Ile-Ife arts, Cornelius Adepegba (1980) noted three stylistic differences, all of which are premised on the presence or otherwise of facial marks and scarification patterns. In general, Ife facial marks and scarifications change with the ruling dynasties. At first, under Obatala's dynasty, people were plain-faced. The later facial markings during the reign of Oduduwa's dynasty showed long cicatrization. Adepegba's (1980) argument is supported by Ife's oral traditions, which note that a band of foreigners led by Oduduwa overthrew the Obalufon/Obatala group. Another tradition states that Oranmiyan, the grandson of Oduduwa, left Ile-Ife for Benin and later went to Oyo-Ile. It was consequently argued that Oranmiyan introduced facial marking to Oyo-Ile, from where the practice diffused to other parts of Yorubaland.

Given Oyo's sociocultural and political dominance over the region, the assumption that facial marking diffused from Oyo to other parts of Yorubaland seems acceptable. Supporting this proposition is the fact that during the Atlantic slave trade, *Alabaja*, i.e., anyone with the *Abaja* facial marks (discussed below), were excluded from enslavement. Hence, most communities under Oyo's influence, especially their kings and nobles, adopted the *Abaja* marks for identification and therefore escaped enslavement (PRO 1882).

Whatever the origin of scarification and facial marking in Yorubaland, Lander, in his account of Captain Clapperton's expedition, emphasized that scarification and tattooing are some of the means "by which the different races in Africa are distinguished from each other much more easily than by any natural peculiarity in the color of the skin, or their general appearance" (Lander 1830: Vol. 1, 215).

4.3 Body Art and Decoration in Yoruba Identity Construction

As the following popular saying makes clear, body arts and decoration are not only for identification, but also for beautification: *"Bi a sa Keke, ti a wo Gombo; Aajo ewa naa ni"* (Whether we are marked with Keke or with Gombo, facial markings are for adornment).

As noted by Clapperton, facial markings were given to every Yoruba child from age six or seven as a form of identification and membership in different Yoruba communities (Lander 1830: Vol. 1, 217). Of the different groups in Yorubaland, facial marking is predominant among the Oyo, Egba, Ijebu, Owu, Ife, Ondo, Ijesha, Ila, Igbomina and Yagba people (Adeoye 2005: 179). However, Clapperton noted further that tattooing and facial marking are not peculiar to Yorubaland alone, but are a general practice from Badagry to Sokoto.

Although the traditions are fast dying out, facial marking, body scarification and tattooing are still practiced in Yorubaland today. Before the colonial intrusion, five forms of body marking existed in Yorubaland. These were facial marking (*Ila-Oju*), stomach or torso marking (*Ila-Inu*), incision (*Gbere*), tattooing (*Soju*), and the use of antimony (*tiiro*) and henna (*lile-laali*).

In most literature, circumcision is mentioned as part of body scarification and tattooing. This is however misleading, as circumcision has ritual significance among Yoruba people, and cannot be grouped together with body beautification. In fact, a boy could get his head broken for calling another an *alatoto* – an uncircumcised! Circumcision is left out in this discussion because it relates more to health and hygiene, in addition to being a private affair, which cannot be known simply by looking at an individual.

Torso scarification has been described in some literature as a type of tattoo; however, scarification involves cutting or making an incision into the skin, which when it heals, leaves behind a permanent scar. Tattooing is different from scarification in many respects. Importantly, it must be asserted that, of the five mentioned forms of body marking, facial marking and torso marking symbolize ethnic identity while incision, tattooing and the use of henna/antimony are matters of fashion and therefore could overlap in their various designs.

There are different types of facial marks: *Keke, Gombo, Pele, Abaja, Baramu, Ture, Mande, Jamgbadi* and so on. This popular saying serves to illustrate the pervasiveness of facial marks among the Yoruba: "*Pele oju kan l' o ko; Abaja oju kan l' o bu, E ko r'aye oni Gombo!*" (He was marked *Pele* on one cheek and *Abaja* on the other; what a life for them that have *Gombo*!)

Generally, there are two main classifications of Yoruba facial marks: *Abaja*, which predominated in Oyo and all the other communities that came under Old Oyo's sociocultural and political influence, and *Pele*, which originally began as a single mark predominating in eastern Yorubaland and underwent enormous changes with the advent and influence of Islam on Yorubaland.

From the above, it could be argued that Yorubaland could be divided into an *Abaja* axis and *Pele* axis, with the *Abaja* sphere of influence being from Old Oyo toward the coast and *Pele* being from the eastern direction toward the kingdom of Benin. Within these two broad classifications, a variety of facial markings are to be found, as we discuss below. Figure 4.1 presents artistic reproductions of some of the facial marks prevalent among the Yoruba people of Nigeria.

Abaja, ostensibly the most important and famous facial marking among Yoruba people, is exclusively reserved for the Oyo royal family and a few of the chiefs, especially the *Basorun*. *Abaja*, contrary to Johnson who maintained that it comprised three or four parallel lines, describes between six and 12 lines placed either vertically or horizontally on the two cheeks. *Abaja* is of four kinds: *Abaja Omo Oba, Abaja Basorun, Abaja Olowu* and *Abaja Oro*. Of these, *Abaja Omo Oba*, which contains six lines cut horizontally into the two cheeks, remains the most famous. *Abaja Basorun* consists of three vertical lines on the right cheek and four horizontal lines on the left cheek. *Abaja Olowu*, also known as *Abaja Mefa*, has on each cheek three lines placed horizontally with a set of three vertical lines above. *Abaja Oro* (vertical *Abaja*), as the name implies, is a set of three lines set in an upright position cut into each cheek. This is common among the Egba people and differs from *Pele* only in length. While the lines in *Pele* are short, in *Abaja Oro* they are longer.

While *Abaja Omo Oba* and *Abaja Basorun* are popular in Oyo, *Abaja Olowu* and *Abaja Oro* apply only to the Egba people of Abeokuta, Egbado, Owu and their environs. *Abaja Omo Oba* is also called *Mefa-Mefa* or

Mefa-Ibule, which describes both the number (six) and the horizontal positioning of the lines. In addition to these three types of *Abaja* are four others: *Mejo-Mejo, Merin-Merin, Merin Pelu Baramu, Mokanla-Mokanla* and *Meje-Meje*. These forms of *Abaja* are commonplace in eastern and western Yorubaland, especially in places like Ofa, Ilorin, Ajase-Ipo and so on. Although all these forms of *Abaja* are used by many families in Yorubaland, *Abaja Omo Oba* was the most respected because of its being the royal facial mark.

Although *Abaja Omo Oba* was also given to royal home-born slaves, it must be stated that three broad marks, called *Eyeo*, were cut on the arms and thighs of both male and female members of the ruling family in order to differentiate them from others in the royal household. Only those with *Abaja Omo Oba* and *Eyeo* could ascend the throne. It must be noted that all the *Alaafin* who have ruled Oyo have these important facial and body marks. The above totally differs from Ojo's claim that even royal home-born slaves received *Eyeo* (Ojo 2008: 365).

Besides *Abaja*, there are also *Keke* and *Gombo*: these consist of four or five perpendicular and horizontal lines placed at an angle on each cheek, the design of which fills the entire cheek. There are three types of *Gombo*: *Gombo*; *Gombo and Towoboju*; and *Gombo and Baramu*. The first type comprises four horizontal lines serving as base, and four vertical lines that appear as continuation of the horizontal lines that break at a right angle, projecting vertically quite close to the ears. Three more vertical lines are cut over the cheekbones. The second type differs only in the addition of two vertical, but smaller lines above and parallel to the original four vertical lines. The third has, in place of the three vertical lines on the cheekbones linking the nose with the eyes, a single horizontal line that terminates on the ridge of the nose.

Keke, on the other hand, comprises three long vertical lines, placed beside 15 horizontal lines. Thus, altogether 18 lines are cut into each cheek. Given the nature of these facial marks, many Yoruba people are wont to taunt those who have them: *"Mo sa Keke, mo mu re 'le Ado; Mo bu Abaja, mo mu re Idi Ape"* (Keke is synonymous with Ado people, and Abaja with Idi Ape people).[5]

Two other facial marks of importance are *Pele Egba* and *Ture*. In addition, there are *Mande* and *Jamgbadi*, both being exclusively used by the non-Yorubas who have settled among the Yoruba.

It must be noted that the above does not represent the totality of facial markings in Yorubaland, but only the most important ones. In fact,

---

5   Idi Ape is the part of Oyo where the *Alaafin*s are buried.

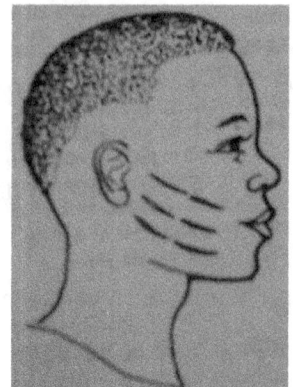

Abaja Omo Oba

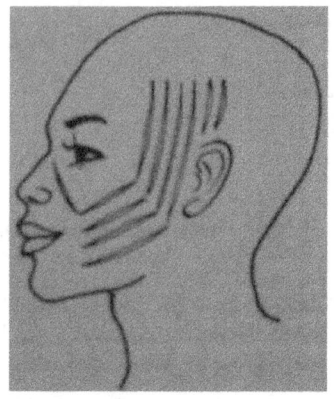

Gombo Pelu Baramu

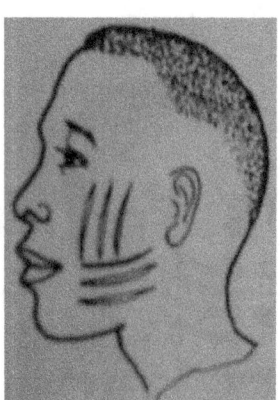

Abaja Olowu

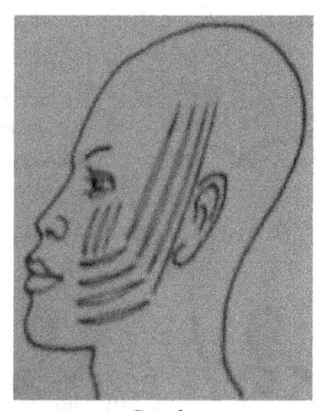

Gombo

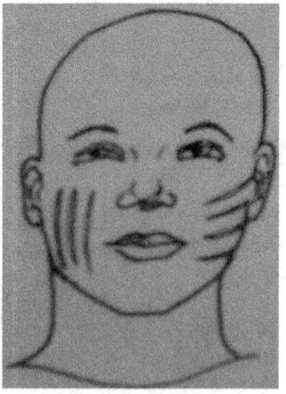

Abaja Basorun

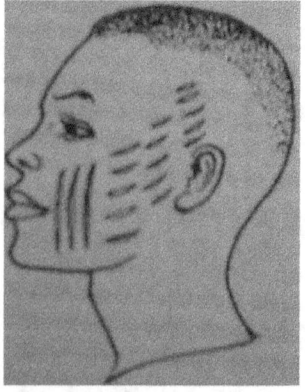

Keke

Body Arts and Identity in Yorubaland 85

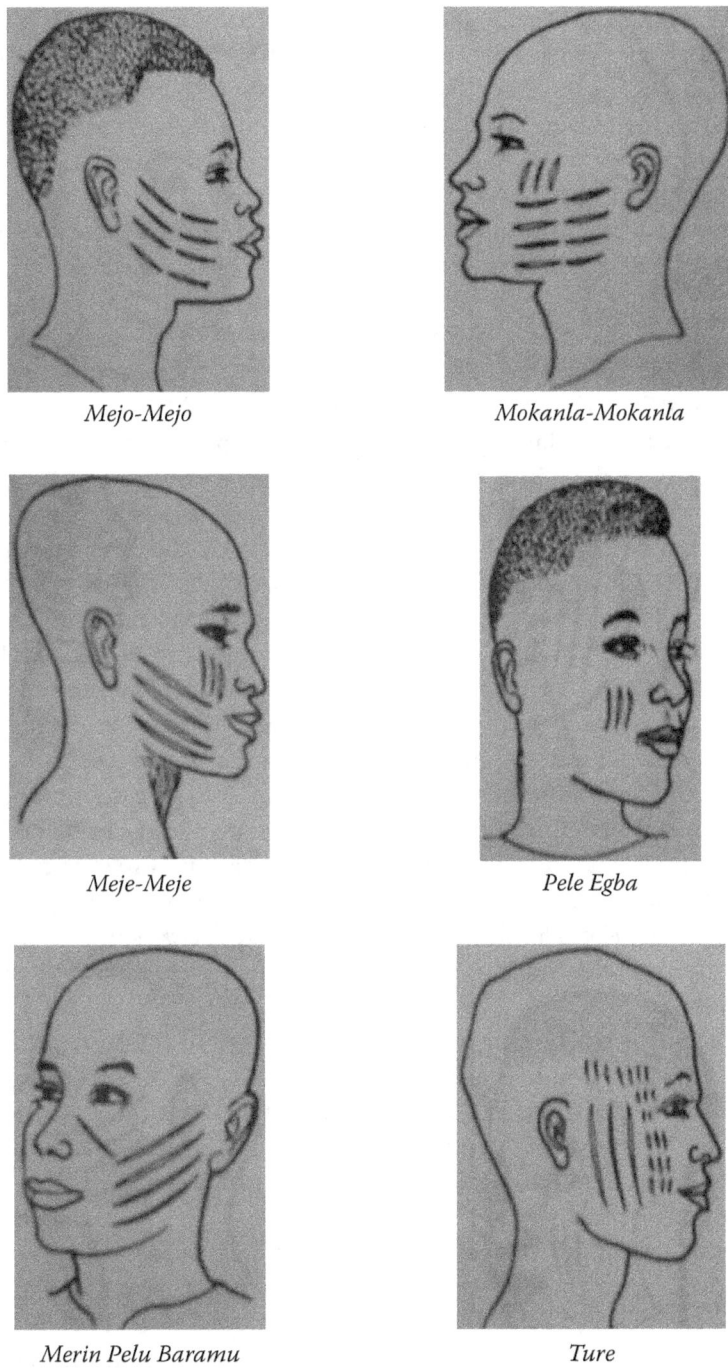

Figure 4.1. Facial marks in Yorubaland.
Source: Adeoye (2005: 180).

variations of the above abound in different parts of Yorubaland. Although both males and females are given facial marks, these are patrilineal, children being given the same facial marks as their fathers. By implication, married women would have facial marks that are different from the rest of the family. However, in the case of royal marriages two patterns of facial markings ultimately evolved. In the case of the children of a marriage between a royal family and the family of either a warrior or a powerful man, the facial marks of the royal family is cut into one cheek and that of the other family into the other cheek. Where a royal marries a commoner, the paternal facial mark is given to the "fruits" of such a marriage. When this happens, the Yoruba are wont to say *"Jemureke! Olowo pade omo olola."* (Stop press! The powerful has collided with the royal.)

On the whole, facial marking among Yoruba people is comparable to a national passport, an insignia of membership, a badge of identity or a uniform for all individuals of the same group, village or lineage; and therefore differs from one community, group and sub-ethnic group to another (Ojo 2008: 368). Facial marking is done either between the ages six and seven as a signifier of membership of a particular family, lineage and community; or given to adult non-members when they become part of a particular family, as a symbol or a mark of naturalization into the family, lineage and town.

Irrespective of when it was done, the facial marking was given uniqueness through the length, positioning and number of strokes. Through the addition of pigment to the scarification's opening to give it a shining black color, this ethno-political marking was transformed into a thing of fashion and beauty. It must be added that the beautification of markings through pigmentation also reflects wealth and status, as the following Yoruba folksong suggests: *Kor'Owo ko 'la; O gbe bembe eke R'Oshogbo* (He could not afford the cost of procuring [colored] marks, he therefore went plain-faced to Oshogbo).

In general terms, body markings (especially facial), are strong citizenship identity markers. And, as already noted, when given to adults, especially plain-faced adults from outside Yorubaland, it allows for the incorporation of strangers or foreigners into a family, a lineage and a community. The cases below help to illustrate the saliency of body marking as it relates to identity in Yorubaland.

On March 18, 1898, one Okolu, an Ijesha man, accused Otunba of Italemo ward, in Ondo, of seizing and enslaving his sister Osun and his niece – mother and daughter. Osun and her daughter had been enslaved by the Ikale in 1894 and had, in 1895, escaped and fled from their master, but as they headed toward Ilesha, Otunba seized them. As the mother claimed, Otunba forced her to become his wife and to hoe his farm, and gave her daughter one deep, bold line (Ondo facial markings) on each cheek. At the trial, Otunba and his witness, Itoyimaki, denied the enslavement charge, but proudly asserted that he had prevented Osun and her daughter from being taken away as slaves by Soba, another slave dealer, and also that he had taken Osun as his wife and given her daughter the Ondo mark to bestow on her Ondo identity.[6] While it must be admitted that the event took place in the 19th century, it however reflects the general trend of things, especially the place of marriage, identity and aesthetics in ethnic configurations across precolonial Yorubaland.

Another example is the case of Osundina, a 1892 baptismal candidate in Ondo, whose mother had been enslaved at Ile-Ife, where Osundina was born. Because he was born far away from Ondo, he was plain-faced. With the end of the Yoruba civil war and the eventual incorporation of Yorubaland into the vortex of colonialism in 1893, domestic or internal slavery was abolished and many who had been enslaved in different parts of Yorubaland and Nigeria became free and returned home. Osundina's mother returned to Ondo, but Osundina stayed behind at Ile-Ife.

When in 1894 Osundina rejoined his mother in Ondo he was daily treated as a slave and not as an Ondo citizen for the simple reason that he had no facial mark. So, to *"remove the scandal that he is a slave,"* Osundina was given the Ondo facial mark.[7] Osundina's plain face had symbolized his "alien" origin and noneligibility for Ondo citizenship rights, thus reducing him to the status of a slave.

There was widespread displacement and dislocation of peoples as a result of the Yoruba civil war, when refugees, slaves and defeated soldiers converged on Ibadan, Ijaye and Abeokuta to continue the war, and especially to curb the menace of the Fulani Jihadists from Ilorin. This development brought about the mixing of peoples from different families, lineages and communities in Ibadan. This medley of peoples formed the nucleus of the Ibadan army, and one of the implications was that facial markings no longer served to differentiate these soldiers from those of the other side. At the campaign of Osogbo where Ibadan recorded a resounding victory over the Jihadists in 1843, and later in 1878 at Ikirun where another Ibadan victory was also recorded, Ibadan had to invent a password or a code, which

---

6   Nigerian National Archives, Ibadan (NAI), Albert Erhardt, *Journal*, March 18 and 22, 1898, Ondo Division 8/1.
7   Nigerian National Archives, Ibadan (NAI), Phillips 3/5, *Names of Baptismal Candidates, Ondo, 1892*. See also Paul Lovejoy, "Scarification and the Loss of History in the African Diaspora," paper presented at York University, Toronto, July 2005, pp. 7, 14.

was known only to its soldiers and not to any others who might have the same facial marks as the Ibadan warriors. When there was a need to differentiate between the real Ibadan soldier and a "suspicious" character who might want to infiltrate the Ibadan camp, the question asked was "*Elo ni owo Odo?*" which means "How much is the fare to cross the river?" This was the amount the Ibadan warlords paid to ferrymen who brought Ibadan soldiers across the Osun river; it was impossible for anybody not involved in the campaign to know that the payment was 2,000 cowries.

The import of the above is that the mixing of people occasioned by the 19th-century conflict-induced displacement rendered identity or citizenship based on facial marking difficult for the communities that received displaced Yoruba peoples during the period. It must also be noted that Ibadan, owing to its policy of assimilating and integrating slaves and foreigners into its city during this period, became a kind of a melting pot where facial marking, as a symbol of citizenship, was not recognized.

On the use of facial marking to confer citizenship by naturalization, the example of the Egba nobles is illuminating. Rev. James Johnson of the Christian Missionary Society recorded the widespread practice of adoption and outright purchase (for the purpose of adoption) of thousands of child slaves by rich and childless Egba nobles and chiefs immediately after peace was restored in Yorubaland in the 1880s. A similar practice was reported among Owo nobles and chiefs. In the case of the Egbas, the noble or chief would give such an adopted child the facial mark of his or her new family. David O. Asabia and J.O. Adegbesan (1970) argued that the prevalence of Ijesha facial marks in Owo towns was a result of sexual liaisons between Ijesha soldiers and Owo women during the decade of Ijesha military campaigns in northeastern Yorubaland in the 1870s. This points to the problem of command sex or sex-for-safety, which is common even in modern wars and conflicts.

However, these adopted children, as they bore the facial marks of their new families, lineages and communities, were bestowed with the same status as that given to home-born slaves and enjoyed fairly good treatment. They could also own family properties in their own right; a privilege that non-home-born slaves did not enjoy (Ojo 2008: 370).

As a badge of citizenship, scarification must have imposed a great liability on the various Yoruba peoples during the 19th-century Yoruba civil wars. Rev. Richard Henry Stone, the Baptist Pastor of Abeokuta between 1859 and 1861 who mandated that all Yoruba converts must wear European dress, noted that facial marking, owing to its visibility and ease of identification of where the wearer was from, made it:

impossible for strangers to conceal their identity and slaves rarely escape to the interior. The fugitive is compelled to follow the roads leading through the towns and the gatekeepers recognize them by their face marks and their scanty outfit, and they are captured and returned to their masters... . Gatekeepers are thoroughly posted in this kind of lore and they know the nationality of every one passing through their gates. (Stone 1899: 30–1)

It must be noted that Rev. Stone compiled an eye-witnesses account of Yoruba cultures and customs as well as what he witnessed in Yorubaland during the period of war in the late 1850s and again during the first years of the American Civil War. He was an intelligent, reflective and reliable observer, which makes his works important sources of information on Yoruba society before the European colonialism. *In Africa's Forest and Jungle* is a rare account of West African culture, made all the more complete by the additional journal entries, letters and photographs included in the new 1988 edition.

In addition to the above, Clapperton described how facial markings and tattooing were also used to punish criminals and offenders:

When a Yoruba person perpetrates ever so trivial a crime, the tattoo mark of his nation is so crossed by other incisions, inflicted upon him by the ministers of justice, that it becomes utterly undistinguishable, and the impression of another people is substituted on the other side of the face in its stead. With this brand, which can never be erased, the offender is disenfranchised and must therefore quit his native country, as even a toddler constantly looks upon his facial mark as "a mark of scorn." In most cases, offenders, thus treated, normally leave their communities, as their immediate family members usually reject them out of shame. They therefore wander to another, but far community where they could not be traced and live quietly until they die, unpitied and unknown. (Lander 1830: Vol. 1, 217)

Facial marking was also used as a form of punishment not only for erring slaves, as the tale of *Alaafin* Sango above demonstrates, but also for captured warriors, as the example of the famous Ijesha Chief Ogedengbe illustrates.

Ogedengbe, who was captured by the Ibadan forces in about 1860 when he would have been 60 years old, was accused of violating his oath not to attack Ibadan warriors after the truce of Iperu. When he was captured, Chief Ogunmola of Ibadan ordered that Ogedengbe be given rough facial marks that formed a broad patch and gave him an appearance of a Bunu man, which many writers noted when they met him in the 1880s (Johnson

1920: 377; Lander 1830: Vol. 1, 217). With this branding, which could never be erased and was looked upon as a *"mark of scorn,"* Ogedengbe quit being a native of Ijeshaland. He was said to have died, unpitied and unknown, in a foreign land (ibid.).

Invariably, scarification, especially when "meted" out as a form of punishment, became some kind of a tracking device through which friends were differentiated from foes. When this happened, Olatunji Ojo argues, the punishment amounted to disenfranchisement of the individual concerned. Ogedengbe, for example, had his "citizen's passport" defaced and re-branded from that of a Yoruba man of Ijesha extraction to that of a Bunu man.

The predominance of facial marking waned considerably during the 19th-century Yoruba civil wars, during which many suffered untold hardships. From the 1850s, the number of plain-faced Yoruba people increased, as the end of the war made only certain ethnic identities fashionable. Social change occasioned by British imperial rule in Yorubaland further reduced the allure of facial marking, as being plain-faced became synonymous with modernity, civilization and Christianity; while having facial marks was regarded as conservative, backward and encrusted in the past.

Tattooing (*Soju* or *Ara-fifin*), among the Yoruba, is done both for aesthetics and for health reasons. Incisions of different kinds are also common as health care involves not just the oral use of herbs of different kinds to cure diseases, but also the rubbing of concoctions of different kinds into incisions cut into the body with sharp objects. Incision use varied widely with class, age, gender and fashion.

As part of the initiation rites of kings and chiefs in Yorubaland, hundreds of incisions are cut into the head, arms, and bodies of kings and chiefs and herbal concoctions are rubbed into the open wounds for the body to absorb the vital ingredients in the concoctions. During the installation of the *Are-Ona-Kakanfo*, the Field Marshal of the Oyo army, 201 incisions are usually cut into the head of the officer and charms of different kinds are rubbed into the open wounds to make him fearless, courageous and impervious to iron weaponry and bullets.

Ojo (2008) described the scars of the wounds from these numerous incisions as *"living symbols."* He also noted that tattoos that are strictly tied to fashion move with time based on generational preferences.

Given the conceptualization of dress as including all forms of body art and decoration, how do facial markings, body scarification and tattooing interface with identity? In relation to their eclectic usages, how do such markings project, establish and reinforce identity? These and other questions are examined in our concluding section.

4.4 By Way of Conclusion

Dress, broadly conceived, is any addition and/or supplement to the human body. Body art and decoration are therefore forms of dress that are part of ancient tradition in Yorubaland. Some forms are permanent, like facial markings, while others are temporary, e.g., the use of henna. Whether permanent or temporary, body art and decoration interface with identity in very many ways. Essentially, they help other items of dress to create, reinforce and project affiliation and membership, status and values, among other things. Put differently, body art and decoration are some of the ingredients through which Yoruba people build, sustain, project and reinforce their individual and group identity.

Dress, whether broadly or narrowly defined, communicates. More often than not, dress takes preeminence over the other means through which we create and communicate identity. As far as the Yoruba are concerned, individual and group identity revolves around social categories such as family, clan, lineage, society, guild etc. So, in social and interpersonal relations, many things, including body art and decoration, differentiate individuals and members of the same social group from others. In this way, while individuals and groups create identity using different materials, body art and decoration help in reinforcing these identities. For instance, body art and decoration help to reinforce the sense of membership in a community, family, clan or lineage. *Pele*, for instance, gives Ijesha and Ondo people their unique identity as Yoruba people, and separates them from Ogbomoso people who cut *Baramu*. In the same manner, *Abaja Omo Oba* and *Eyeo* separate members of the Oyo royal family from others who also cut *Abaja* on their faces. As this is true of facial markings, so it is about body scarification and tattooing.

Within Yorubaland, as in other human societies, body art and decoration announce, reinforce and establish individual and group identity in much the same way as (religious) names, dress, etc. help in identifying and separating, for instance, Christians from Muslims today.

From the foregoing, therefore, it can be argued that body art and decoration contribute to the process of identity making or construction and help individuals or groups to develop their distinct personalities or characteristics. While this deals essentially with the individual and/or group's relation with and to others, it also helps in the construction of taxonomic sameness and difference. For instance, *Abaja*, *Pele* or *Baramu* helps people from the same area to recognize their sameness and build community feelings of relatedness in much the same way as it separates the different groups from one another.

Understood in this way, body art and decoration contribute to individual and group efforts at negotiating between similarity and alterity. They help the individual and group to cultivate a sense of continuity, a sense of uniqueness and a sense of difference from others. They contribute, in no small measure, to how individuals express a sense of affiliation among themselves.

Sociological analysis of body art and decoration, as shown above, underscores the importance of both the biological and symbolic interaction theories in any analysis of dress in Yorubaland. While the biological theory asserts that dress use results from the need to provide for the human body, the symbolic interaction theory shows that Yoruba dress does not only cover human nakedness and protect the body from the unsolicited gaze and vagaries of nature, but also communicates values, status, affiliation etc. Hence, while the biological function of Yoruba body art and decoration cannot be denied, they relate more to the social function of dress, i.e., dress as a communicator of values.

As this chapter has shown, individuals occupy a number of social positions and thus exude a number of identities, all of which contribute to the self-configuration of the individual or group as a whole. While some of these art forms and decoration are permanent, e.g. facial marking, others are not and therefore serve Yoruba people admirably well as they negotiate different social positions. Although enormous changes have occurred between the pristine and contemporary usages of body art and decoration, the tradition still finds relevance among Yoruba people of today. Among other things, it helps in identity construction and the transmission of the materiality of dress as a strategic resource for the making, remaking and unmaking of persons and identities.

References

Adeoye, C.L. (2005). *Asa ati Ise Yoruba*. Ibadan: University Press PLC.

Adepegba, C. (1980). Yoruba art and art history. In D. Ogunremi & B. Adediran (eds.), *Culture and Society in Yorubaland*. Ibadan: Rex Charles/Connell Publications.

Akinjogbin, I.A. (2009). *Milestones and Concepts in Yoruba History and Culture*. Ibadan: Olu-Akin Publishers.

Akinwumi, M. Tunde. (2006). Oral tradition and the reconstruction of Yoruba dress. In Toyin Falola & Ann Genova (eds.), *Yoruba Identity and Power Politics*. Rochester, USA: University of Rochester Press.

Asabia, David O., & J.O. Adegbesan. (1970). *Idoani Past and Present: The Story of One Yoruba Kindgdom*. Ibadan: Ibadan University Press.

Egharevba, J. (1960). *A Short History of Benin*. Ibadan: Ibadan University Press.

Ereduawa, I. Omo N'Oba. (2004). *I Remain Sir, Your Obedient Servant*. Ibadan: Spectrum.

Johnson, S. (1920). *The History of the Yorubas from the Earliest Times to the Beginning of the British Protectorate*. Lagos: CMS Bookshops.

Kriger, C. (2006). *Cloth in West African History*. Lanham: Alta Mira Press.

Lander, R. (1830). *Records of Captain Clapperton's Last Expedition in Africa*. 2 vols. London: Routledge.

Lovejoy, P. (2005). *Scarification and the Loss of History in the African Diaspora*. Toronto: York University.

Meskell, L. (2002). The intersections of identity and politics in archaeology. *Annual Review of Anthropology*, 31(1), 279–301. http://dx.doi.org/10.1146/annurev.anthro.31.040402.085457

Nigerian National Archives, Ibadan. (1892). *Phillips 3/5, Names of Baptismal Candidates*. Ondo.

Nigerian National Archives, Ibadan (1898). *Albert Erhardt Journal*, March 18 and 22. Ondo Division 8/1.

Ojo, O. (2008). Beyond diversity: Women, scarification, and Yoruba identity. *History in Africa*, 35, 347–74. http://dx.doi.org/10.1353/hia.0.0015

Oyeniyi, B.A. (2010). *Mobility and Social Conflicts in Yorubaland: A Socio-Historical Reinterpretation*. Berlin: Dr. Muller Verlag.

PRO (Public Records Office). (1882). FOn147/48, statement made by His Majesty, Owa Agunloye-bi-Oyinbo, January 12, 1882, enclosure 10 in Rowe to Kimberly, March 14. London: PRO.

Roach-Higgins, M.E., & J.B. Eicher. (1995). Dress and identity. In M.E. Roach-Higgins, J.B. Eicher & K.K.P. Johnson (eds.), *Dress and Identity*. New York: Fairchild Publications.

Stone, G.P. (1962). Appearance and the self. In A.M. Rose (ed.), *Human Behavior and the Social Process: An Integrationist Approach*. New York: Houghton Mifflin.

Stone, Richard Henry. (1899 [1988]). *In Africa's Forest and Jungle: Six Years Among the Yorubas*. USA: Religion and American Culture.

Young, R.J.C. (1995). *Colonial Desire: Hybridity in Theory, Culture, and Race*. New York: Routledge.

5
Bodies in Motion: Gestures and Performance of Identity in Tess Onwueme's *Shakara*

Maureen N. Eke[1]

5.1 Introduction

If as the introductory chapter suggests "the body is a site bearing multiple signs of cultural inscription," it would seem that artists deploy the body in a variety of ways either to articulate various positions of power or to negotiate states of identity, belongings and relationships. One such example is Nigerian playwright Tess Onwueme who infuses her plays with dramatic movements and gestures that signal the cultural location of her characters and of her plays. Using a combination of feminist, cultural and performance theory/criticism, this chapter examines Onwueme's play, *Shakara: Dance-hall Queen* (2000), paying attention to how the playwright uses her characters' bodies to register their socio-economic and political marginalization as well as to protest such disempowerment. In almost all of her plays, Onwueme uses movement, especially dance, as a trope to interrogate her women characters' identities, thus engaging in what Helen Gilbert describes as "an active self-constituting process" (2009: 304). This chapter examines how in *Shakara* the body becomes representative of the site for cultural (colonial and postcolonial) struggles of identity and "authenticity." It further explores how and what the body signifies either verbally or nonverbally through gestures, which include dance, facial expressions or looks, hand motions, dressing and body movements.

1 Maureen N. Eke is Professor of English in the Department of English Language and Literature, Central Michigan University. She is the Associate Editor of *African Literature Today*, the Annual Series Editor, African Literature Association and the Chair of the Human Rights Committee, African Literature Association.

If successful national progress and development are measured by the productivity of the national citizenry and the youth, then, according to several of Onwueme's plays – for instance, *Then She Said It* (2002), *What Mama Said* (2003) and *Shakara* (2000) – the nation of Nigeria has failed. Her plays project a depressing image of the national body, especially in its provision of development options for the youth. Onwueme's characters deploy their body to perform identity, be it socio-political as in gender or economic as in class. Thus, Shakara reads her body as a significant instrument and capital that she exploits to survive in a postcolonial nation reeling from its encounters with globalization and failed national/international developmental and economic policies, as well as glaring class and gender inequities.

Onwueme's plays suggest that postcolonial Nigeria suffers from the disease of cultural imperialism and neo-conservative religious revivalisms, an acute sense of social alienation and disengagement of the youth. Indeed, according to Onwueme's plays, the nation is caught in the throes of acute identity crisis or national schizophrenia. In *Shakara*, for instance, we encounter a young generation that in order to survive has been forced to grow up too soon, and that must persist only through a dramatic reworking of its identity. Here, the performance of one's identity – name, sexuality and gender – becomes an existential act; it is seen as central to survival. For Shakara, the central character for whom the play is titled, a reconstitution of her identity becomes necessary for her survival in the urban milieu in which she lives. Reading herself as "the sole author of my life" (*Shakara*: 21), Shakara engages in a series of acts, including dance, to exercise agency, representing herself as oppositional to her mother or to the society in general. According to Marvin Carlson (2009: 310), "the constitution of the self through social performance is viewed as a dynamic simultaneously coercive and enabling." Thus, the performance of the self can be a double-edged sword, empowering on the one hand and disruptive on the other. I use performance here as a communicative act, a language, aimed at representing identity and meaning through various acts – verbal and nonverbal. Such acts or gestures may also include body movements – dancing, head-shaking, body rocking – and facial expressions.

In the play to be discussed, as in most of Onwueme's plays, dance, movements and gestures serve as modes of communication (verbal and nonverbal); they function through "systems of representation" in what Stuart Hall (2003: 5) has described as "a signifying practice." According to Hall, these "systems of representation" function like language "not because they are all written or spoken (they are not), but because they all use some element to stand for or represent what we want to say, to express or communicate a thought, concept, idea or feeling" (2003: 4). His definition of language is expansive and includes spoken language, musical language and "the language of the body" which uses gesture. I read performance through Hall's expansive lenses as "the language of the body." Thus, broadly speaking, performance as it relates to the body and as used in this chapter can be read as signifying all acts (movement, that is, postures and gestures) that entail the deployment of the body to signify meaning. In examining the various characters' performance and interrogation of gendered identities, I am also informed by Judith Butler's theorizing of gender as socially constructed and performative. In her book *Gender Trouble: Feminism and the Subversion of Identity*, Butler posits that

> If gender is the cultural meanings that the sexed body assumes, then a gender cannot be said to follow from a sex in any one way. Taken to its logical limit, the sex/gender distinction suggests a radical discontinuity between sexed bodies and culturally constructed genders.... Assuming for a moment the stability of binary sex, it does not follow that the construction of "men" will accrue exclusively to the bodies of males or that "women" will interpret only female bodies. (2006: 6)

In other words, gender as an identity is fluid and can be performed. This discussion also explores how the characters' culturally defined gendered bodies become representative of the site of contestation and negotiation of "new" identities, mediated by postcolonial national/cultural and global urgencies, as well as various forms of marginalization and silencing. I will attempt to address the following question: How does the body signify identity or self through verbal and nonverbal acts, including voice and movements such as dance, facial expressions, hand gestures, the placement of the body in space and other motions?

Onwueme's play *Shakara: Dance-hall Queen* interrogates the cultural or social constructions of identities (gender and class) and power through several female characters who directly or indirectly confront the structures which they believe oppress them. Certainly, these characters do not necessarily theorize gender, but through various actions, informed by their readings and "performances" of "gendered" identities, the women claim agency and redefine their identities as well as roles in a postcolonial society fraught with economic, political and social challenges. In the play, several characters reject their traditionally prescribed status as the "Other" of maleness by problematizing the patriarchal and cultural/social association of gender (power) with sexed bodies, particularly male bodies. In claiming agency, they vigorously challenge and, perhaps, seemingly "overthrow" what is perceived as male authority, albeit temporarily. Other characters, however, seem to invest these sociocultural assumptions of gendered identity with more vigor, activating the stereotypical alignment of certain gender or sexed bodies with particular social roles and power.

5.2 Interrogating Girlhood: "I am the sole author of my life"

With these words, Shakara declares her agency – first to her friend Dupe, then to Omesiete, her mother. But, Shakara's agency and ability to fully control her own life is constrained by her economic disempowerment, gender and age, thus undermining her mantra, "I am the sole author of my life." In scripting this play about mothers and daughters, Onwueme explores specifically the performance of a young woman's identity as it is mediated by postcolonial urbanization. As Carole Boyce Davies (1994: 8–9) correctly observes:

> If following Judith Butler the category of woman is one of performance of gender, then the category Black woman, or woman of color, exists as multiple performances of gender and race and sexuality based on the particular cultural, historical, geopolitical, class communities in which Black women exist.

Onweme's *Shakara* belongs to the genre of "bildungsroman," although rendered through drama. It is a coming-of-age story about a young girl's journey of self-exploration in an urban setting. Although the play can be cast as a work about youth disillusionment as represented by the intersecting lives of three young women and their mothers, it is the particular experiences of the central character Shakara that drive the action. Throughout the play, the teenage Shakara attempts to interrogate her subjectivity as a young "black woman" and, principally, the cultural and social gendering of that identity. What does it mean to be young, black and female, particularly within an African (Nigerian) urban context? Shakara reads her identity within this context of urban space as one of containment and acute abjection. She is the second daughter of Omesiete, a poor (working-class) single mother, who has been abandoned by her husband because she could not produce a male child. Omesiete and her two daughters, Kechi and Shakara, live in a rented, broken-down house located in a "'shanty' in advanced stages of disrepair." In the United States, someone like Shakara's mother might rely on a government assisted program to support her family. But, since Nigerians do not have such options, Omesiete must raise her children on the meager income she earns from hawking produce on the street beside her home in this urban squalor. She also serves as the "caretaker" of the weeds of her drug-dealing landlord Madam Kofo, whose daughter Dupe is Shakara's best friend.

In the first stage direction of the play, Onwueme establishes the urgency that dominates the life of her central character – a desire to transgress social class and to escape her ethnic/racial identity by transforming herself:

> In her red hot-pant suit, Shakara now sits on the tree stump opposite her friend and starts mounting her altar/shrine of cosmetics. These include: lip-sticks, mirrors, bleaching creams, soaps, pressed powder, a blonde wig and fashion magazines glazed with erotic cover-pictures of sexy models. Now and again, Shakara looks at the sexy magazine cover-girl, holds up a mirror to look at her face, then sighs. Not satisfied with herself, she scrubs her face and body with mixed bleaching cream, then lifts and pinches her wide nose into a cute "v", with a nod and a smile at the magazine model. (1)

In this scene, Shakara's performance of her identity and sexuality/gender underscores a questioning of various perceptions of self – as the subject of a narrative which the character is (re)inscribing, or the object of a gaze (Shakara's and an unidentified audience/public's). The conflation of subject production and objectification in this scene is articulated in the various paraphernalia Shakara employs to transform herself. On her "tree stump" altar of self-transformation, one notes several things that underscore Shakara's sense of self-disgust or hate – a "blonde wig" and "bleaching creams" to transform herself from black to white or "yellow" as the legendary Nigerian Afro-pop musician, Fela Anikulapo-Kuti described it. These items collectively serve as a mask for the performance of a new identity, writ white, which to Shakara seems to be the ideal. Indeed, Onwueme's stage direction underscores her character's preoccupation with escaping her black (African) identity. In scrubbing "her face and body with mixed bleaching cream," Shakara actually destroys her skin, erasing or rubbing off the pigmentation, thus, symbolically "altering" her racial identity. As such, she figuratively attains the "beauty," whiteness, which she desires or imagines. The act of pinching "her wide nose into a cute 'v'" fulfills a similar psychological purpose. In this gesture toward whiteness, Shakara, in disgust, targets her body as the site for the articulation of her anxieties about her racial inferiorized self, which she perceives as ugly. Indeed, Shakara's reading of racial identity in this scene points to self-hate or internalized racism. Such internalization is indicative of cultural colonization; it is a symptom of the Manichean struggle which the colonized subject experiences – a psychological schism, stemming from a mental acculturation which reads black as ugly and white as desirable or beautiful.

Truly, Shakara's preoccupation with whiteness as symbolizing beauty is not only a consequence of the colonial legacy which did not value blackness, but also representative of a larger historical and cultural negation of blackness by Western culture, which either exoticized blackness or tried to erase it. Indeed, Shakara has fore-sisters in Toni Morrison's Pecola (*The Bluest Eye*) who prays for blue eyes to make her beautiful and Wallace Thurman's Emma Lou Morgan (*The Blacker the Berry*) who finds her black skin so threatening that, like Shakara, she tries to erase or mask it. It is worth noting also that many black and African diaspora women have a love-hate relationship with their hair. Therefore, it is not uncommon to find black women hating their tightly textured hair, referring to it as bad or "nappy" and opting for straightened hair or a wig, especially since the dominant culture has generally defined "good" hair as straight and, possibly, light-colored.[2] India Arie's song "I am not my hair" (*Testimony: Vol. 1 Life & Relationship* 2005) speaks to the hair question and although the song may have universal appeal, the hair experiences cataloged by the song – adventures with jerry (Jheri) curls, relaxed or straightened hair, braids and dreadlocks – underscore black women's hair stories.[3] Really, 17-year-old Shakara's donning of a Western wig to cover her African hair, because she perceives it or herself as ugly, is outside the boundaries of what her family and friend Dupe see as normative. According to bell hooks, "[t]hat the field of representation remains a place of struggle is most evident when

---

2   I want to acknowledge that not all black women hate their hair or wear wigs because they have "hair complexes." It is important to recognize the diverse ways in which black women treat their hair. Many black women braid or (dread)lock their hair and this is becoming a growing trend amongst them. Some shave it off completely, while others navigate between braids and straightened hair or wigs. Some black women opt to wear wigs because it is expedient, especially when they are confronted with the length of time it takes to braid their hair in readiness for work or social engagements. Other women wear wigs because they have experienced an illness, such as cancer, whose treatments often lead to hair loss. However, Shakara's use of a wig does not fall into any of these categories.

3   India Arie (Simpson) has performed different versions of this song with various singers, including Pink and Akon. The version with Akon chronicles the persona's experience of pain because of her/his hair – nappy hair, jerry curls, relaxed hair, dreadlocks, braids, etc.

we critically examine contemporary representations of blackness and black people." She adds that she was

> painfully reminded of this fact when visiting friends on a once colonized black island. Their little girl is just reaching that stage of preadolescent life where we become obsessed with our image, with how we look and how others see us. Her skin is dark. Her hair is chemically straightened. Not only is she fundamentally convinced that straightened hair is more beautiful that curly, kinky, natural hair, she believes that lighter skin makes one more worthy, more valuable in the eyes of others. (hooks 1992: 3)

In Shakara's case and that of the teenage daughter of bell hooks' friends, it is the black woman's body that is scarred and becomes the signifier of the cultural colonization and psychic dismemberment of blacks. Indeed, the two young girls have targeted their bodies as the sites and representations of imagined and socially constructed "otherness," negation and ugliness. Ironically, the skin bleaching and hair straightening which they read as corrective gestures further negate the girls' racial identities. While hooks' friends' daughter has "internalized white supremacist values and aesthetics, a way of looking and seeing the world that negates her values," Onwueme's Shakara actualizes that perception and negation by bleaching her skin and donning a blonde wig, and in the process, scarring her body. Ironically, to Shakara, the racial difference (whiteness) which she desires represents progress, modernity, social mobility, which she believes would liberate her from her abjection. It is this internal psychic rupture that her friend Dupe observes when she tells Shakara that the latter has a "color-complex" (5), again underscoring the symbolic role which Shakara's body plays as a site of cultural contestation.

But, Shakara's yearning to escape her spatial and social locations is not limited to her submergence into whiteness. She will not be white regardless of how much she bleaches her skin or tries to pinch her nose into a "cute 'v'." Perhaps, her acute awareness of the finality of her racial status adds to her desperation. As such, she finds succor in the cultural productions of other African diaspora groups. References to reggae, rap, hip-hop, the blues and other African diaspora musical traditions abound in this play. On several occasions, Shakara and her friend Dupe articulate their anguish or states of mind through music, especially the music of African diaspora cultures. In the opening scene, which I cited earlier, Shakara is listening to rap music from her "boom-box," playing it "loud enough to offend anyone who doesn't like that kind of music" (1). Shakara not only listens to music that she sees as transgressive, but she also indulges in dances such as "'Electric

Shock', 'Break-Dancing', 'Moonwalk' and 'Buddy-Call'" (1) that are associated with new world African diaspora cultures.

While the songs and dances point to Shakara's writing of her body as a signifier of either cultural displacement or encroachment, the references to these cultural productions represent Onwueme's location within African (Nigerian) and new world African diaspora contexts. In this play, she pays homage to these cultures. Onwueme defines her use of "shakara" in this play as "'Sassy' – the bluff/show off." The word or idea was made famous by Afro-pop king Fela Anikulapo-Kuti in the early 1970s with his song titled "Shakara Oloje." In the play, a sassy Shakara tells her mother and sister that she won the moniker "Shakara: Dance-hall Queen" because of her prowess and popularity in the dance clubs. While the name may be apropos for the character, it is a mélange of cultural productions: one Nigerian (Fela's song), and the other, the Jamaican dance-hall culture.[4] Thus, Onwueme's Shakara embodies the cultural links between African and new world diaspora cultures. Like the dancers in Fela's musical extravaganza or carnival, the Jamaican dance-hall queen can be provocatively gaudy, erotic and carnivalesque. In both instances, as with Onwueme's character, the body and its gestures or motions are central to the performance of Shakara's identity, name or title as dance-hall queen. It is through the body that the social position is achieved, gestured, danced into existence, stabilized and/or sustained. It is, therefore, through the bodily representations or enactments of the character that the identity is transformed and her new name or identity comes into being. Thus, for Shakara, the dancing or bodily gestures represent an existentialist position, her own articulation of agency, resistance, or of self-gestation and/or birthing. In other words, according to Shakara, she figuratively gives birth to herself, as in "I am the sole author of my life" (2).

5.3 What's in a Name?

Omesiete named her second daughter Nwaebuni to articulate resistance against her husband's masculinist ideas about progeny and birthrights. So, Shakara's given name, Nwaebuni, means "the child uplifts" (14), but Shakara does not uplift her family; rather, she abandons it, rejecting it in

---

4   Onwueme's title and character's dance-hall prowess may also have been influenced by the 1997 Jamaican independent film *Dance Hall Queen* (1997). A simple search of the internet will reveal a plethora of erotic pictures and poses all associated with the Jamaican dance-hall queen.

pursuit of instant gratification in the social clubs and dance halls she visits, or sexual trysts with "wealthy" men in big cars, "Mercedes Benz 500." While her mother tells her that she is "much more precious than all [her gangster friends] put together," advising her to stay away from "trouble-trouble-trouble" (14), Shakara brags about her escapades in clubs with esoteric names: "Gondola, Caban Bamboo, Labamba ... Where the real life is ... with the guys: Italian, Lebanese, French, American, English, Portuguese, Spanish ..." (15), places which to Omesiete underscore her daughter's alienation. Indeed, whereas Omesiete interprets her daughter's name as signifying the child's responsibility to her family and community, Shakara construes it narrowly and believes that her obligation is only to herself, and like Icarus, whose spirit she often invokes, flies toward the sun. Unlike Omesiete who believes in the cultural significance of her daughter's name,[5] Shakara calls it a "bush name," suggesting that it is not modern. Consequently, she renames herself "Shakara, Dance-hall Queen." In the end, like Icarus who did not heed Daedalus's warning, Shakara flies too close to danger and eventually is trapped and destroyed by her involvement in Madam Kofo's drug trade.

The scene between Shakara and her mother is important, because it provides Onwueme, as playwright, an opportunity to engage in a performance of storytelling through her character. In telling her daughter about her name, Omesiete narrates a story of origins, betrayal, abandonment and disempowerment (13–17). Through this narrative, she tells Shakara about her birth and the origin of her name; Omesiete also tells her children about herself, a young Omesiete, who like Shakara ignored her parents' warnings about the untrustworthiness of her spouse. In other words, the narrative becomes a fable with didactic purposes. The performance also enables Omesiete to perform her role as a good mother, who is concerned about her family. This scene, therefore, represents Omesiete as a foil to Madam Kofo, who does not seem to care about her only child Dupe. As such, Omesiete possesses the qualities that are lacking in Madam Kofo. Unlike Omesiete, who cares for her two daughters (31), Madam Kofo, the drug-dealing landlady, spends little time with her only child. Instead, she is preoccupied with her wealth and brutalizes her daughter and employees. Where Omesiete is affectionate, motherly, nurturing, ethical and patient Madam Kofo is brash, immoral, unethical, "power hungry" and unmotherly. Consequently, it is Omesiete's acts of kindness that endear her to Dupe, Madam Kofo's only

5   Most African cultures believe that names have significance and that a person's name guides that person through life. So, when a child does something perceived as wrong, he/she may be urged by elders to recall the significance of his/her name or to live by his/her name.

child. While the portrayals of these two women may be dramatic, their representation collapses into binary opposition, invoking stereotypes about women.

Still, despite Omesiete's piety and affection for her children, Shakara remains resistant. Responding to her friend's criticisms and attempts to dissuade her from indulging in self-hating acts, Shakara insists on declaring her independence and individuality, believing that she controls her life and that she can "change [her] destiny" (101). She states to Dupe:

SHAKARA.	Girl, I'm the sole author of my life. Nobody rules it.
DUPE.	(Still laughing.) You? A mere brat competing with God? You and my mother. You'll never learn.
SHAKARA.	(Wincing.) Leave that woman alone. What is there to learn?
DUPE.	A lot, my friend. A lot. (Pointing.) The hot comb spoke it loud and clear. Listen!
SHAKARA.	(Dismissing her with a wave of the hand.) Girlfriend, you're letting them cripple you ... Yeah. You've been infected with that moral epidemic. (Dupe replies with loud laughter. Shakara resumes her erotic dance.) I am free. What does prophet Marley say? (Briefly sings: "Don't let them fool ya!"). (2)

This exchange between the two young women is telling, because it reveals Shakara's mental state as well as Dupe's awareness of her friend's estrangement from her family and community. At 17, Shakara is impatient and preoccupied with materialistic needs and instant gratification. She desperately desires money, eager to leave with any man who may offer her some attention. It is safe to say that she consequently engages in sex trafficking, for in several scenes, she chases after "the beast," the Mercedes Benz 500, which constantly plies her street. In a dramatic performance of rebellion in the penultimate "Eighth Stage," which marks the climax of the conflict between Shakara and her family, she denounces her mother and sister, berating her mother for not seizing a "life-time opportunity, standing there in front of you ..." (98). Announcing to her sister and mother: "I can't help ... can't help myself anymore. But for good or bad, something's got to be done. And I'm ready. If I succeed, good. If not, goodbye to you, mother and sister" (98), Shakara abandons her family for a life with Mama Kofo as a drug mule.

For Shakara who sees Omesiete, her mother, as a failure, Madam Kofo's life and drug trade represent a world of luxury and materialistic potentialities. In a gesture suggesting her subordination to Madam Kofo, Shakara "curtsies," stammers and trembles before her idol (99). Even when Madam Kofo threatens her by calling her dog to attack Shakara, a "terrified" Shakara pleads, "Madam, please!" and chants, "Take me. Take me! I'm tired. I'm dead" (100). Despite the allure of Madam Kofo's wealth, Shakara's embrace of the former comes at a cost – specifically, the threat of self-annihilation. Ironically, in an earlier scene, a brazen Shakara tells her mother: "I'm not here to inherit anybody else's failures, but mine" (16). But, the Shakara before Madam Kofo seems to be only a ghost, a shadow of the defiant child who dares her mother to stop her, and who despite her mother's warnings against the illusory nature of Madam Kofo's wealth, is determined to negate the significance of her name. Consequently, Omesiete calls her appropriately, "Eneke-nti-mkpo," which is a caution that says "The fowl which refuses to listen hears inside the anus of the wolf" (17), foreshadowing Shakara's fate at the end of the play.

5.4 Rewriting Gender and Power

For Shakara, power is liberating and the performance of sexuality or a sexualized body grants women power. In a moment of desperation she asks her mother: "Why should I be so young and so ashamed of myself? ... When am I ever going to have a chance to live like my mates?" (18). Later, she complains, "Mama, I'm tired. Tired of being ridiculed and laughed at by other girls who're not even as pretty as myself. The way they look down on me, my clothes as if I carry shit on my body" (18). Although these comments underscore a degree of agency and defiance, Shakara sees her body as a signifier of her class position. Despite her mother's stoicism and acceptance of her poverty, believing in the possibility of change one day, Shakara is not convinced. Rather, she finds a model of female empowerment in the figure of Madame Kofo, who has amassed a lot of wealth through her illegal drug business and by terrorizing her employees. To Shakara, Madam Kofo is "A great woman. The envy of the world! Princess and jewel among her peers!" (6). But, who are these "peers"? They do not exist, except in Shakara's imagination of Madam Kofo's financial empire. She describes Madam Kofo as "very smart." She is "the kind of women we want nowadays" because "they're the best survivors" (52). Later, she gloatingly tells Dupe, "You should have seen how she cruised into our place with that chief after you left... . You should see her strides ... (Imitating). Oh girl, that woman walks with confidence" (53). Ironically, the encounter which Shakara describes is one in which her family is humiliated by Madam Kofo.

But, Shakara reads it as a performance of power. Indeed, this reading is in keeping with Madam Kofo's display of her stature as presented at the opening of "The Sixth Stage." Onwueme describes the scene: "Madam Kofo in her ornate sitting room. She is richly dressed, her long blonde wig mounted right in front of her.... [S]he is discussing a business deal with some partner on the telephone. A bottle of whiskey is sitting by her side" (46).

Ironically, what Shakara reads as a means of social empowerment reinscribes women's identities in stereotypical terms: woman = gender = female sexed body = powerless. Therefore, only by either transgressing those normative women's roles through some public performance of power, like Madam Kofo, or subscribing to and performing them within defined traditional contexts, like Omesiete who sees herself as the good mother, are women able to acquire social recognition. In either case, one is confined or limited to the performance of a particular gendered role or identity, informed by one's sexual identity, as a woman. Madam Kofo succeeds because she is able to exploit her sexuality, specifically in her relationship with certain men in powerful positions, as well as engage in the drug trade. While Shakara is preoccupied with her life as a young woman, Onwueme's women, in general, seem to agree that women are not valued by their society. In fact, Omesiete confirms this perspective when she informs her daughters that: "Your father lost interest in me because he expected male children" (17). Then she tells Shakara, "You should have seen the spiteful look in his eyes when he saw you, my baby-child. He just hissed and mumbled something about the house filling up with ra ... rats. Rats!" (17). Omesiete's comments suggest that gender is associated with the sexed body and, consequently, being and power. According to Omesiete, then, it is the sexed body, the possession of a particularly "important" anatomical part that privileges individuals, endows them with power, social importance. That body part signifies their subject positions as persons – embodied. By implication, women or girls, because they are not privileged with that "particularly important" anatomical part seem to occupy secondary locations within their culture or society. And, because Shakara is acutely aware of her status as a second-class citizen or marginal figure, a consequence of her sexed body, she believes that to counter the various layers of oppression women encounter and claim space (read social status), women have to perform their sexuality/gender. According to Onwueme, Shakara is "the underclass youth restless to wrest her sordid life from the gripping jaws of poverty. Failing, she yields her own body to the vampires of the marketplace" (Onwueme 2011: 63).

In exercising power over all her employees, Madam Kofo challenges the patriarchal location of power in a male body. Hence, she is often described as "chief" or "cobra." Interestingly, these are terms which are often associated with men. One would venture to claim that Madam Kofo, therefore, occupies an interstitial location. While corporeally she is encased in a space read as female, she performs publically as male. In fact, Dupe signals her mother's interstitiality when she refers to her as godlike – that is, all-powerful. Her floating identity is in keeping with Judith Butler's position that gender is performative and floating. According to Butler,

> The presumption of a binary system implicitly retains the belief in the mimetic relation of gender to sex whereby gender mirrors sex or is otherwise restricted by it. When the constructed status of gender is theorized as radically independent of sex, gender itself becomes a free-floating artifice, with the consequence that *man* and *masculine* might just as easily signify a female body as a male one, and *woman* and *feminine* a male body as easily as a female one. (2006: 6)

Patriarchy generally empowers men and disempowers women. Onwueme's characters recognize their subordination, especially in a postcolonial "modern" environment with entrenched traditional practices. The characters occupy locations where various competing layers of social structures become disempowering. While the women we generally find are marginalized by a male-dominated society, some women are also disempowered by other women. Indeed, the relationship between Omesiete and Madam Kofo is an example of the latter power relation and reproduces the dominant patriarchal male/female tension and hierarchy, where Madam Kofo assumes superiority or privilege, although through class. In fact, Madam Kofo's assertions of power become threatening and disempowering even for the men. Although she claims that her trading in drugs is an act of survival, the Police Officer who arrests her sees it otherwise. To him, Madam Kofo's actions have "gone beyond surviving." He tells her, "All you want now is to have it all, stay on top and run down everybody" (109). To him and the law (or society), Madam Kofo has become "A very dangerous criminal" (108). Interestingly, the Police Officer suggests that had Madam Kofo stayed within certain limits which did not threaten his survival, she may have been safe. In this case, the Police Officer's comments imply that Madam Kofo might have been safe had she performed her gender role, that is, by accepting her subordination. This perception is underscored earlier when a frightened Madam Kofo puts on a mask of humility and attempts to seduce the Police Officer with drinks. Onwueme writes the encounter:

MADAM KOFO:	Nothing. Nothing to declare. (Smiling, offering him a drink.) Officer, you work so hard. And in this heat? Have a drink. Let's go inside and talk.
POLICE OFFICER:	(Turning, inspecting the bags.) Madam. I'm ok. But thanks anyway. I said, anything to declare?
MADAM KOFO:	(Seductive, but nervous.) Officer, I said have a drink on me ... I mean anything. I'll be too glad to give ... just anything to make you comfortable. (105)

Madam Kofo's transformation into a "temptress" signals her awareness of the power of sexuality. In this scene, and threatened by what she perceives as male siege, Madam Kofo becomes dissembling. She puts on various masks, first as seductress, then as a woman in despair by becoming hysterical, and finally as a concerned mother. These gestures are meant to neutralize the threat and secure her safety.

5.5 Closing

Onwueme's plays in general are replete with characters, especially women and youth, who constantly struggle against oppressive forces. Shakara's protest against her social status is justified as it underscores the economic and social disparities in her environment. Like her mother and Madam Kofo, Shakara is acutely aware of the limited economic opportunities available to the poor, and especially women. She tells her mother that education no longer secures a better future or progress, for the educated roam the streets in search of jobs. Indeed, the national leadership has failed the citizens. Therefore, for Shakara, her survival depends on her assertion of agency, her ability to create those opportunities for herself. In declaring her independence from her family at age 17, Shakara transgresses accepted cultural practices which privilege the family and parents' nurturing their children. Indeed, Onwueme's play asserts that the pressures of postcolonial urban (Nigerian) society undermine the survival of families, especially women-headed households, represented by those of Madam Kofo and Omesiete. Both women and their daughters are subordinated by society because of their gender, but whereas Omesiete finds strength in her stoic belief in the power of religion and morality, Madam Kofo and Shakara believe in the power of the individual to control his/her fate or life. For Shakara, survival entails the ability to perform one's identity or self, transforming the self as an act of defiance against societal restrictions and expectations. One must fly high like Icarus, wrench power from the gods so to say. As her friend Dupe puts it, Shakara is "one of those who want to run before they can even learn to walk" (2). Dupe's comment underscores Shakara's impatience, and ironically signals her Promethean temperament. But, like Icarus, Shakara, too, must learn moderation.

References

Butler, J. (2006). *Gender Trouble: Feminism and the Subversion of Identity*. New York: Routledge.
Carlson, M. (2009). Resistant performance. In Bill Ashcroft, Gareth Griffiths and Helen Tiffin (eds.), *The Post-Colonial Studies Reader*, 2nd ed. (pp. 309–12). London and New York: Routledge.
Davies, C.B. (1994). *Black Women, Writing and Identity*. New York: Routledge. http://dx.doi.org/10.4324/9780203201404
Gilbert, H. (2009). Dance, movement and resistance. In Bill Ashcroft, Gareth Griffiths and Helen Tiffin (eds.), *The Post-Colonial Studies Reader*, 2nd ed. (pp. 302–5). London and New York: Routledge.
Hall, S. (ed.). (2003). *Representation: Cultural Representations and Signifying Practice*. London: Sage Publications.
hooks, b. (1992). *Black Looks: Race and Representation*. Boston: South End Press.
Onwueme, T.O. (2000). *Shakara: Dance-hall Queen*. San Francisco: Africa Heritage Press.
Onwueme, T.O. (2011). If you want justice, work for truth: Fonlon Nichols Award or Call to Action. In L. Losambe & M.N. Eke (eds.), *Literature, The Visual Arts and Globalization in Africa and its Diaspora*. African Literature Association Annual Series, Vol. 15 (pp. 55–64). Trenton, NJ: Africa World Press.

Part Two:
Nonverbal Communication and Cultural Diversity

Shadowy walk 3. By Augustine Agwuele, 2014.

6
The Convergence of Language and Culture in Malawian Gestures: Handedness in Everyday Rituals

Karen W. Sanders[1]

6.1 Introduction

Natural language is produced through multiple modes of utterances, including spoken words and gestures – the meaningful movements of the hands and other parts of the body (Kendon 2000; McNeill 2006; Enfield 2010). In addition to its primary locutionary function, language in its spoken and non-spoken forms also transcends cultural expectations by producing acceptable structures and contents. For example, using the appropriate form of the second person, *tu* or *vous*, to express familiarity or formality respectively, produces a socially acceptable outcome in French-speaking communities. In ciTonga,[2] a language spoken on the northern lakeshore of Malawi, politeness and inclusivity are also expressed through different forms of pronominal reference.[3] In this chapter we explore the symbolic and practical significance of handedness, the choosing of one or both hands to carry out activities in Malawian daily interaction, especially during "everyday" rituals. We argue that handedness plays a major role in displaying important cultural values such as respect and inclusiveness, but this is meaningful only when it takes place in a publically visible setting,

---

1 Karen W. Sanders holds a PhD in Linguistic Anthropology from Tulane University. Her primary research interest includes the structure and function of visible expressions in everyday, face-to-face interactions.
2 The *ci-* in *ciTonga* refers to the noun "language." *Tonga* is adjectival, referring to "of the Tonga." The plural noun *aTonga* refers to "people of Tonga," in which *a-* is the noun prefix for plural people.
3 Two of the person noun classes in ciTonga represent singularity, *wa-*, and plurality, *a-*, but also informal and impolite, respectively.

and when the interlocutors are less familiar with each other. In addition to noting the pragmatic and semantic values of handedness in spontaneous activities, we also use this opportunity to provide a description of three Tonga everyday rituals that have not yet been documented. We observe that handedness is closely associated with the opposing cultural values of generosity and selfishness, strength and weakness, and skillfulness and clumsiness. This association is not only explained by particular aTonga whom we interviewed, but also observed in many spontaneous activities in Malawi that we shall describe below. Despite this perception, we still note many incidents where the left hand is used dominantly in activities that are typically right-handed, such as greeting, and exchanging objects. We investigate here why the left hand is sometimes allowed to act dominantly, and in what contexts it is allowed to do so. Does using the left hand communicate anything significant about the gesturer, about the relationship between the interlocutors? To answer these questions, we survey multiple forms of gesture within three everyday rituals – access, exchange and dining rituals – because each has been studied in detail in other cultural contexts but lacks significant description in ciTonga-speaking communities, and each is popularly perceived in Nkhata Bay and Northern Malawi as right-hand-only activity. In the next section, we provide an ethnographic background of the aTonga in Malawi, showing that left-handed actions are perceived negatively in the society. In section 6.3, we define everyday rituals and explain how they differ from rituals in general along with some of the structures and contents that make them different from other daily activities. We then offer documentation of three Tonga everyday rituals to show the significance of handedness in these activities.

6.2 Ethnographic Background

CiTonga is a Niger-Congo, Narrow Bantu language spoken by the aTonga people residing on the northwestern shore of Lake Malawi. It belongs to N10 of the Niger-Congo, Narrow Bantu language family, sharing linguistic ancestry with ciTumbuka (N20), its language neighbor to the north, and its southern neighbor ciChewa (N30), the national language of Malawi (Lewis et al. 2015). According to the 1998 Malawian demographic census, ciTonga is the second most widely spoken language in the northern region (11 per cent), behind ciTumbuka, spoken by 65 per cent of the population (National Statistical Office 2011). According to Van Velsen (1964), there are at least five distinct peoples called "Tonga" in the Central African region. Here we are discussing the Tonga residing in Nkhata Bay, Malawi.

In Malawi, as in most African countries, there seems to be strong pressure against left-hand activities. For instance, people in the Ivory Coast usually call the left hand "the bad hand," and consider it improper to give directions or give an object to another person with the left hand, with such an action being interpreted as a sign of contempt (De Agostini et al. 1997). In Ghana, some gestures produced by the left hand are considered obscene (Kita & Essegbey 2001) and pointing with the left hand is restricted. In Nigeria among the Yoruba speakers, the left hand is associated with bathroom activities or is reserved for neutralizing evil forces in traditional medicine (Orie 2009). Particularly in Muslim countries, there are strong social pressures against eating with the left hand and more generally for using the left hand to perform any action related to food. Alternatively, the use of the left hand seems to be culturally recommended for "unclean" activities such as blowing one's nose or wiping oneself after defecation.

Handedness preference is a result of physiological determination and cultural and environmental socialization. The preference for using one hand over another is common across societies, with right-handers as the majority, roughly 90 per cent, and left-handers in the minority, 8–12 per cent (McManus 2004). A small percentage of the population, about 2 per cent, are ambidextrous, using both hands with equal facility. This distribution has not changed in 50 centuries (Coren & Porac 1977), but within it there are varying levels of handedness, ranging from someone who is strongly right-handed to someone with a weak right hand but strong left hand. The asymmetry of hand use is a characteristic of human populations (Perelle & Ehrman 1994). The cause of handedness is not necessarily correlated with brain lateralization, as fetuses demonstrate handedness in the womb without a well-formed spinal cord (McManus 2004). People tend to associate positive thoughts with the side of their dominant hand (Casasanto 2009).

In general, informal or permissive cultures, such as many in North America and Europe, have liberalized attitudes toward left-handedness and apply little cultural pressure to changing the hand preference of children (Coren & Porac 1977), whereas formal or culturally restrictive societies, such as found in much of Africa, Asia and Latin America have strong anti-left-handed prejudices and practices (Zverev 2006). According to Coren & Porac (1977), such differences in cultural orientation to handedness might account for up to 23.5 per cent of the cross-cultural variations in handedness patterns. Although in some African societies like Ghana and Nigeria, writing with the left hand is no longer prohibited (personal communication with Orie & Essegbey), in Malawi schools remain opposed to allowing left-handed children to write with that hand.

During our research, we interviewed many native ciTonga speakers on handedness and gesture preference. One speaker commented, "I believe that left-handed [people] are greedy people who can't give to others." The left hand is also directly correlated with the word for "bad" as in the idiom *wachitazakumazere*, literally translated as "You have done left things," but meaning, "You have done bad things."

Even though the physiological aspect of handedness preference is similar across cultures, the perceptions and allowances made to using the left hand are not. Strong cultural sentiment is enforced through education and socialization, a learning process where an experienced member trains a novice in the appropriate social behaviors for specific situations (Garrett & Baquedano-López 2002; León 1998; Schieffelin & Ochs 1986). This process often includes, but is not limited to, linguistic communication, the sense of physical comportment and posture (Geurts 2002), the consumption of food (Mintz & Du Bois 2002), and clothing and dressing (Hansen 2004). During fieldwork, we often observed adults correcting toddlers at home and in nursery schools in order to enforce right-handedness.

6.3 Ritual and Everyday Rituals

Ritual refers to a set of socially recognized activities that are conducted to represent social values, ideologies and expectations; as well as setting a standard for how to behave (Geertz 1977). Rituals are orchestrated to reinforce the dominant ideologies of a community through a symbolic manipulation of the body and voice, and sometimes objects (Turner 1995). The performance of rituals commonly projects societal norms onto the performer and/or the audience, which includes not only the immediate participants, but also anyone who sees or hears the performance (Bell 1984). Rituals are also used to signify transition from one life stage to another – for example, rite of passage rituals for transition from youth to adulthood (Turner 1995) – or restore stability, as in the case of witchcraft rituals to identify thieves or unfaithful romantic partners. A central element in ritual interaction is the psychological commitment and training of the agent actor, who at the very least needs to possess fluency in the semantic and expressive aspects of his/her community of practice. For the actions to be considered rituals they must be produced in a particular order and fashion.

Some rituals may take place at certain times and places – for instance the Malipenga dance performance that takes place in the afternoon of July or August in designated spaces – and others can take place at any time. Rituals repeat socially significant values and practices, ranging from patterns of speech, to ways of spatially organizing the location of people inside the house (Enfield 2009). Sometimes the reason for a chosen technique is because it simply facilitates the completion of a task, while at other times the technical significance appears unclear or is explained as having cultural value. Ritualized activities include everything from subtle actions like the pace of walking to highly organized activities like celebratory dance performances. Rituals sustain relationships between people and maintain standards of behavior. This chapter also takes the view from Basso and Senft (2009: 2) that everyday rituals are inherently multimodal, in which the human body, temporalization and formally categorized spatial settings all play crucial roles. Analyzing the linguistic and non-linguistic actions in ritual communication shows that the symbolic power of the ritual is dependent not only on the expressive competency of the actor, but also his/her devotion to the role assigned. The division between formal and informal rituals is often blurry.

It is apparent that giving and receiving rituals depend heavily on the use of the hands, and here, we focus specifically on the flexibility of handedness in carrying out selected everyday activities and how handedness plays a role in reinforcing cultural standards. The consideration of handedness is prefaced by the fact that, across societies, there is a strong physical dominance of the right hand. The body has been frequently partitioned as a micro-representation of a culture's ideology, and the selection of a certain part of the body to carry out a ritual task often has symbolic meaning that is given considerable importance.

6.3.1 Access Rituals

Access rituals are the everyday bodily and verbal actions that individuals exchange to initiate a social encounter (Duranti 1997). Ameka (2009) expanded this to also include the routines used to terminate an encounter. So a greeting is an action that is only part of a larger access ritual; it fulfills the function of a ritual in that it allows the expression and reinforcement of social relationships. The hands are dominant actors in access rituals. While a handshake appears to be the dominant form of greeting around the world, some societies have traditionally preferred other activities such as bowing (Japan), *hongi* or forehead touching (Maori), and the *bissou* or cheek kiss (France).

The form of greetings in Tonga Malawi is determined by whether the interlocutors are seated or standing. Seated greetings are typical of prearranged meetings in Malawi and are much longer in duration, usually from morning to afternoon. Standing greetings typically involve interlocutors in passing and take place outside of the home. They may take place without any verbal exchange, or they may turn into longer conversations and recruit more members as other passersby stop and join the conversation. Formality can be expressed during both forms of greeting, but the spatial nature of seated greetings causes the host party to have more power and control over the proceedings. Though it does set the overarching tone of the interaction, the power dynamic may vary frame by frame, and interlocutors may use subversive strategies to contest it (Goffman 1974). The two types of greetings also have termination rituals relative to the duration of the event. Fleeting greetings do not need a termination, while the end of a seated greeting may include the host escorting the visitor to a bus terminal or a junction in the main road where the visitor will then go his or her own way.

(A) Single-hand Handshake

Handshakes in Tonga Malawi are slightly different from handshakes in Western societies. In both cases, the right hand of the greeter is used to grasp the right hand of the visitor, but in Malawi, the left hand also participates by supporting the right forearm (Figure 6.1). A person of senior status, whether the visitor or the host, can show affection by extending both hands to hold the other's right hand or place the left hand on the other's shoulder. If the right hand of the visitor or the greeter happens to be occupied – for instance, if while being approached, they have already started eating a snack – the right wrist is offered for handshake and in this case the left hand does not hold the right forearm.

Handshakes in Nkhata Bay typically last a bit longer than in Western societies. Often the handshake continues during the first few verbal greeting rituals. During handshakes, the right hand is used to detect the physical wellness of one another. In addition to the firmness and warmth of the palms, one can also detect the amount of physical labor that the hands have endured. Dryness or thickly calloused hands suggest that the person might work in the field, while a softer hand reveals that the person perhaps works in an office. Soft hands on a woman suggest that she either does not cook, or cooks on a stovetop. Thus, the prolonged Malawian handshake communicates important information about social status.

Language and Culture in Malawian Gestures

Figure 6.1. Shaking hands with the right hands but supporting and holding with the left hands.

Handshakes, however, are not universal and are not observed across all African societies. In Nigeria, especially among the Yoruba, handshakes are not commonly practiced (Orie, personal communication).

(B) Thumb Handshake

After the hands come in contact in a typical handshake, the participants may rotate their wrists pivoting at the web of the thumb and hold onto each other's thumbs using the remaining fingers (Figure 6.2). Since the handshake is always made with the right hand, this subsequent motion also continues to be performed by the right hands. The thumb handshake is typically used for consoling the sick or the family members of the deceased at a funeral. If one wishes to provide small monetary contribution to the

Figure 6.2. Thumb handshakes are common when paying condolences.

ill, one may include a folded bill in the curved palm and subtly transfer it to the recipient. When a folded bill is detected, the receiver will shake the hands of the giver repeatedly to show gratitude. We must note here that bribery or other forms of secret money exchanges are not carried out through the thumb handshake.

(C) Tickle Handshake

The tickle handshake is a right-hand handshake where one of the participants tickles the palm of the other using his right index or middle finger. The tickle of the palm is quick and fleeting, but the sensation is enough to surprise the tickled. Typically, a man gives the tickle handshake to a woman. This action communicates a wish to make a sexual advance to the one being tickled.

(D) Handholding

A handshake can be extended to turn into a handhold, when one or both of the participants of the same gender want to show affection (Figure 6.3). Handholding does not have a fixed hand conformation, so long as the right hands are touching. When the interlocutors have an exciting topic to discuss, they can swing their handholding arms and continue to chat. The duration of handholding is typically less than in an access ritual. The hands are released mutually, as it is considered rude and unwelcoming if one pulls one's hand away before the other.

In addition to the access ritual, it is not uncommon for good friends of the same gender to hold hands while they walk and talk, or for a friendly

Figure 6.3. Shaking and holding hands to show familiarity.

local to hold the hand of a visitor while the former directs and escorts the latter to the desired destination. The person standing on the left will extend the right hand, while the person on the right extends the left hand. ATonga also hold hands for a similar reason when they are not greeting. For example, two colleagues of the same gender may lightly hold hands and walk together. The duration of handholding depends on the amount of affection one wants to share with the companion. Non-access handholding does not have a hand preference because it typically takes place while a pair of friends are walking and facing the same direction. A male American teacher in Nkhata Bay narrated that his local friend held his hand for the entire duration of a 20-minute walk. This prolonged hand contact allows people to show their friendship to others and include them in the community. While the hands are touching, there is also an exchange of the tactile sensation of each other's palms and fingers. The warmth, dryness and state of muscle relaxation are detected directly through handholding. This kind of prolonged contact also signifies that the individuals are at ease in each other's company and are in no rush to leave.

(E) Handclasp

When a physical barrier separates people, whether that barrier is a distance or other people seated in between, a handclasp may be substituted for a handshake. There is no fixed way that the hands must be clasped together. Either the right or the left hand can assume the top position, depending on personal preference. A handshake can be replaced by a handclasp when it is evident that the greeter cannot physically meet the hands of every person present. The handclasp is the preferred form of greeting when one person greets a group of people or when appearing in front of an audience. For example, when giving a public speech during a village meeting, the greeter is expected to give a verbal greeting and handclasp to every member present to show humility. In this situation, the hands are re-clasped as one moves on to greet the next person, in the form of a light clap.

We have observed a woman giving a handclasp greeting to an audience attending a village meeting for the purpose of distributing toy donations from a foreign donor. The woman clasps with her right hand on top. However, the hand that is positioned on top is variable. In another event, a village memorial celebration, an older man handclasps with his left hand on top (Figure 6.4). Unlike the handedness in asymmetrical quotable gestures and handshakes where people consistently use the right hand, handedness in handclasps displays varying patterns.

Figure 6.4. Older man clasping his hands to greet a female friend, with his *left* hand on top.

There are two alternative functions of the handclasp outside of the greeting ritual: quotable gestures with the meanings "excuse me" and "thank you." The placement of the hands appears to depend on personal preference. The preference for which hand goes on top, in these contexts, seems more related to a different kind of hand dominance – the same kind of handedness that determines which arm is on top when arms are crossed in front of the torso and which thumb is on top when the fingers interlock. Handedness in greeting handclasps is not related to hand dominance in writing, eating and tool use.

(F) Hugging

A quick hug or a tap on the back is used during greeting between interlocutors of the same gender, more often between women than men (Figure 6.5). Both hands perform hugs but typically the right arm is used for embrace. Tonga men and women do not hug each other, but younger residents, especially those with friends from Europe, North America or Australia, will receive and sometimes initiate hugs with foreigners of the opposite sex.

Figure 6.5. Hugging is common between female friends.

(G) Hand Slap and "Sharp"

When two familiar individuals meet in passing, a quick hand slap may be exchanged. Alternatively, younger aTonga often use a thumbs-up gesture called "sharp." There appear to be no restrictions on which hand should be used for hand slaps and "sharp" gestures, as they are fleeting gestures between good friends. Figure 6.6 (left) shows two women with head-loads

Figure 6.6. Hand slapping with right and left hands.

greeting each other by extending their right hands for a quick hand slap, combining a hello and a goodbye. The bodies come in contact momentarily and the hands do not hold.

When the bodies of greeting participants are visibly restricted, the left hand can be used. In Figure 6.6 (right), a woman bids goodbye to her male friend who happens to be riding in the back of a pick-up truck. The man raises his left hand to wave good-bye but is met with the left hand of his friend. Left hands are used in this greeting because of the restricted body orientation of the man.

If one is carrying something it may be difficult to use one's hands to greet another. Women and children typically carry their *katundu*, bundled traveling baggage, on the head, but adult men, who carry objects by hand or slung over the shoulder, may have to unload the *katundu* to use their hands in greeting. Women and children unload their *katundu* only if they sense that the conversation being initiated will be long, and if the party with whom they are conversing has the physical strength to help them reload the *katundu* on their head afterwards. Individuals carrying head-loads bend their knees slightly to greet or show respect to another. They are exempt from extending their hands for handshakes since the size of the *katundu* may prevent close contact or the object may spill.

The hands do not perform additional symbolic actions at the termination of the encounter. Young aTonga, likely due to European influence, often wave at the guest with either hand, sometimes even using both hands, to say goodbye. Adult Tonga men and women rarely wave their hands to say goodbye, except when one of the parties is departing in a vehicle, particularly on the back of a pickup truck. The two parties will typically wave to each other until they can no longer see each other. Visits in Malawi often conclude with the host giving the visitor a *chibwaila*, a wrapped parting gift, containing washed harvested crops such as bananas, peanuts, potatoes or rice. A member of the host party will be sent to *kulinda*, to escort, the guest and carry the *chibwaila*. At the parting point, interlocutors do not shake hands or exchange hugs. Instead, they leave the encounter space by lowering the body slightly and walking backward for a few paces, hand-clasping as they move away.

The hand clasp is the only hand gesture that is used to bid farewell to a guest. In farewell gestures, handshakes do not occur. Instead, both host and guest make a hand clasp a few times to show gratitude. If the visit takes place at someone's home, a *chibwaila* is prepared and the hosts will escort the visitor(s) to the nearest road junction or bus stop.

As we have seen, the default, or "unmarked," hand used for greeting is the right hand. Handedness in access rituals is strict when only one of the hands is extended. However there are several contexts, both physical and social, where this restriction can be broken. A sense of friendliness and rapport must be established before the right-hand restriction can be relaxed and interlocutors can feel at ease using their left hand in access ritual gestures.

6.3.2 Exchange Rituals

Members of any community need to share material resources, sometimes distributing and at other times receiving. Giving and receiving are basic activities that keep society moving. As in the West, in Malawi a present is dressed in wrapping paper; but, in addition, the gift can also be dressed by the delivery style, choice of hand gesture and which hand performs the gesture. These giving and receiving rituals are more elaborate than in the West and involve much more than a simple transfer of the object. The ritual of giving is so important that, even when there is nothing to give, sometimes the gesture of giving can replace the actual object.

Giving and receiving, or simply "exchanging," is a ritual activity that has different purposes. For example, in Tonga Malawi, the *chipongo*, or sister-friend relationship, is maintained by annual kitchen top-up parties. A top-up party is a celebration in which women and their sisters and friends share kitchenware, such as cups, basins and towels. A kitchen top-up party is one instance in which exchange rituals facilitate crucial social interactions.

There are four gesture conformations for giving, and two for receiving. The giving configurations include two ways of giving with both hands, giving with the right hand only and giving with the left hand only.

(A) Giving with Both Hands

In this ritual, the most polite way to give an object is with two hands. There are two configurations that are used in free variation, depending on the size and the weight of the object being transferred. For smaller, lighter objects, the right hand is used for giving and the left hand holds the right forearm, as in the polite handshake. Therefore, the left hand has two functions: support and symbolic politeness, because using two hands is considered more polite than using one hand in Malawi. Figure 6.7 shows an adult man receiving a hand-washing basin from his young cousin. The basin is light enough to be handed over with just one hand, but the cousin nonetheless extends both her hands out of respect.

124 *Body Talk and Cultural Identity in the African World*

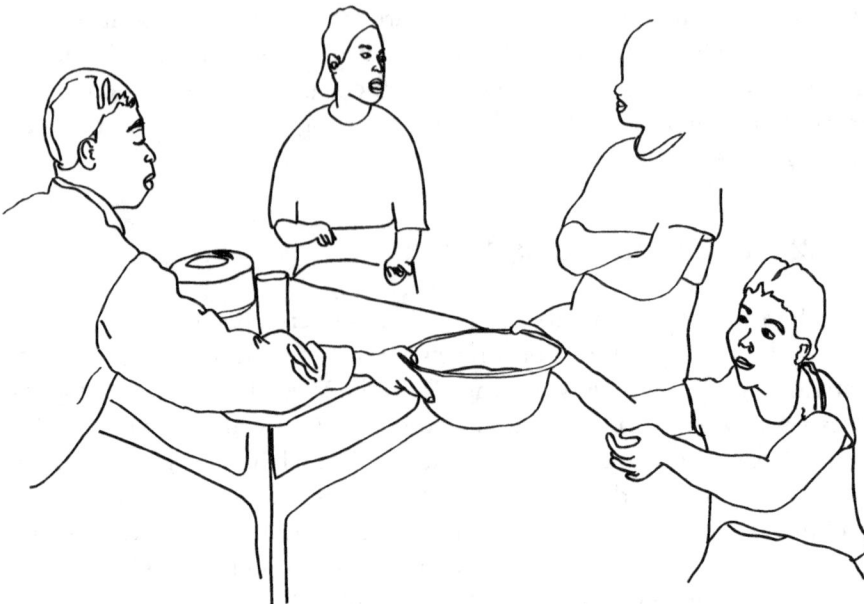

Figure 6.7. A woman handing over a basin with her right hand, but also extending the left.

Unlike the greeting ritual where a power relationship is pre-established, the giving and receiving ritual features a power relationship that is relative to the context. The giver is in a more powerful position while the receiver is less advantaged. Because not exhibiting graciousness may reduce the chance of receiving again, the receiver has an incentive to use the most formal gesture possible.

In Figure 6.8, a visitor has brought fish that he has purchased for the family. The daughter-in-law passes the gift of fish to her mother-in-law who receives the present with both hands. The younger woman too demonstrates her appreciation of the gift as she hands over the present with her right hand, while her left hand holds onto her right forearm.

As mentioned above, sometimes the giving gesture can even be used in when one has nothing to give. During a church service in Malawi, when the collection basket is sitting on the front altar, people walk up in lines to donate money to the church. Everyone will walk up to the collection basket, regardless of whether they have money to give or not. With their left hand holding onto their right forearm, they will dip their right hand into the collection basket, moving the hand as if it is dropping money, even if they have nothing to donate on that particular Sunday.

Figure 6.8. Giving and receiving with both hands.

(B) Giving with the Left Hand

While use of the left hand has never been observed in formal single-handed access rituals, the left handed taboo may be broken in giving rituals. There are two conditions in which the left hand is used for giving. First, familiarity must be mutually acknowledged. Second, the right hand must be visibly occupied. For example, we have observed an instance when a young man has just returned from working in the fields. His right arm and hand are occupied, carrying a hoe, while his left hand holds a handful of cassava. He offers the cassava to a group of visitors, older gentlemen who live in the neighborhood. The young man, who in this case must give with his left hand to an elder, still shows a respectful Malawian method of giving. He lowers his torso by bending his knees, thus compensating for the use of the less respectful left hand (Figure 6.9, left).

Among familiar friends, the left hand can be used when it is the most convenient hand, such as when the left hand is in the closest receiving position. For example, many household items such as pots, baskets and salt, are shared among close friends and relatives. When these items are exchanged between close relatives, either hand is used for the sake of convenience, not politeness.

The convenience hand can only be used among familiar parties or when the giver is in a higher social status than the receiver. In Figure 6.9 (right), a

Figure 6.9. It is possible to give with the left hand in exceptional circumstances.

businessman gives a female friend a card containing credit for a cellphone. The female friend graciously receives the "top-up units" with her left hand holding her right forearm, even though she carries notebooks in her left hand.

6.3.3 Eating Rituals

While many societies prefer to use cutlery while eating, there are some that do not. Societies that not use cutlery have an overwhelming preference for using the right hand as the dominant hand for eating. Meals in Malawi take place at three set times daily: morning "tea," midday *nsima* and evening *nsima*. *Nsima* is a thick porridge made of polenta (maize flour), but it is often used to refer to the main meals of the day – lunch and dinner – even if the porridge is made with another starch. In Nkhata Bay, many families prefer *kondoole*, the porridge made from cassava, but they still use the term *nsima* to refer to their meal. In addition to the *nsima* or *kondoole*, typically two side dishes are also served along with a relish: a protein dish or *ndendi*, usually beans but on special occasions eggs, chicken or fish, and a fiber dish, usually pumpkin or cassava leaves. The aTonga rarely consume food outside of meal times because it would require one to take time away from work to prepare extra food or it would mean spending money on snacks; besides, it shows that one cannot control hunger.[4] While we focus on the manual laterality of meal consumption, in this section we will also briefly outline other physical movements involved in the eating ritual.

4   However, snacking while one is riding in public transportation is quite common, because public transportation is slow and travel often overlaps with meal times. Men are more likely to purchase snack foods than women. Bananas are

In a typical household in a rural area, the woman with the most physical strength prepares the meal. The food is typically divided for serving two groups of people: the men and older boys sitting in the *mphala* (men's quarter), and for the women who will eat by the kitchen with the girls and boys under the age of four. Once prepared, the *nsima* and the *ndendi* are brought to the two designated dining spaces and put on a mat laid over the hardened red mud ground. The men sit around the food on *kaduli*, short wooden stools, while the women sit on the mats in their own space. The woman who has cooked the meal or other females in the family carry their food to the space near the kitchen where they will eat, while a young boy comes to pick up the food for the *mphala*. After the food is brought, the woman who has cooked the food (or the host) hands the washbasin to the most honored person in the group, either the most senior member or an honored guest, out of respect for them since the first person using the basin gets the cleanest water. The water in the washbasin may be cold or warm, depending on the time available and the demands on the family. In the kitchen, the cook rations the food into individually sized portions. If *kondoole* is prepared, a large volleyball-sized sphere is made and put in the middle of the dining space for everyone to share. If *nsima* is served, several four-inch semi-spherical patties are piled in a medium-sized bowl. An adult typically eats two or three patties during the meal.

(A) Sitting

When Tonga women sit on the ground, they use a posture that allows them to sit for a long duration while modestly covering their legs – thighs are considered an adult's private parts. The body forms an "L"-shape where the legs are extended directly in front of the body with one ankle crossed over the other. Once seated, the woman will remain in this position for the entirety of the event, occasionally alternating the positions of the ankles to facilitate blood flow. Young girls and female visitors from other countries are frequently reminded to sit properly, making sure that no parts of their legs above the knee are visible. During meal time, women sit around the food facing clockwise, with their bottom closest to the food and the feet pointing away. In this way, the food is accessible on the right side of everyone's body, allowing them to use their right hand to reach for the food. Since men wear trousers and almost always sit on an elevated chair

---

the preferred snack foods, followed by citrus fruits (equally economical but less filling) and roasted peanuts. People with disposable income may purchase factory-baked breads or sometimes even skewered meats.

Figure 6.10. Correcting the child to position the food on the right side of the body.

or stool, they sit with their knees apart and reach forward and downward for the food.

Sitting "properly" in Tonga Nkhata Bay not only requires that the legs be close together, but also that they are positioned in the correct clockwise orientation. In Figure 6.10, a group of young girls sit in a circle to share their portion of food. In an extended family like the one shown in the picture, children from all households eat together under the supervision of an adult woman. Children are divided into smaller groups if there are many or if the children belong to separate age groups. In the midst of the meal, the aunt of young Mphatso tells the three-year-old that she is sitting *uheni* – horribly. Mphatso immediately puts her legs together and sits in the L-shaped posture, but this does not satisfy the aunt who gets up from her seat, lifts up Mphatso and reorients her body so that the food is on her right side. Dining etiquette among the aTonga not only requires the use of the right hand, but also requires that the food be placed on the right side of the body.

(B) Tasting with the Right Hand

The right hand is the only hand that should be used for eating during *nsima*. According to an aTonga parent of a left-handed child, eating and writing are the two tasks that he forces his daughter to perform with her right hand. A study carried out in Blantyre, the largest urban city in southern Malawi, shows that eating with the right hand is mandatory (Zverev 2006). Across the world in societies that eat with the hand, eating with the right hand is almost universal. When gesturing the eating activity, the right hand is also faithfully used (Figure 6.11). Thus, the cultural preference of handedness is obeyed not only in daily ritual activities, but also in some aspects of visible languages, such as the word-like or "quotable" gestures (Brookes 2004; Kendon 1992).

Language and Culture in Malawian Gestures **129**

Figure 6.11. The quotable gesture for eating reflects ritual handedness.

The right hand serves not only as means of transporting the food to the mouth, but it is also one of the organs used for "tasting" the food. Similar to how the right hand is used for touching another person during handshakes, the right hand is used for sensing the warmth of the *nsima*, kneading it to test its texture, and forming and re-forming the *nsima* so that it can soak up the soup of the relish without bits dropping into the common relish bowl. "Ritual is not just something done but something experienced in the doing" (Basso and Senft 2009: 3).

(C) Snacking with the Left Hand

The left hand may be used for eating food outside meal times. For example, during teatime, the right hand holds the teacup while the left hand is used to hold a boiled potato, a common teatime food in Malawi. The dominant hand is used to hold the more difficult object, a hot liquid in

Figure 6.12. It is possible to eat and touch teatime food with the left hand.

an open container, while the subordinate hand is used to hold the easier object. We have observed a woman picking up a piece of chicken that she has accidently dropped on the ground and because this chicken is not eaten as a meal, she can use her left hand to perform this task. The right would have been used if she were eating it with *nsima*. Figure 6.12 shows a man eating *mandazi*, a fried donut common in East Africa, with his left hand, while his right hand stirs tea. Even though food should be consumed with the right hand, this hand may also be assigned to another task that is more difficult.

To sum up, when food is consumed during lunch or dinner, and in formal settings, the right hand is used to signify respect for one's eating comapnions and graciousness toward whoever prepared the food. In addition to serving as the transporting organ, the right hand is also used for tasting *nsima*, the porridge staple in Malawi. At breakfast or when snacking alone, the left hand can used to bring food to the mouth.

6.4 Summary

In a Tonga access, exchange and eating rituals, the right hand takes a dominant role. Using both hands is considered most polite in giving and receiving rituals, while the dining ritual not only has a preference for right-hand use, but also produces an environment that facilitates right-side dining. In Table 6.1, we provide a summary of handedness as it relates to the number of participants. When the number of people interacting is two or more, such as in public, using both hands is considered the most polite in access, exchange and eating rituals. The least polite is using the left hand only, but using it will not be considered impolite between intimate friends.

Table 6.1. Summary of hand preference in access, exchange and eating rituals.

Number of persons	Rituals	Both hands	Right held by left	Right only	Left only
Two or more	Access	Most polite	Most polite	Familiar	If right not available
	Giving	Most polite	Most polite	Familiar	Familiar or if right not available
	Receiving	Most polite	Most polite	Familiar	Familiar
Single	Dining	Not applicable	Not applicable	Most polite	Not allowed

In conclusion, handedness in Tonga everyday rituals is enforced in most circumstances. However, activities that are not considered formal rituals have more flexibility. Because the right hand is associated with positive social values – strength, dexterity and sensitivity – it is also used in public and highly visible interactions, regardless of the biological handedness of the individual.

References

Ameka, F.K. (2009). Access rituals in West African communities. In G. Senft & E. Basso (eds.), *Ritual Communication* (pp. 127–51). Oxford and New York: Berg Publishers.
Basso, E. & G. Senft. (2009). Introduction. In G. Senft and E. Basso (eds.), *Ritual Communication* (pp. 1–21). Oxford and New York: Berg Publishers.
Bell, A. (1984). Language style as audience design. *Language in Society*, 13(2), 145–204. http://dx.doi.org/10.1017/S004740450001037X
Brookes, H. (2004). A repertoire of South African quotable gestures. *Journal of Linguistic Anthropology*, 14(2), 186–224. http://dx.doi.org/10.1525/jlin.2004.14.2.186
Casasanto, D. (2009). Embodiment of abstract concepts: good and bad in right- and left-handers. *Journal of Experimental Psychology: General*, 138(3), 351–67.
Coren, S., & C. Porac (1977). Fifty centuries of right-handedness: The historical record. *Science*, 198(4317), 631–2. http://dx.doi.org/10.1126/science.335510
De Agostini, M., A.H. Khamis, A.M. Ahui, & G. Dellatolas. (1997). Environmental influences in hand preference: An African point of view. *Brain and Cognition*, 35(2), 151–67. http://dx.doi.org/10.1006/brcg.1997.0935
Duranti, A. (1997). Universal and culture-specific properties of greetings. *Journal of Linguistic Anthropology*, 7(1), 63–97. http://dx.doi.org/10.1525/jlin.1997.7.1.63
Enfield, N.J. (2009). Everyday Ritual in the Residential World. In G. Senft and E. Basso (eds.), *Ritual Communication* (pp. 51–80). Oxford and New York: Berg Publishers.
Enfield, N.J. (2010). Jürgen Streeck, Gesturecraft: The Manu-Facture of Meaning. *Pragmatics & Cognition*, 18(2), 465–7. http://dx.doi.org/10.1075/pc.18.2.11enf
Garrett, P.B., & P. Baquedano-López. (2002). Language Socialization: Reproduction and Continuity, Transformation and Change. *Annual Review of Anthropology*, 31(1), 339–61. http://dx.doi.org/10.1146/annurev.anthro.31.040402.085352
Geertz, C. (1977). *The Interpretation of Cultures*. New York: Basic Books.
Geurts, K.L. (2002). *Culture and the Senses: Bodily Ways of Knowing in an African Community* (Vol. 3). University of California Press.
Goffman, E. (1974). *Frame Analysis*. New York: Harper & Row.

Hansen, K.T. (2004). The world in dress: Anthropological perspectives on clothing, fashion, and culture. *Annual Review of Anthropology*, 33(1), 369–92. http://dx.doi.org/10.1146/annurev.anthro.33.070203.143805

Kendon, A. (1992). Some recent work from Italy on quotable gestures (emblems). *Journal of Linguistic Anthropology*, 2(1), 92–108. http://dx.doi.org/10.1525/jlin.1992.2.1.92

Kendon, A. (2000). Language and gesture: Unity or duality. *Language and Gesture* (August), 47–63. http://dx.doi.org/10.1017/CBO9780511620850.004

Kita, S., & J. Essegbey. (2001). Pointing left in Ghana: How a taboo on the use of the left hand influences gestural practice. *Gesture*, 1(1), 73–95. http://dx.doi.org/10.1075/gest.1.1.06kit

León, L.D. (1998). The emergent participant: Interactive patterns in the socialization of Tzotzil (Mayan) infants. *Journal of Linguistic Anthropology*, 8(2), 131–61. http://dx.doi.org/10.1525/jlin.1998.8.2.131

Lewis, M., M. Paul, G. Simons & C. Fenning. (2015). *Ethnologue: Languages of the World* (18th Edition). Dallas, Texas: SIL International. http://wwwlethnologue.com

McManus, C. (2004). *Right Hand, Left Hand: The Origins of Asymmetry in Brains, Bodies, Atoms and Cultures*. Cambridge, MA: Harvard University Press.

McNeill, D. (2006). Gesture and communication. In Keith Brown (ed.), *Encyclopedia of Language & Linguistics* (2nd edition). Oxford: Elsevier. http://dx.doi.org/10.1016/B0-08-044854-2/00798-7

Mintz, S.W., & C.M. Du Bois. (2002). The anthropology of food and eating. *Annual Review of Anthropology*, 31(1), 99–119. http://dx.doi.org/10.1146/annurev.anthro.32.032702.131011

National Statistical Office and ICF Macro. (2011). *Malawi DHS, 2010: final report*. Zomba.

Orie, O. (2009). Pointing the Yoruba way. *Gesture*, 9(2), 237–61.

Perelle, I., & L. Ehrman. (1994). An international study of human handedness: The data. *Behavior Genetics*, 24(3), 217–27.

Schieffelin, B.B., & E. Ochs. (1986). Language socialization. *Annual Review of Anthropology*, 15(1), 163–91. http://dx.doi.org/10.1146/annurev.an.15.100186.001115

Turner, V.W. (1995). *The Ritual Process: Structure and Anti-structure*. Chicago: Aldine Transaction.

Van Velsen, J. (1964). *The Politics of Kinship: A Study in Social Manipulation among the Lakeside Tonga of Nyasaland*. Manchester: Manchester University Press.

Zverev, Y. (2006). Cultural and environmental pressure against left-hand preference in urban and semi-urban Malawi. *Brain and Cognition*, 60(3), 295–303.

7
Nonverbal Communication Codes among the Hamar: Structures and Functions

Moges Yigezu[1]

7.1 Introduction

The Hamar of southern Ethiopia use an elaborate system of nonverbal communication in order to convey various social, cultural and political meanings that are largely conscious and deliberate. A person's social status, political rank, cultural values, norms and expectations are communicated through a range of nonverbal codes, which are socially constructed and as such have socially shared meanings. This chapter examines how the Hamar speak without "voice" in order to communicate the various social, cultural and political meanings.

The Hamar are an Omotic-speaking people living in the plain lands of the semi-desert region of the rift valley in southern Ethiopia. Their territory stretches from the lower Omo valley in the west to the rift valley of Chew Bahir in the east. To the south, their border coincides with that of Kenya, and to the north they share borders with their closest kin – the Benna and the Bashada, which themselves are bordered by the mountainous region of Bako. The area of the Hamar is poor in rain; topographically it is quite diverse with a wide valley, a dry arid land and rugged mountains.

According to the 2007 national census, the population of the Hamar is 46,532. Their economy is both pastoralist and shifting agriculture. They keep cattle near the Omo valley and mostly depend on milk and cow-blood. They take blood by pricking the jugular vein of the cow with an arrow, and

1   Moges Yigezu is an Associate Professor of Linguistics at the Department of Linguistics, Addis Ababa University. His research interest includes phonetics and phonology, comparative-historical linguistics, sign linguistics, mother tongue education and higher education. Currently he is working on developing the orthography of Hamar language and the description of its grammar.

mix this with fresh milk to make a drink. This is supplemented by *kurkufa*, a kind of porridge made of corn or sorghum flour. The Hamar are a famous tourist attraction in the region because of their cultural practices such as bull jumping, Evangadi dance, clothing, hairstyle and body decoration.

The nonverbal communication systems among the Hamar include body decoration and object language (clothing, hairstyle, necklaces and decoration with animal skins) among others. However, this study focuses on the structure, function and meanings of nonverbal codes related to the transition to manhood, womanhood, marriage and legal parenthood. Furthermore, it will explore the impact of modernity, tourism and global economy on Hamar nonverbal codes.

The methodologies employed in collecting the relevant data include review of secondary sources on the ethnography of the people, as well as observation and interviewing selected resource persons on the types, uses and meanings of the nonverbal codes.

7.2 Transition to Manhood, Womanhood, Marriage and Parenthood

In Hamar society there are various initiations and rituals associated with the transition from boyhood to manhood and from girlhood to womanhood. This transition is also tied to the right to have legitimate children and becoming a full member of the society. Every boy and girl must pass through various stages of initiation to earn the right to participate in all the social, cultural and political activities of the society. We shall briefly describe the major events and activities that relate to the recognition of boys and girls as adults and their integration into the mainstream society.

7.2.1 Becoming *Donza* – a married man

Among the Hamar, as well as their closest kin, the Bashada and the Benna, the transition to manhood involves several steps of rituals. In order to become eligible for initiation, seniority is a prerequisite. Junior males have to wait until their seniors have been initiated (Bruderlin 2005; Epple 2010; Zigita 2013). On the other hand, the initiation is conducted on an individual basis; there is no collective initiation or ritual related to manhood or marriage. As a result, the age of initiates may vary significantly, ranging from 20 to 30 years (Epple 2010: 160–1).

Uninitiated males are called *marid*, a term that seems to be derived from the verb *mara*, which means "to stop from," "not to allow." The *marid* are, therefore, males who are required to pass through different steps of initiation in order to become adult men and to be eligible to marry a woman (Epple 1995: 43). Then a *marid* becomes an *ukuli*, an initiate, a term which also refers to the impurity of the initiate's childhood and to the sexual taboos imposed on uninitiated boys. Uninitiated boys are expected to stay away from girls and women and not to have sexual contact with them (Bruderlin 2005: 44). Literally *ukuli* means "donkey," a term that alludes to the impurity of males during childhood and adolescence (Epple 2010: 165). Whether a boy should be initiated or not is decided by his seniors. "Once his senior male relatives have agreed that a *marid* (uninitiated male) should be initiated, he is given the *boko*, 'initiate's staff.' Once he has been given the *boko*, a *marid* changes his status to an *ukuli*, an 'initiate'" (ibid.).

The *boko* is a short carved wooden stick, which signifies that the boy is going to undergo initiation in a specified time. The boy also ties a string to the *boko* stick with knots to indicate the days remaining for his initiation (Figure 7.1). Holding the *boko* stick, the boy visits friends and relatives and invites them to the ritual ceremony.

The change of status from *marid* to *ukuli* leads to changes in the external appearance of the initiate. "On the day he takes the *boko*, the initiate's

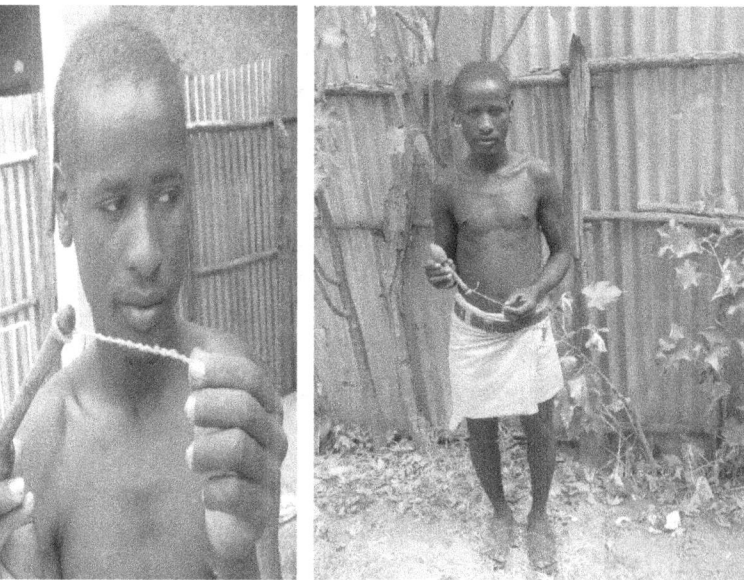

Figure 7.1. An *ukuli* holding the *boko* stick with a knotted string tied to it.

hair is shaved above his forehead and on the lower part of [the] back of his head. The remaining hair is braided until the day of the initiation" (ibid.). Furthermore, as compared to a *marid*, the *ukuli* is expected to behave differently, leading a subdued lifestyle. For instance, he has to give up all his belongings – his beads, earrings, arm rings, his loincloth and shirt – and stop decorating himself. Generally, he keeps a low profile and lives "a monk's life," having no property and wearing a rag as a loincloth, until he has leapt over the cattle, the final ritual that prepares him for marriage (Lydall & Strecker 1979: 195, 37).

During the period of initiation the *ukuli* is supported and escorted by the *maz*, initiated men who have not married yet. They help him to carry out the necessary rituals and keep the cattle standing still for him to leap over. After the leap, the *ukuli* himself becomes a *maz* and is allowed to marry and have a family (Bruderlin 2005: 45). Among the Hamar, Benna and Bashada, adult married men are called *donza*, a term probably derived from the verb *donsha*, which can be translated as "to be self-controlled" and "to keep one's emotions to oneself," attributes that an adult man is expected to possess (Epple 2010: 211). For Strecker (1976: 58) "Donza means to have become a man, to have married and begotten children, to have shown oneself competently in everyday life, to be responsible, to be learned, to deserve respect and – above all – to have the right to participate in all the politics and decision-making that are of public concern." According to Epple, Strecker's definition entails two aspects of male adulthood – a status that is ritually performed and a status that is socially defined. Ritually a male reaches the status of a *donza* through marriage. Once a male has performed the marriage ritual he raises his status from a *maz* to a *donza*. By marriage, a man assumes the right to build up his own herd, lead his own homestead, and to father legitimate offspring (Epple 2010: 211–12).

7.2.2 Becoming *Uta* – a bride

Among the Hamar both little girls and adolescent girls are called *anza*. Just like males, females have to pass through various initiation rituals in their transition to womanhood and motherhood. Marriage for a girl takes place at early age. After marriage both the girl and her future husband continue to live in their respective homes until the girl becomes old enough to go to her husband's home and assume responsibility. Once she has moved to her husband's homestead, she is not a "married girl," but an *uta*, a "bride" (Epple 2010: 117). *Uta* is both the term of reference and the term of address for a bride. Literally it means to leave, to come out and to go up, and may refer to the fact that the bride has left her parents' home. A woman is called an *uta* at least until she has had a child or two (Lydall & Strecker 1979: 207).

"The period of bridehood signifies the most drastic change in the girl's life. She must leave her parents behind and live from then on under the supervision of her husband and especially of her mother-in-law" (Bruderlin 2005: 49). During this period she is very reliant on her new mother-in-law. It is the mother-in-law who ritually prepares the *uta* for her future role as a wife and a mother. During the first three months of bridehood the *uta* has no contact with her husband or any other person besides her mother-in-law. During this time, and later in life, the *uta* receives instructions from her mother in-law on what to do and how to behave (Bruderlin 2005: 50).

The transition from girlhood to bridehood is additionally made visible by a transformation in the physical appearance. In other words, there are nonverbal codes or artifacts that are displayed on a woman's body to indicate that she is an *uta* (Figures 7.2 and 7.3).

Figure 7.2. An *uta*, "bride."

Figure 7.3. An unmarried girl.

Epple (2010: 182) describes the external appearance of an *uta* among the Beshada as follows:

> When a girl moves to her husband's family, she becomes an uta, "bride": her head is shaved, the head and body are rubbed with butter and ochre and her girl dresses are taken away. Instead, she is given the uta's dress, a woman's front skirt (korba) and a long cape (karke) that hangs from her shoulders over her back and is fastened around her waist

Lydall & Strecker (1979: 140–1) give the same description for the Hamar *uta*. In Hamar too, a mother-in-law shaves the *uta*'s head and rubs her with red ocher and butter. All her girlhood belongings are taken away and in return she later receives a new *karke* cape and a married woman's skirt, *aizi*. The *aizi* is long so that it can cover most of the body, particularly the legs, while the girl's skirt is shorter and it clearly shows her legs and the sides of her thighs. Hence there is an essential difference between the *uta*'s skirt and that of an unmarried girl.

7.2.3 Making the *Binyere* – the neckband worn by first wives

The *binyere* is an artifact that is worn around the neck only by first wives and it distinguishes them from co-wives (Figure 7.4). It is the symbol of the status and special position that first wives enjoy within the society. For instance, they perform all rituals with their husbands and have a special power and authority over co-wives. First wives are viewed as seniors by the co-wives who address them by the term *imisho*, "elder sister." If the husband dies, the first wife inherits all his belongings, so the co-wives become dependent on her (Epple 2010: 175).

> Hence, for every first wife a *binyere*, a special neckband made from the leather of dik-dik antelope, is made. It is made from twisted dik-dik skins, one from a female and another from a male dik-dik. The dik-dik leather has special meaning in this context, as the dik-dik antelope is monogamous and therefore represents a lifelong partnership. The object symbolizes that the man and the woman are couples for life. The dik-dik leather is bought by the husband and tanned by his sisters. Then the expert who

Figure 7.4. A woman wearing a *binyere*.

makes the *binyere* and the husband sit together on a special cow hide in the cattle kraal to prepare the *binyere*. After the leather has been twisted, a small piece of *baraza* wood is pressed into the pointed end of the neckband. (Bruderlin 2005; Lydall & Strecker 1979)

The *binyere* is inherently linked to a young man's initiation and his first marriage. As a sign of his new status, the *maz* wears a *binyere* belt around his waist made from the bark of the *baraza* (*Grewia mollis* Juss.) tree. Afterwards, he goes in search of dik-dik antelopes to make a belt from their skin. Then he wears the leather belt made of the skin of the dik-dik antelope in place of the bark one until his wedding day, at which time he gives the belt to his bride (Verswijver & Silvester 2008). When he marries the belt is loosely tied around his wife's neck, and when she moves to his homestead, a proper *binyere* will be prepared by a specialist for her (Epple 2010: 178–9). A woman will only take the *binyere* off when her first son becomes an initiate, when her eldest daughter gets married, or when her husband dies.

7.3 The Structure and Functions of the Nonverbal Codes

The structure of the nonverbal codes regarding a *donza* include the change of physical appearance such as hairstyle, clothing and objects (the *boko* stick) which show the person's status in the society and signify that he is an initiate and is in the process of transition to manhood and eventually to fatherhood.

Becoming a *donza* is all about a man's status and integration into the society as well as his right to legitimately reproduce and keep his lineage. To become a *donza* does not only require passing through initiation and marriage, but also fathering a legitimate child. Without legitimate descendants, a man does not become a full member of the society. "A man who dies without fathering a legitimate son is not going to have the same mortuary rites as a man who has fathered legitimate sons" (Lydall & Strecker 1979: 64). At the same time, as a married man and a father, a *donza* has to fulfill many expectations. He will be watched closely by his seniors and neighbors as to whether he shows responsibility for his wife and children. If he fails to do so, he will be reprimanded to stop behaving like an adolescent (Epple 2010: 213). So there is monitoring and reinforcement even after his transition to adulthood, which is a way of sustaining the tradition as well as the nonverbal codes established in the society.

As a responsible family man, a *donza* has multiple tasks to accomplish (ibid):

(a) He has to work carefully and responsibly.
(b) He should always ensure that his family has enough food and drink, and therefore he needs to establish social networks with relatives and friends.
(c) He must sensibly handle his cattle and small stock, and clear fields big enough to feed his family, and also relatives and friends who may need his support when they are in trouble.
(d) A *donza* must be able to plan for the future, a capacity that children and women are believed to lack.

The term *donza* has political as well as social meanings and it also entails serious obligations and rewards. It does not only increase the political influence of a married adult but it also has a great impact on his social position. By being initiated, a male person gains the right to marry and father legitimate children and ensure the continuity of his lineage.

Similarly, the structure of the nonverbal codes regarding the *uta* involves the transformation of the physical appearance of a girl, the change of attire and ornaments followed by a prescribed way of life that is fundamentally different from her lifestyle before marriage. All these nonverbal codes communicate the new social status of the girl as a woman and mother and her right to bear legitimate children.

The process of preparing, coaching and guiding the *uta* also signifies the power and authority of women in ensuring the continuity of the family and its lineage. It is in the context of guiding, controlling and mentoring the *uta* that the power of elderly women over others is clearly demonstrated. Although this is a patriarchal society, it is the mother-in-law who ritually gives the bride (her daughter-in-law) to her own son, reflecting unusual power relations in Hamar. Moreover, "After the bride has been kept away [from her future husband] for a certain time and has physically separated herself from her former life [i.e. from her parents], the mother-in-law symbolically gives birth to her, reintegrating the *uta* into the social life and ritually preparing her for her future role, the role of being a married woman" (Bruderlin 2005: 51). The ritual preparation of the daughter-in-law is a very significant source of pride for elderly women in Hamar, Benna and Bashada. The women themselves are very much aware of their position and the power they have over their sons by way of their sons' wives (ibid.: fn. 92).

7.4 The Linguistic Meanings of the Nonverbal Codes

The nonverbal codes discussed in the preceding sections are displayed in public regularly and consistently. According to what Guerrero & Floyd (2006) call "the message orientation" of the nonverbal communication, following Burgoon (1980), the codes in use in the social and cultural life of the Hamar can be considered as communicative since: (a) they are displayed with intent in order to communicate certain social, cultural or political messages, (b) they are interpreted as intentional and (c) they are regularly used and have consensual, shared meaning within the culture. Hence, they are linguistic codes with socially shared meanings that are exchanged between a sender and a receiver (Guerrero & Floyd 2006: 14).

How these nonverbal codes and their meanings are prescribed at social and cultural levels and how people come to acquire them can be seen in light of the sociocultural paradigm developed by Guerrero & Floyd (2006). According to this paradigm, which encompasses a number of models and theories, nonverbal behaviors and their meanings are learned through observation and direct instruction and people learn or teach what is culturally considered appropriate (ibid.: 28). In particular, the social learning theory (Bandura 1977, cited in Guerrero & Floyd 2006: 28–9), asserts that "learning occurs most effectively when people observe the enactment of behaviors by others in a social situation and take stock of the consequences of those behaviors." The theory further considers learning "as a socially embedded process" and argues that "the ability of social learning to instigate behavior change depends on two important aspects of the learning process: modeling and reinforcement" (ibid.: 29).

The social learning theory further posits that "social roles are only learned when they are modeled by groups and individuals" and "effective modeling requires four conditions to be met" (Guerrero & Floyd 2006: 29). These conditions are, according to the same theory: (a) that sufficient attention be paid by the learner, (b) that adequate retention of the information be made by the learner, (c) that sufficient motor ability of the learner be ensured to replicate the observed behavior and (d) that there be motivation to do so.

Within the Hamar society, the learning activities pass through a range of compulsory rituals and initiation ceremonies that involve modeling, observation and direct instruction augmented by reinforcement by way of either reward and recognition or punishment. For instance, the girl has to go through a rigorous training under the strict supervision of her mother-in-law for her future roles of wife and mother. Likewise, a male *maz* has to go through similar intensive training through role modeling, observation and direct instruction by his seniors, who also help him in performing all the necessary rituals up to the final ritual of leaping over cattle that prepares him for marriage. Even after a man has become a *donza*, he will be watched and monitored by his seniors and neighbors to see that he is fulfilling the expectations of the society and accomplishing the multiple tasks expected of him as a fully integrated adult in the mainstream society. The reward for fulfilling the expectations of the society, for a man, is to be recognized as a full member of the society where he takes part in any decision-making process of public concern. Failing to act like a *donza*, as a responsible adult married person, would also have its own negative consequences. The two important social learning processes – namely, modeling and reinforcement – are strictly observed in the enactment of the codes that have socially shared meanings.

Within the sociocultural paradigm, the fact that nonverbal codes are socially constructed and have socially shared meanings has been emphasized by the social meaning model (SMM) of Burgoon & Newton (1991). This theory asserts that nonverbal codes "acquire their meanings through social consensus within a given social or language community," with some nonverbal codes consisting of "a socially shared vocabulary of relational communication" (ibid.: 31). Accordingly, a specified nonverbal code within a given culture should have a fairly consistent meaning for all receivers and observers. Hence, the sociocultural paradigm concludes that most nonverbal codes are learned and not innate and that social learning usually occurs through the processes of modeling and reinforcement.

The SMM further stipulates that within a given culture some nonverbal codes have consensual social meanings and are therefore perceived and interpreted by all members of the community in a similar way (ibid.: 55).

7.5 Impacts of Globalization, Modernity and Tourism

There are major factors that are affecting the culture of the Hamar in present times, namely, the expansion of formal education, the development of infrastructure and establishment of mega projects in the area, and the growing tourism industry. A recent study by Zigita (2013) assesses the impact of formal education on the socialization, initiation, marriage and burial rites of the Hamar. The study reports that the expansion of formal education, particularly the agenda of "education for all," which the government is promoting to achieve the millennium development goals, is affecting the cultural practices of the Hamar in a significant way.

During the reign of Haile Sellasie, some 40 years ago, there was only one elementary school in Hamar and formal education was limited to those in urban areas. Very little progress was made under the military regime (1974–91) in terms of formal education. It is only in the last two decades that formal education has expanded and today there are 14 first-cycle, four second-cycle and one third-cycle schools in the Hamar area plus 37 ABE (Alternative Basic Education) schools and three kindergartens. In addition, there are boarding schools that cater for students coming from areas far from the towns (Zigita 2013).

Zigita concludes that the introduction of formal education is causing tremendous changes in the lifestyle of the Hamar, and according to her findings:

(a) Young men who went to school are refusing to participate in major rituals such as leaping over cattle, a final ritual in the transition to manhood and fatherhood.
(b) Young women who are already engaged and whose family has received the bride wealth run away from the village without informing their parents.
(c) Young men who are already initiated and engaged/married also leave their wives with their families and marry girls from other ethnic groups.
(d) Elders believe that formal education has brought all these changes and challenges to their community and this has led to disappointment among the Hamar.
(e) The educational policies of the government do not address the specific features of the Hamar society and as a result parents are refusing to send their children to schools.

Furthermore, the huge infrastructure projects such as roads built in the area in the last 10 years and the establishment of mega projects such as sugarcane plantations and factories and large farms and agro-industries, have led to a huge influx of northerners into the area. This has increased the exposure of the Hamar to a wide variety of people from other ethnic groups. Although no serious study has been done on the effect of tourism in the area, there is little doubt that this has also acted as a catalyst for many of the changes taking place today. Poorly trained guides and a complete lack of local tourism guidelines and controls by the federal or the regional government are reasons cited for this negative impact.

The future of the Hamar culture of nonverbal communication seems to be bleak given the rapid changes that have been observed within the last decade in education, infrastructure and agro-industry development, as well as a constant flow of tourists in search of remote cultural groups. The latter in particular is seen to be undermining the traditional cultures and the perspectives of the people due to a total lack of guidelines on tourism management.

7.6 Conclusions

The Hamar have a robust tradition wherein nonverbal codes are regularly and intentionally displayed with a range of social, cultural and political meanings that are of paramount importance in the life of individuals as part of their recognition and integration into the mainstream society. These nonverbal codes used in the processes of initiation and transition to adulthood, marriage and ultimately to the right to continue one's lineage are socially constructed and have consensual social meanings that are perceived equally by both senders and receivers. Needless to say, this dynamic and vigorous system of nonverbal communication rooted in the traditions of the Hamar is today endangered by the advent of globalization, modernization and tourism.

References

Bandura, A. (1977). *Social Learning Theory*. New York: General Learning Press.
Bruderlin, T. (2005). "The Incorporation of Children into Society: Pre- and Postnatal Rituals among the Hamar of Southern Ethiopia." Unpublished MA thesis. Johannes Gutenberg-Universitat Mainz.
Burgoon, J.K. (1980). Nonverbal communication in the 1970s: An overview. In D. Nimmo (ed.), *Communication Yearbook 4* (pp. 179–97). New Brunswick, NJ: Transaction.
Burgoon, J.K., & D.A. Newton. (1991). Applying a social meaning model to relational message interpretations of conversational involvement: Comparing observer and participant perspectives. *Southern Communication Journal*, 56(2), 96–113. http://dx.doi.org/10.1080/10417949109372822

Epple, S. (1995). "Life in Gunne: Social Relationship in a Village in Bashada." Unpublished MA thesis. Johannes Gutenberg-Universitat Mainz.
Epple, S. (2010). *The Bashada of Southern Ethiopia*. Koln: RudigerKoppeVerlag.
Guerrero, L. and K. Floyd. (2006). *Nonverbal Communication in Close Relationships*. London: Lawrence Erlbaum Associates, publishers.
Lydall, J. and I. Strecker. (1979). *The Hamar of Southern Ethiopia II: Baldambe Explains*. Hohenschaftlarn: Renner.
Strecker, I. (1976). *Traditional Life and Prospect for Socio-Economic Development in the Hamar Adiminstrative District of Southern Gamo Gofa*. Online publication at www.uni-mainz.de/Organisationen/SORC?content view/58/41
Verswijver, G. and H. Silvester. (2008). *Omo People and Design*. Verona: Mondadori.
Zigita, S. (2013). "Assessing the Impact of Formal Education on the Socialization, Initiation, Marriage and Burial Rites of the Hamar." Unpublished MA thesis. Addis Ababa University.

8
So That We Might Find Ourselves: Collective Identity in Yoruba Culture

Abimbola A. Adelakun[1]

8.1 Introduction

One of the outcomes of cultural trauma is that, ironically, it strengthens collective identity. When trauma strikes through the social bonds that unite a people, it impacts their sense of oneness as a community. Members of a collective who experience trauma define their relationship in ways that facilitate solidarity and a stronger sense of collectivity and oneness (Alexander 2004: 1). Group identity responds to other factors such as a cultural reference (ibid.: 10); leads to an interest formation process that is strongly conditioned by self-identification of group members in relation to other groups and the State (Hall 1999: 5); promotes shared ideologies (Alexander 2004: 8); is a precursor to citizenship or political participation (Pierce 2012: 4); and emerges as a response or pushback against oppressive conditions (ibid.: 6). Group identity, in all the stated attributes, revolves around a notion of the *collectivity* of the said group. There is an emphasis on a structured arrangement of the collective around an idea that makes the group a tangible one and, consequently, accountable for the ideologies it canvasses. Also, the palpability of the collective sets it up for a system of reward or, in the negative case, attack by vengeful groups.

In this chapter, I look at emerging collectives that hold up to the above listed attributes and yet, when analyzed comprehensively, resist a structuralist conceptualization. To achieve this, I will be comparing two aspects of

---

1 Abimbola A. Adelakun is a graduate student of African/African Diaspora Studies and Performance as Public Practice at the University of Texas at Austin. Her research interests are culture, modernity, transnationalism, African religion and performance. She is currently working on the theatricality of Pentecostalism in Nigeria.

Yoruba cultural traditions that involve group identification: the practice of body marking and Aso-Ebi (the culture of group dressing). Both cultural practices premise collective identity by using the corporeal body as a vehicle to drive the indicators of unity, but are dissimilar. This work combines my personal experiences – growing up in Ibadan within a family system where body marking was prominent – with my scholarly observations and analysis of texts to study how collective identities are created by a people, the end process of both and how new forms of understanding emerge when a collective does not quite behave as a collective. While the theoretical conception of collective identity applies to the practice of body marking, it becomes shaky when extended to Aso-Ebi. Indeed, the similarities and differences between body marking and Aso-Ebi critique the insinuation of permanence, or cultural continuity, that foregrounds analysis of collective identity.

This sort of *anti-collectivity* of the Aso-Ebi collective makes it hard for the group to be, for instance, harmed by trauma – defined as "the acute discomfort entering into the core of the collective's own sense of identity" (Alexander 2004: 10) – that groups are susceptible to due to their essential nature. If the one major difference of the anti-collective collective is that it does not stay as a group long enough to acquire the traits we attribute to collectives, then what are the socio-political and moral implications of the markers of identity that are rootless, fluid and devoid of commitment to the community? How does contemporary Yoruba culture express this transience through body marking? And how do members of anti-collectives then relate to artifacts that structure their commonality only temporarily? What political and social agencies and possibilities exist for members of collectives whose markers of identity are temporary?

8.2 *So That We May Find Ourselves*

There is a proverb I heard frequently while growing up in the city of Ibadan, the capital of Oyo state in Southwestern Nigeria: *So that we might find ourselves if we get lost, is the reason Ibadan people wear facial marks.*[2] The proverb's specific focus on Ibadan, the home of a sub-ethnic group of the Yoruba ethnic nationality, is rather intriguing since the cultural practice of marking the body is neither exclusive to Ibadan people nor particular to the Yoruba in general. It extends to some parts of Northern Nigeria as well.

2 Throughout this chapter, I use "facial" and "body" marking interchangeably.

The focus on Ibadan, however, is a consequence of the history of the founding of the city and its subsequent growth. Falola (1987: 96) narrates that Ibadan, founded in the late 1820s, was a great military state. From its initial war camp status it grew into a city-state, a metropolis and an empire. The nature of its founding shaped its emergence as a military republic and its economy. The chiefs engaged in wars, brigandage and raiding expeditions to procure slaves who would provide cheap labor to manage the booming agrarian industry. A prosperous agricultural trade would generate much-needed resources to feed the burgeoning population, and also to buy weapons. For Ibadan to manage its political and economic ambitions, it had a reliable military machine and hundreds of soldiers who dominated the political system. Ibadan engaged in many wars, secured thousands of slaves – Falola, citing an observer, noted that the high number of slaves Ibadan secured would outbalance the freemen (1987: 96).

So that we may find ourselves is therefore a throwback to the historical formation of Ibadan, the culture of violence that typified its emergence and the precariousness of life and social status on which its penchant for war rested. The Ibadan of the 19th century must have been eclectic, the pulse of the city throbbing with all the cultural syncretism that created its definitive character and identity. The influx of various enslaved bodies into Ibadan at different periods had other implications: families who had been previously dispersed by war could find each other through their distinctive body markings. For those who had become a part of Ibadan, an empire built on the existential realities of war and chaos, the fear of dispersal, estrangement and permanent severance of blood ties was a credible fear. The practice of body marking was a calculated move to find some order in the midst of social and institutional disorder.

One of the characteristics of war is the aim for the annihilation of a people's entire existence. This could be executed through either physical death, or social death which entails the absolute denial of the humanity of the enslaved conquered people (Patterson 1985). The latter is a state of living death because it entails a natal alienation; the slave is violently severed from the umbilical cord that connects him/her to a culture and a terra firma. This alienation from all formal or legal ties, according to Patterson, makes the slave "the ultimate human tool, as imprintable and as disposable as the master wishes" (1985: 7). Of all the losses associated with war, however, that of kin members must be the very worst because it involves the separation of socially and emotionally conjoined bodies. Death and loss, among the Yorubas, is expressed in *araferaku* – the imagining of or desire for bodily contact which will not be.

Yorubas, in their preoccupation with *the finding of selves*, therefore engage with the notions of loss and the possibility of retrieval through collective identification. The body, with its susceptibility to loss and longing, however, harbors other potentials as well. It signifies the possibility of retrieval. To recover the body is to recover the familial ties, the accumulated history on the body and, overall, one's humanity. This makes the body a viable site for mapping routes of return. The Yorubas thus created a distinct semiotics that marks out families and locale. In each marking system is embedded distinct familial history and culture. Knowing that the rampaging warriors of enemy clans would not let their material culture survive, they worked toward putting the maps in an open vault: the body. The very act of body marking was a preemptive act to forestall, as far as possible, the annihilating tendencies of the enemy.

That the human body carries these marks within the context of a culture is a double signifier. One, that such a body is connected to history, to a people and a culture that resonate in what is etched on the skin. Two, that such a body is also predisposed to natal alienation. The latter is an ontological negation that is counteracted with the map tattooed on the body to signify a rootedness and a belonging within a nexus of consanguine and non-consanguine clan relationships, all within a territory. Through the pragmatic arrangement of collective identification, safety and strength is sought in numbers. The larger the extended family system or settlement, the greater their strength, the better the visibility of their body marks and, therefore, the higher their chances of being reunited if separated. This way, when members of a family are lost to violence, they are *searchable*; and in case of a chance meeting between lost family members, the marks make them *findable* or *identifiable*. Body marking is thus a tracking system that is invested with hopes and perhaps superstitious expectations that the body, if detached from its roots, will use this GPS to find the way back home. Or, if home no longer exists, body marking will remain as evidence that it once did.

The emergence of the Yoruba as one nation, rather than various discrete peoples constantly at war with each other (Peel 2003), cannot be divorced from various cultural artifacts like body marking and its creation of a "synthesis of commonalities" (Coy & Woehrle 2000: 6) that distinguishes them from other groups. The sense of sameness and oneness created by the political economy of symbols like body marking is bolstered by spatial proximities, shared history and an external threat that necessitates banding together to derive strength from numbers. Collective identity, theoretically, is therefore constructivist. The fashioned nature of collective identity is a self-redeeming process as it shapes the emergence and escalation of conflicts, and also opens up spaces for de-escalation and resolution (ibid.). Members of a collective relate to texts, practices and artifacts and they find meaning from their relation to these cultural products (Melucci 1995: 42). The group creates meanings by acting together and the sum total of individual subjectivities thus becomes a self-essentialized identity that risks homogenizing the diversities that are certain to exist in the collective (Bernstein 2002: 85).

8.3 Body Markings: Dead, Dying or Being Reborn?

It is perhaps unsurprising that many people readily speak of facial/body marking in the past tense. It is a culture that is dead, they suggest, because it is no longer necessary in contemporary times. Indeed, a few years ago, when CNN reporter in Africa, Christian Purefoy, produced a news feature on the culture of facial markings in Southwestern Nigeria, he interviewed a few people who still held on to the culture, largely for superstitious reasons, but who confirmed anyway that it was a dying culture. The report noted that facial markings "are becoming increasingly restricted to people in the rural regions" (Purefoy 2010); and that though various governments had unsuccessfully moved to outlaw the practice, its discontinuation by the people themselves made such an executive fiat unnecessary in any case. The report attributed the decline of facial markings to the "displacement of old ways by western influence" (ibid.) but it could be that this pronouncement greatly exaggerated the news of the death of facial marks.

While it is largely true that various African indigenous practices have died out because they no longer find relevance within the evolving paradigms of contemporary culture, it might be too early to conclude that because people no longer mark their faces/bodies to identify their own family members, the practice is dead too. The spirit behind a cultural practice might be realized in some other way if the external circumstances that produced the original practice change or are modified. The interrogation of contemporary cultural activities thus requires a close scrutiny of the social and communal needs that such practices meet, and these should be juxtaposed with the needs met by those activities when they were still mainstream practices, not to compare or to pitch one century against the other as equivalent, but to expand the scope of knowledge on the resilience of cultural practices. Also, a comparison of the social and psychological benefits Yorubas of the 17th–20th century derived from body markings with the ones those who live in the 21st century get from Aso-Ebi goes to the heart of the pliability of the intent behind cultural practices and how they are freshly awakened for successive generations.

The proclamation of the death of the culture of marking the body often fails to question where and when the culture began its dying process. Rather, the death is often celebrated with quiet triumphalism over the melting of one more "ancient" culture in the face of the fiery mission of civilization, modernization and Westernization accelerated by globalization and the wonders the 21st century has brought upon us. The decline of the culture, however, goes much further back. I grew up with my grandparents and extended family members, some of whom were born at the turn of the 20th century, and even as a child, I noticed that some of them had no facial markings. Those who had the marks often jokingly referred to those who did not as being too poor to afford it. Those who did not have the marks said their parents had thought the practice rather unnecessary. From this personal observation, it is perhaps fair to suggest that at least by the early 20th century, and possibly before the onset of colonialism, the act of scarification was already on the decline. The decline is by no means novel and, in effect, challenges the readiness with which the decline of cultural practices is usually blamed on the "eye-opening" effects of "Westernity" (a merging of Westernization and modernity) as if life in precolonial, pre-Westernized Africa did not yield itself to social evolution that engendered changes in cultural patterning.

Another personal anecdote: my mother told me how she and her classmates were repelled when a child they knew underwent facial scarification. It was in the 1970s, and they were teenage schoolgirls who loved to play with the "beautiful" grandchild of their school food vendor. It was noteworthy that they had known the child when she had a plain face, and when they saw her again with facial markings, they could not reconcile the two. As far as they were concerned, the child was no longer beautiful in the cherubic way children are often thought to be beautiful. The plying of scarifying tools on her body was, to my mother and her peers born in a different era, a violation of her sweet innocence rather than an ennobling act promoting the idea of collective identity. My mother told me that she and her friends asked the mother of the child why she had done that to her daughter; they did not see the greater achievement of the beauty, the cultural rooting carved on the child's face.

By the time I was passing through adolescence in the 1990s, the art of body marking – now largely carried out on the face – had become a thing of curiosity, and the proverb about finding ourselves and its particularization of Ibadan did not quite resonate with my generation. Rather, body marking was a burden to be borne. In my secondary school days, we had a classmate with facial markings. She was the only one of us – in a class of 50 or more – who did and we taunted her to no end. We called her names (by which I still remember her even now, having long forgotten her actual name) and asked why her parents had been so unkind as to deface her.

There was another teenage girl, Amina, who came to live with my family for some years. She had a single vertical mark on either cheek and probably never thought of the urban vs rural cultural implications of the mark when she still lived with her parents in their rural home. However, when she moved to the city with us, she became very self-conscious. The city, she must have found, had no use for a preoccupation with home and belonging. To display such earthiness on her face in a space where anonymity and invisibility were the norm made her a body that was instantly hypervisible. In a sense the mark announced her attachment to a territory, and in an urban setting this was an instant signifier of the primitivism associated with rural spaces (Odunbaku 2012: 256). Amina, however, was not alone in her discontent. In a study conducted among three Yoruba communities by the Oral and Maxillofacial Surgery Department of the College of Medicine, University of Ibadan, a survey of 1,800 people revealed that a high percentage of the younger generation were discontented with their facial marks and wanted these removed (Obiechina & Olutayo 2000). Amina was one of those young ones whose attitude was captured in this study. She desperately wanted the marks off her face.

One day, unable to bear it anymore, Amina sent me to several chemist shops (drugstores) to ask if there was a drug she could use to wipe off the marks. At one of the stores, the staff fell into convulsive laughter while I wondered what the joke was all about. One of the laughing staff told me to tell her to get sandpaper and rub the abrasive surface against her skin. The poor girl would have probably done this if she had not been prevented by the adults in my family. Amina returned to her village after years of living with us but I cannot help wondering what became of her and my secondary school classmate, and how the marks gifted to them by parents anxious to for their children to always be found wherever they sojourned on the good earth, became, for them, a scarlet letter they were condemned to bear.

Marking the body, it must be noted, did not at any time have only a single purpose. The Yorubas marked the body not only to enhance belongingness to a group but also for aesthetic reasons. The marks on the body had to be beautiful and desirable, and display sheer artistry. That, in itself, is an ontological irony: the body that could be lost to slavery or displacement must be marked; and to be marked is to be beautiful, aesthetically pleasing and desirable. Drewal (1988) describes a body artist in Yorubaland as a cultural innovator who "contributes his aesthetic sensibilities by embellishing human flesh with beautiful, creative patterns" and says the art of cutting the flesh, to inscribe artful patterns, among the Yorubas is highly prized because of its evocative imagery and the craftsmanship cannot be downplayed. It is a skill that does more than make scarifications, similar to the way the praise poem of Lagbayi, a celebrated Yoruba carver, extols his skills at inscribing the Keke and Abaja marks on wooden carvings to give them not only beauty, but a personality that animates their woodenness (Scharfstein 2009: 258). The very act that redeems the body from death also, paradoxically, enhances it.

The enhancement, however, presumably lies in the eye of the beholder. There is an illustration in the cultural practice of marking an Abiku – a spirit child believed to come to earth only to callously die and be reborn several times – to excommunicate such a child from the assembly of his/her fellow spirit children. When such a child dies again on one of its frequent trips to earth, the parents make marks on its corpse, in the belief that when the Abiku surfaces again among its fellow spirits, the markings of the terrestrial world will repel them. Thus the Abiku, rejected in the spiritual world, will be forced to return to earth and stay with the parents. The myth is that such children, when reborn, carry the marks of mutilation as identifiers of their frequent journey between this world and that of the spirits (Mobolade 1973). The social death of slavery, and the biological death of the Abiku, are both redeemable by body markings that in each case, establish their link to the earth of someplace else. The markings signify the investment of somebody's humanity on their bodies, to make legible the personhood of the corporeal body as a counteraction against the disposability to which it was predisposed. To the slave's captor, as well to the Abiku's fellow spirits, the marks must be repugnant; while to parents of the Abiku, and the family of the enslaved, those same body marks make redemption possible and that must be beauty enough.

Like various cultural practices that existed in times past, it is however, difficult to state which purpose preceded which. Did Yorubas discover collective identity while marking the body for purposes of beautification, or did identification lead to the exploration of the body as a living canvas of artistic virtuosity? Or did both exist simultaneously at first, and then with the changes taking place in the larger world – the end of the transatlantic slave trade and the beginning of colonialism leading to more stable societies where the threat of being captured as slave receded – did the purpose of body marks evolve largely into that of beautification? There are no clear answers but evidence in Yoruba rhetoric (such as proverbs) suggests that body markings still serve a dual purpose in traditional Yoruba societies. Body marking it has been suggested had, and perhaps has, various roles in Yoruba body politics. While its precipitous decline cannot be halted, there seems to be evidence of another form of identification that is replacing it. This is the practice of "Aso-Ebi," and the next section focuses on this transformation of an old culture of bodily markings into one of identity through dress.

8.4 "Old" Culture, Evolving Forms: The Semiotics of Aso-Ebi

The practice of Aso-Ebi has been extensively documented in sociological, anthropological and popular literature (Barnes 1986; King-Aribisala 1998; Olajubu 2003) and is largely popular within the ambit of Yoruba contemporary culture. Though the practice developed in Nigeria among the Yorubas it has spread extensively to other African countries and is even practiced by Africans in the diaspora, on festive occasions. Aso-Ebi translates inadequately as "family cloth" or "cloth for the members of the (extended) family." It may also be understood as "group-dressing" (Chiavetta 2008: 98) or "family dress" since the same fabric design is worn by a social group to project "oneness." Aso-Ebi, very much like body marking, is premised on collective identification of family members and a projection of communal oneness signified, this time, by the clothes. It, of course, must demonstrate beauty and glamour as an expression of these as traits of the members of the collective who choose it. The process of selection is democratic; family members must be informed ahead and a fabric is collectively chosen which everyone who identifies with the family should buy. In advance of a special occasion, the family members select delegates who go to market to find a suitable fabric for the Aso-Ebi. When they find a colorful pattern which they believe matches the family character, they take samples to show the rest of family who decide on the aesthetics and whether it is befitting the family. If the family members agree, the representatives go back to the seller on the price for a sufficient quantity to go round. They make a deal with the cloth seller to keep the cloth exclusive to the family until after the function. They buy the fabric in bulk and sell members of the family the quantities they require (Ogundipe 2012: 209). This process of obtaining Aso-Ebi thus subjects members of the collective to exploitation through overpricing, over-privileging the material to the point of making it into a gate pass at events, and turning it into an in-group identity marker at events such that those who do not wear the outfit are excluded from certain privileges. There is a popular saying that is descriptive of the exclusionary process: *Eni ti o wo Ankara o je semo*. That is, anyone who is not wearing the Aso-Ebi material will not be served *semovita*, a local delicacy.

When dozens, sometimes, hundreds of people wear the same outfit, the effect is spectacular and "often very charming, and symbolizes strikingly the unity of the family" (Marris 2005: 31) The Aso-Ebi has been described as a "social uniform" because of its role in fostering "group identity, solidarity, a sense of being special" (Ogunyemi 1996). In the crowded party scenes in Nigeria, family members not only need to be distinct, they display their strength – numerical and financial – by donning Aso-Ebi. Visitors are thus able to identify the celebrant's family or those who belong to the same social or religious group as the celebrant (Asakitikpi 2007: 105–16). Familusi (2010), like several other scholars, premises the collective identification of a people with the person of the celebrant as the sociological significance of Aso-Ebi, which at times overlooks the ideological underpinning of such gatherings.

Some historical documents suggest the Aso-Ebi has not always existed but developed in Lagos – Nigeria's commercial and, arguably, cultural center – sometime in the 1920s when the post-war trading boom hit Nigeria (Olukoju 2004). It has survived and evolved over the years to take up an identity, not as a legacy of the boom that followed World War I, but from an ethnic Yoruba culture to a national one. Another account says that the Aso-Ebi culture started with an agrarian people who wanted to have some entertainment with much pageantry and special dress (Little 1974) and a third version is that the Aso-Ebi rose to replace the older practice of Aso-Egbe, the uniform dress worn by members of a social club (Olukoju 2004).

Over the years, Aso-Ebi has broadened its influence and it is no longer limited to expressing familial ties. Non-consanguine members pay for the privilege of sharing the same fabric to signify close friendship, association (Little 1974) and identification with the celebrating family. It is a pragmatic relationship as it obliges the celebrants to extend the same courtesy to any of the members of the group who buy the Aso-Ebi in their honor as they would to their own family. Yorubas say, "*Ebieniniasoeni*," that is, one's (extended) family is one's clothing. The clothing is also a metaphor for the person and one's social perception playing the role of aesthesizing the body as well as the body aesthesizing the cloth (Drewal 1979). Thus while Yorubas recognize that "cultural markers like scarification, tattoos or brands serve as physical representations of kinship protection and social currency" (Shillington 2004), juxtaposing clothing materials with family is evocative of nearness, of beauty, of protection, of identification and other similar functions which clothing serves. This is not always ideal as, sometimes, family rivalries and politics also play out in the Aso-Ebi culture when factions within the same family either refuse to buy the Aso-Ebi material with everyone else or select their own distinct fabric to communicate intra-family differences.

Some writers criticize Aso-Ebi since it presumes a certain economic and social equity among different members of an extended family who are forced to show a belonging they may barely be able to afford. To show their family identity, people feel obliged to devote a substantial amount of money to Aso-Ebi (Falola & Adebayo 2000). One of the persistent criticisms of Aso-Ebi revolves round the practice as a fructification of the convergence of culture, commerce, commodification, capitalism and consumerism. Ajani, in her critique of the commercial bent that Aso-Ebi has undergone, points out that commodification erodes the social and moral essence of a culture (2012). This devaluation is further evident in the widening of the social sphere of those who can purchase Aso-Ebi to include non-family members. Her argument, however, presumes that Aso-Ebi endows the people who practice it with its essence, rather than the other way round – that is, people collectively identify through Aso-Ebi, thus making the culture. The economic critique of Aso-Ebi, often with dense moral undertones, misses the point that the survival of the practice is owing to the capitalist culture that drives it. Aso-Ebi might be commodified but it owes its survival, its spread beyond Yoruba culture to all of Nigeria, West Africa and even diaspora Africa, to the dynamics of international trade. While the Aso-Ebi might be imported, it is re-signified within local communities that build a cultural economy around it and make it suitable to local tastes (Nwafor 2011).

In some instances, Aso-Ebi is about color and not about the fabric itself (Balogun 2011). Thus, when for instance the color gold is chosen, all the members of the assembled family are at liberty to wear what they please as long as it is of this color. Unlike its precedent, facial marking, Aso-Ebi allows individuality and self-expression through diverse tailoring styles, patterning and adornments. Individuality based on aesthetic taste, body type and even financial standing is integral to the Aso-Ebi, thus reflecting "evidence of will, agency, and the democratic cultural instinct of its originating milieu. Asoebi is a cultural open sesame to a world where genius meshes with style, aesthetics and democratic agency" (Adesanmi 2011). While affirming identity and group cohesion (Smith 2010), Aso-Ebi also expresses sartorial differentiation of class. However, Nigerians have found an all-class bridge in the Dutch wax-print, popularly called Ankara. In the past decade, Ankara, formerly labeled as working-class/semi-rural wear, has seen a resurgence, and emerged as the choice textile in social gatherings in Nigeria (Oyedele & Babatunde 2013). Though fewer and fewer Yoruba children, especially those in urban areas, grow up with facial/body marks, they are co-opted into the culture of Aso-Ebi with its twin attributes of culture and collective identity.

One of the defining characteristics of Aso-Ebi in contemporary Nigeria is its de-essentialization of the collective labeling and institutionalization of practices. The very performative act of using clothes to express identity and identification as evinced in Aso-Ebi is counteracted by its transience as the cloth can be shed and wears out before any defining ideology can take root. The impermanence of Aso-Ebi, metaphorized in the cloth and quite unlike body marking in ancient Ibadan, suggests an easy detachability from the skin.

8.5 Aso-Ebi and Collective Identity: The Case of Olabode George

The Aso-Ebi is a cultural practice that signals collective identification and beauty through body decoration but at the same time transcends consanguine relationships and territorialization of identity which can be mutually reinforcing of each other (Howell 2001). Quite unlike body markings that tie you to a people and a place, Aso-Ebi is not binding beyond a certain moral obligation. This fluidity that enables people of all shades and characters to momentarily identify as a collective, rather than stressing the *finding of selves*, actually encourages dispersal when the ceremony/occasion ends. A sort of dis-identifiable identity creation is enabled by the nature of Aso-Ebi – something to be put on and taken off – as against the culture of body marking that is more static and rather inescapable. When family members are tied to each other through body markings, it fosters a certain level of moral responsibility among individuals who know that what affects one person in the collective can have a domino effect on them. The familial and territorial connection of body markings to the body makes the individual findable within a milieu of social and moral behavior. The culture of Aso-Ebi is however antithetical to this. When the definition of whom you can identify with is loose – and this ambulatory nature of Aso-Ebi is enabled by urbanity – it divests people of certain social and moral obligations as they can escape the responsibility of the ideology their group canvasses.

This attitude manifests in Nigeria particularly in various gatherings like political campaigns and public demonstrations where crowds of people are hired, given Ankara or any other sort of colorful Aso-Ebi to wear so as to create a spectacle, and then paid to support an ideological stand. The performers know that Aso-Ebi as a form of body marking does not commit them to any community of ideology beyond the moment, as the clothes can be easily bought off the market and are neither peculiar to family nor to territory or even ideology. People who collectively identify as a group and take up Aso-Ebi can far more afford to go against social mores than those who have their family identity inscribed on their body. When their performative act is over, the crowd is paid; they disperse to the various locations they were sourced from, and may never rejoin again. These groups have been caught on camera several times, sharing out the money and gifts they received. A few times, fighting has broken out as they dispute over the distribution of the remuneration for a job they did as a collective. None of them can be held to any account, and their participation in the collective can be very easily denied if necessary.

The case of the Nigerian politician, Chief Olabode George, was one that shocked the nation, in showing the extent to which the celebratory nature of Aso-Ebi could be employed to counter the social and moral values of a society. Chief George, former Chairman of the Nigerian Ports Authority, was accused of corruption and was being tried by the Nigerian legal system. While his trial was ongoing, his supporters would gather wearing Aso-Ebi – dressed in *buba* and *iro* (blouse and wrapper) with matching headgear, men and women, some of them singing and playing drums, would follow him to court. They would set up a tent, serve food and generally turn the court into a festive site. These actors would sing the praises of Chief George and disrupt the court atmosphere. That a cultural practice was being violated in such a manner was shocking to a number of Nigerians. Unlike the moral economy implicated in the culture of body marking, that of Aso-Ebi could be subjected to abuse because of its nature as removable from the body. Aso-Ebi enables both the creation of an identity capacious enough to absorb all persons, causes, ideas and ideologies, tactile materials and aesthetics; and the disbanding of these without any permanent commitment. Identity is performed only for a moment through this vehicle of fashion and clothing.

References

Adesanmi, Pius. (2011). Aso-Ebi on my mind. *Sahara Reporters* (February 19).
Ajani, O.A. (2012). AsoEbi: The dynamics of fashion and cultural commodification in Nigeria. *Journal of Pan African Studies*, 5(6), 108–18.
Alexander, J.C. (2004). Toward a theory of cultural trauma. In: Jeffrey C. Alexander (ed.), *Cultural Trauma and Collective Identity*. Berkeley: University of California Press. http://dx.doi.org/10.1525/california/9780520235946.003.0001
Asakitikpi, A.O. (2007). Function of handwoven textiles among Yoruba women in South Western Nigeria. *Nordic Journal of African Studies*, 16(1), 101–15.
Balogun, Hairat. (2011). *To Serve in Truth & Justice: An Autobiography*. Bloomington, IN: AuthorHouse.
Barnes, S.T. (1986). *Patrons and Power: Creating a Political Community in Metropolitan Lagos*. Manchester: Manchester University Press.
Bernstein, M. (2002). The contradictions of gay ethnicity: Forging identity in Vermont. In: David S. Meyer, Nancy Whittier and Belinda Robnett (eds.), *Social Movement: Identity, Culture and the State*. Oxford: Oxford University Press.
Chiavetta, E. (2008). Clothing and alienation: Karen King-Aribisala. In M.F. Borch & A. Rutherford (eds.), *Bodies and Voices: The Force-Field of Representation and Discourse in Colonial and Post-colonial Studies*. New York: Rodopi.
Coy, P.G., & L.M. Woehrle. (2000). Introduction: Collective identity and the development of conflict analysis. In: Patrick G. Coy & Lynne M. Woehrle (eds.), *Social Conflicts and Collective Identities*. Lanham, MD: Rowman & Littlefield. http://dx.doi.org/10.1016/S0163-786X(00)80032-4
Drewal, Henry John. (1979). Pageantry and power in Yoruba costuming. In: Justine M. Cordwell and Ronald A. Schwarz (eds.), *The Fabrics of Culture: The Anthropology of Clothing and Adornment*. Chicago: University of Chicago Press.
Drewal, H.J. (1988). Beauty and being: Aesthetics and ontology in Yoruba body art. In: Arnold Rubin (ed.), *Marks of Civilization*. Los Angeles: Museum of Cultural History, UCLA.
Falola, T. (1987). Power relations and social interactions among Ibadan slaves, 1850–1900. *African Economic History*, 16, 95–114. http://dx.doi.org/10.2307/3601271
Falola, T., & Adebayo, A.G. (2000). *Culture, Politics & Money among the Yoruba*. Rutgers, NJ: Transaction Publishers.
Familusi, O.O. (2010). The Yoruba culture of Aso Ebi (group uniform) in socio-ethical context. *LUMINA*, 21(2), 1–11.
Hall, R.B. (1999). *National Collective Identity: Social Constructs and International Systems*. New York: Columbia University Press.
Howell, D.L. (2001). Territoriality and collective identity in Tokugawa Japan. In: Shmuel Noah Eisenstadt, Wolfgang Schluchter & Björn Wittrock (eds.), *Public Sphere and Collective Identities*. Rutgers, NJ: Transaction Publishers.
King-Aribisala, K. (1998). *Kicking Tongues*. Ibadan: Heinemann Press.
Little, K. (1974). *African Women in Towns: An Aspect of Africa's Social Revolution*. Cambridge: Cambridge University Press.

Marris, P. (2005). *Family and Social Change in an African City: A Study of Rehousing in Lagos*. Florence, Kentucky: Psychology Press.
Melucci, A. (1995). The process of collective identity. In: Hank Johnston and Bert Klandermans (eds.), *Social Movements and Culture*. Minneapolis: University of Minnesota Press.
Mobolade, T. (1973). The concept of Abiku. *African Arts*, 7(1), 62–4. http://dx.doi.org/10.2307/3334754
Nwafor, O. (2011). The spectacle of Aso Ebi in Lagos, 1990–2008. *Postcolonial Studies*, 14(1), 45–62. http://dx.doi.org/10.1080/13688790.2011.542114
Obiechina, A.E., & A.O. Olutayo. (2000). Attitude to facial marks in South Western Nigeria. *Odonto-Stomatologie Tropicale*, 91. http://www.santetropicale.com/Resume/39103.pdf
Odunbaku, J.B. (2012). The use of tribal marks in archaeological and historical reconstruction: Isale abandoned settlement as a case study. *Research on Humanities and Social Sciences* (online), 2(6).
Ogundipe, P.J. (2012). *Up-Country Girl: A Personal Journey and Truthful Portrayal of African Culture*. Bloomington, IN: AuthorHouse.
Ogunyemi, C.O. (1996). *Africa Wo/Man Palava: The Nigerian Novel by Women*. Chicago: University of Chicago Press.
Olajubu, O. (2003). *Women in the Yoruba Religious Sphere*. Albany, NY: State University of New York Press.
Olukoju, A. (2004). The "Liverpool" of West Africa: The dynamics and impact of maritime trade. In: *Lagos, 1900–1950*. Trenton, NJ: Africa World Press.
Oyedele, A.M.T., & O. Babatunde. (2013). The resurgence of Ankara materials in Nigeria. *Journal of Education and Practice*, 4(17), 166–70.
Patterson, O. (1985). *Slavery and Social Death*. Cambridge, MA: Harvard University Press.
Peel, J.D.Y. (2003). *Religious Encounter and the Making of the Yorubas*. Bloomington, IN: Indiana University Press.
Pierce, A.J. (2012). *Collective Identity, Oppression, and the Right to Self-Ascription*. Lexington, KY: Lexington Books.
Purefoy, Christian. (2010). Tribal scars custom drying up in Nigeria, CNN.com, July 10.
Scharfstein, B.-A. (2009). *Art Without Borders: A Philosophical Exploration of Art and Humanity*. Chicago: University of Chicago. http://dx.doi.org/10.7208/chicago/9780226736112.001.0001
Shillington, K. (2004). *Encyclopedia of African History, Vol. 1*. Boca Raton, Florida: CRC Press.
Smith, F.T. (2010). Ceremonial and festival costumes. In: Valerie Steele (ed.), *The Berg Companion to Fashion*. Oxford: Berg.

9
Nonverbal Message: The Yoruba View of "Deviant" Male Hairstyles

Augustine Agwuele[1]

9.1 Introduction

A day after his 74th birthday, *The Hollywood Reporter* (*THR*) visited the actor Morgan Freeman for a Question & Answer session. *THR* asked Mr Freeman if he had met President Obama. In response, Freeman said, among other things: "I've noticed that he has a *Chicago walk*. Watch him when he walks up to the podium. He doesn't walk up one, two, three, stop. He goes one, two and one, two. He's got a little bit of *a beat to it*."[2] Apparently, walk is not mere locomotion; how we walk contains certain personal information that others interpret. Societies judge and profile individuals by their body "movements." Analogous to walking, the space between two people could lead observers to describe them as a couple. The way individuals are clothed could make others describe them as professional, shabby or slutty. Hairstyle, the smell of cigars or garlic, a smile or frown, a limp or firm handshake elicits various interpretations from observers. All these signals, known as nonverbal communication signals, frame our interactions and influence the messages we convey, but they are not the message itself.

As you travel through cultures, opinions about hair "brutally remind us of their importance when we consider the passions, the polemics, the taboos, and the violence that they can arouse" (Broomberger 2008: 396). All over the world, hairstyles are sported and perceived as markers of

[1] Augustine Agwuele teaches in the Department of Anthropology, Texas State University, San Marcos. He is interested in experimental phonetics, language, culture and society, and the peoples and cultures of Africa. He studies closely the Yoruba people of Nigeria and in the African Diaspora, as well as the Amhara people of Ethiopia.

[2] http://www.hollywoodreporter.com/news/morgan-freeman-barack-obama-he-196667, accessed September 9, 2011 (emphasis mine).

social identity, forms of presentation of the self and means of identification by Others. The interpretations of hairstyles, as nonverbal statements of social personhood, are culturally rooted and specific. They reflect varied and sometimes ambiguous approaches to cultural globalization. In the same way that people may be judged based on their clothing as hip, modest or loose, hairstyles serve to typecast individuals as sports professionals or regular Joes, rabbis or skinheads, exotic or home-grown, marginal or integrated, mad or sane, thereby framing interactions with and decisions that are made about such individuals. Studies of African hair and bodily adornment have been conducted for over a century. The subject has generated numerous cross-disciplinary, theoretical and popular cultural interrogations.

This chapter explores the message presumed to be conveyed by hairstyles – specifically, cornrow and dreadlocks – among Yoruba people from an experiential perspective. From a theoretical standpoint, it makes use of the concept of social hegemony put forward by Antonio Gramsci (1891–1937). As *adarihunrun*, "the species that grows hair primarily on the head," that is, human beings (Lawal 2000: 95), Yoruba people have strong views on hair and fervent reactions to hairstyles considered deviant, more so because hair is located on the head, the place of life. Unlike bodily attire, hair is both alive and dead, both inside and outward of the person; it is liminal, forming a conduit from the physical to the spiritual and vice versa. It resurrects itself on the head when it is cleanly shaved. It functions as a key "ethnic signifier." Caught on the cusp between self and society, nature and culture, the malleability of hair makes it a sensitive area of expression. All of these somewhat binary features, especially the aliveness and deadness of hair, encompass two significant spheres influencing the Yoruba worldview that includes their perception of a person based on the hairstyle of that person.

Nonverbal communications are a medium for expressing thoughts and converging feelings; they are not the thoughts or the feelings. Like many linguists, I subscribe to an integrative study of communicative language without discriminating the verbal from the nonverbal; thus I accept the view that they form a single underlying process of utterance production (McNeill 1992). Kendon (1972: 443) suggests that there is only communication, because it does not make sense to speak of verbal or nonverbal. In studying language, attention could be given to any aspect of this communicative system, and regardless of area of focus, such a study must have a way of uncovering the interaction of the mind with eyes, ears, skin, nose and mouth. Thus this chapter focuses on the affective reactions of Yoruba people as gleaned from their verbal and nonverbal responses to messages that they perceived to be encoded by cornrow and dreadlock hairstyles.

In this chapter I take snippets from a more comprehensive ethnographic study (titled Politics and culture of representation: A case of deviant hairstyles in Yorubaland) whose goal was to make sense of the attitudes and reactions of Yoruba people toward male hairstyle, using key sociocultural features such as worldview, language use and socio-political configuration as means of investigation. The chapter is divided as follows: section 9.2 describes the Yoruba people in their environment and their traditional hairstyles; in section 9.3 is a narration of my encounters with friends, colleagues and a religious organization, and the responses to me because of my hairstyle; section 9.4 discusses the basis of Yoruba responses to deviant hairstyle and explicates aspects of the Yoruba cosmology and culture that informs their "perception" of persons; and section 9.5 compares Yoruba and African American responses to "deviant' hairstyles.

9.2 The Yoruba World and Hairstyles

Sir Alfred Moloney, one-time British Governor of Lagos, described the Yoruba as a people who owe their origin to community of language (tongue), communal interests and the necessity of self-protection (Moloney 1890). The Yoruba were separate feuding nations during the 18th century that somehow created a narrative of common ancestorship, constructing their ethnicity from their common political, religious and economic practices and finally becoming unified as a nation (Falola 1987). This nationhood can also be seen as a very large socially coherent body, a community of practice, consisting of people with shared outlook and communicative patterns. Yoruba people have always been agrarian people, they dwelled mostly in large homesteads with surrounding farmlands known as oko-ile (home farm) mostly outside city limits, and they operated a hierarchical form of societal organization. Along with their primary occupation as farmers, they had a series of specialized professional guilds such as hunters, blacksmiths, and various practitioners of divination and worship of the legions of gods whose pantheons number 401. They still follow an elaborate monarchical system of government with the king at the head, and a supporting cast of chiefs and lords who wield power over their different offices. Socially, Yoruba people are extremely polite, and jealously guard their position and status. There is a strong bond of interdependence engendered by the mode of subsistence, kingship and religion. This bond occurs within the family, and percolates to the homestead, the community and to the city under the king. One of the marks of this bond is conformity, unflinching adherence to established codes of conduct and societal injunctions. The Yoruba peoples' view of deviant hairstyles and appearances draws its reference from the conceptualization of a society in which conformity and cohesion are fundamental factors of social organization. Altogether, the goal of the Yoruba nation is the production and reproduction of the material basis of its own existence (Afonja 1981: 304) as well as the maintenance of the requisite social and organizational structures necessary to achieve this goal (Agwuele 2009). In this connection, social hegemony trumps every other consideration. The aforementioned concept of social hegemony (Antonio Gramsci's) is invoked in order to reiterate, and understand, the ways that Yoruba people portray themselves, their ideas, beliefs, conception of the purpose of their earthly existence, power, values and the Yoruba identity to which individuals are expected to subscribe. To Yoruba people, the aesthetically beautiful is a visual outpost for values and morals, and most significantly a sign of integration, rootedness and belongingness in the Yoruba community. While individual uniqueness is acceptable, it is within a corporate identity to which everyone consents; thus to appear other than in a fashion acceptable to the community is to be ostracized, one of the highest forms of punishment among Yoruba people. The ostracism that is meted out to people with deviant hairstyles such as dreadlocks is not mainly a reaction to the wearer going against prescribed norms, but is heightened into violence, as will be argued later, due to the religious worldview that sees in such appearance an omen of the destruction of the very essence of Yoruba existence.

The phrases social hair (Hallpike 1969) and social body (Turner 1993) are useful conceptualizations pertaining to "body talk." Hair, like cloth, touches the body and projects outward; it is at once personal and social, individual and collective; and with increasingly diminishing social-cultural barriers, it fuses the personal, local, regional, national and international in all its outrageousness. Apart from physique and apparel, hair is the most visible aspect of self-presentation in the ordinary course of life. Physical appearance, especially attire, receives significant modification in order to draw admiration, compliment and favorable disposition. The German saying *"Kleider machen Leute"* (Clothes make people) is a maxim expressed in every continent. For Yoruba people, the same sense is conveyed by the saying *"Irinisi ni isenilojo"* (Hospitality is determined by perception).

Presentation of the self was an invaluable cultural value in the ancient Yoruba nation, and the body ornamentation and hairstyle of native Yoruba people have long been a subject of interest and interpretation.

Contemporary readers will find funny some of the descriptions of Yoruba hair by writers of the colonial era. For instance, "The people of Ijesha have a wilder aspect than is common to Yorubans, produced perhaps by an increased amount of negro beard, and a practice of wearing calabashes for head coverings; the females wear a saucer-shaped button, the shank inserted in a hole in the left nostril" (May 1860). While there may not be any correlation between facial hair and aggression, it is nonetheless the case that a person's hair has always influenced individuals' and society's view of him or her. People adorn, style and treat their hair for various purposes; to them, grooming of the hair is an invaluable part of normality, while uncultivated hair is a sign of madness (Sieber and Herreman 2000).

Hairstyles: Travelers have provided observations concerning the hairstyles of Yoruba people even before colonial times. For instance, Astley in his travelogue (1968 [1745]) noted about the men of Benin kingdom (part of the Yoruba nation): "Men content themselves with letting their Hair grow in its natural form except bunching it in two or three places, in order to hang a great Coral at it." Aside from such observations, there are three kinds of traditional hairstyles for Yoruba males:

(a) Completely shaved head: Except in special cases, a Yoruba baby will have its head shorn of hair about a week after birth, immediately following the official naming ceremony. Thereafter, as the child grows, the head of a male child is completely shaved about once a month. Where this is not the case, a very short cut is maintained, with the edges of the hair carefully trimmed.

(b) Different hairstyles as required by (i) guiding deities or (ii) profession: There are numerous deities in Yorubaland; the deities Sango, Esu, Osun and Oya are just four of them. Each deity may require their priests to wear a specific hairstyle to project certain features of the deity. For instance, *osu*, a patch of hair in the middle of head, more like a tuft, is often worn by Esu priests. Sango priests, regardless of sex, wear different styles such as *agogo*, *suku* or *kolese*, *bayanm*i (Drewal & Mason 1998: plate 55), these are different stylizations of cornrows. Osun priests also wear *suku* cornrow braids, similar to a king's crown (Apter 1992: plates 5, 7). Aside from these religiously informed hairstyles that identify practitioners with their guiding deities, there are hairstyles that identify profession. For instance, *jongori*, a strip of hair comparable to the Mohawk hairstyle runnning in the middle of the head from the front to the back, with the sides completely shaved, is sported by priests. There is also the *àáso*, a hairstyle worn by hunters to showcase their spiritual powers (*juju*). This style consists of three round patches at the front, center and back of the head. The style called *ilari* is worn specifically by the king's messengers, a single round patch toward the front of the head.

(c) *Dada*: This is the appellation for children born with knotted hair. They are considered to be special children of blessing, and the gifts of the gods. Until the 1800s cowry shells were legal tender for all transactions across most of Yorubaland. European travelers used them as well. The knotted hair of these children is reminiscent of the cowry, that is, riches, wealth. Having children with such hair is believed to attract wealth, thus their heads are not shaved as is the case for other children (Houlberg 1973: 377; Lawal 2000). *Dada* are also believed to have supernatural powers in their hair, since they are presumed to have taken after the mythological King Dada whose hair was matted. Special panegyrics called *oriki dada* are offered to honor them, for instance:

> Dada Awuru
> The one who wears a crown of money
> The one who owns an embroidered dress
> The one who carries a leaded staff of office
> You carry a big crown of money to the market. (Lawal 2000: 97)

In general, Yoruba male hair could be summarized along the lines described by Stone (1899: 30) in spite of the examples of unspeakable rudeness and wanton ignorance that abound in the book. "Woolly heads are never seen among the men, who shave not only the face, but also the head and even the eyebrows and nostrils. Some leave a strip of hair from the forehead over the head to the back of the neck. Others leave little patches as marks of devotion to some particular deity, but such patches are concealed by the tight fitting cloth cap or the turban." The reality for Yoruba people is that, unlike female hair, the aesthetics of male hair is of little value; hygiene is paramount. "If your hair is poorly looked after, you may be called a lunatic, an outlaw, a witch doctor, an evil person" (Niangi 2000: 26). There is also a magico-religious underpinning for hairstyles across the Yoruba nation, as is the case for most of Africa.

9.3 Encounters

There may be construal disputes about observable events, since certain categories that we use to codify events may implicate not only their meaning but also our understanding of them. Being mindful of this, the three encounters narrated below are presented as accurately as I experienced them. The narration includes experience with friends, with professionals outside of Nigeria and with a religious organization (Scripture Union) in Ibadan, Nigeria.

9.3.1 Acquaintances and Friends

The first stage in my self-experimentation involved growing out my hair. This was my afro stage. Comments of concern indicated that it was becoming noticeable and perhaps that the length of my hair was exceeding the "acceptable" norm. *Afro laye tun gba bayi ke*? (Is afro now the reigning style?) *Se ise ni o je ki o ri aye barber ni*? (Have you been so busy that you have no time to go to the barber?) These comments, though uttered in jest, insinuate disagreement with my appearance. They follow the Yoruba saying that *igba ere laa mo ooto* (playful moments unravel the truth) and the practiced use of politeness face-to-face (Matsumoto 1988).

With the increasing length of my hair, the next step in managing it was to plait it into cornrow. Sporting a cornrow hairstyle was a critical step for a Yoruba male; skepticism and suspicion suddenly emerged from within my circle of friends and acquaintances. A prominent and highly celebrated professor of Yoruba origin in the United States said during a gathering: "If I did not know you and admire your integrity and scholarship before you started this hairstyle, I would avoid you, and would not have anything to do with you."

In 2006, a friend with a doctorate in engineering, whose wife holds a master's degree in linguistics, organized a dinner in honor of their family friend from Nigeria whose child had graduated from the University of Texas at Austin. The family friend belongs to the Nigerian elite; they reside in Nigeria, but their children are in American schools and they visit the USA up to four times a year. They have a home in Lagos; they work in Abuja, the capital city of Nigeria, and fly back to Lagos every weekend. This background information is to illustrate their socio-economic status and their cosmopolitan upper-class lifestyle. The Yoruba woman from Nigeria (NYW) was friendly and warm right from the moment I walked into the residence of the Engineer-Linguist couple where the formal dinner was organized. I did the rounds, making some new acquaintances and saying hello to those I already knew. NYW introduced herself, while her husband was reserved. NYW asked if I was from Jamaica, to which I responded in Yoruba. She said, "You speak Yoruba very well," and the other guests, those who knew me, laughed at her response. The conversation during the dinner was mostly in Yoruba and English. At one point the conversation generated some Yoruba proverbs to which I provided the cultural context and explanation. NYW's friendly view of me as an exotic foreigner who spoke Yoruba changed. The fact that I was Yoruba meant that I now required prayers. She started singing spiritual songs of prayers to ward off evil, and to ask God for protection for herself and her family. Finally she said that she would intercede on my behalf so that God would destroy the demonic influences over me.

9.3.2 Professional Colleagues

During a coffee break at an international conference on Africa at the University of Texas at Austin, a group of us sat around a table with our snacks. Suddenly, a man approached our table with his plate of food in his hands. Without saying hello to anyone at the table, he pointed his index finger at me and asked: "Where do you come from?" A little taken aback, I hesitated. He repeated the question, "Where are you from?" Everyone at the table fell silent as I responded in Yoruba: *"Se ojuyi o gun rege to ni?* (Is this visage not convincing enough?) At this, they all started to laugh, enough to cause him embarrassment. Unperturbed, he asked the same question the third time. An old acquaintance of his and a member of faculty at UT rebuked him: "What is your problem? He is from Ibadan, just like you." Just as abruptly as he had come, the man turned around and walked away without another word. He had broken every Yoruba code of public conduct and politeness.

9.3.3 Scripture Union, Ibadan

In 2007, I was on my way to the University of Ibadan campus. Just about a kilometer from campus, we arrived at the Scripture Union headquarters. This is a religious center with a printing press and a bookstore. Having worked in the building as a teenager and gone there on a fellowship for almost 10 years, I was gripped with nostalgia and curiosity. So I stopped on the spur of the moment and went in. At first I was barred from entering the building because I had no previous appointment. I pointed out that there was a bookstore in there that was also open to the public. So, I was allowed to register at the gate, and I was issued a number tag. I walked in, and strolled around with excitement and curiosity. I said hello to the office workers upstairs and went over to the bookstore. Then, I noticed that I was being followed, closely monitored. Finally, one of the people started quizzing me: "Who are you? Why are you here? Do you know anyone here? Whom do you want, what do you want, identify yourself...." An onlooker will quickly recognize this line of questioning as synonymous with that of the Nigerian Police Force. It is a series of questions designed to hang a crime on an innocent person rather than adjudicate or actually find out anything of value. Irked by the barrage of questions and incessant insinuations, I pushed back with: "Please leave me alone, this is a public space and a religious center." Big mistake! The director of the Scripture Union Nigeria, apparently apprised of my presence, sent the day-guard to beat me up. In vain I tried to speak with the director; I was physically assaulted. So, I left the building. Three hours later, I came back with an expatriate colleague who was staying at the University of Ibadan. We met the director just as he was driving out of the premises with his wife. Seeing that he could not evade us, he finally consented to speak with us. I confronted him with my experience and his behavior and demanded to know why I had been thus treated. When he became aware of who I was, and perhaps as I was bolstered by my European colleague, he began a series of apologies. "I am sorry, I truly am. Please accept our apologies. I take the responsibility and I offer you my sincere apology." His wife showed her support with the customary plea for forgiveness. The guard who had beaten me up bowed in apology, this time with "sir" accompanying every bow and plea. However, I still wanted to know what it was that had led to the assault. He eventually succumbed: "Well, since you persist so remarkably in asking for a reason, I will answer you. You see, unlike others, I have been to Kenya and Tanzania; I am familiar with your hair. But it is against our culture. We do not consider this hair appropriate. It is not the normal hairstyle, you see. If your hair was normal, nobody would suspect you of anything. Our culture does not tolerate this hairstyle."

9.3.4 Summary of Observations

- Yoruba people accommodated me when they viewed me as a stranger and gave me the exotic specimen treatment.
- When they saw me as a Nigerian, they often continued under the belief that I was not Yoruba, hence an ignoramus.
- When it became inevitable for them to accept that I was Yoruba, I was seen as a as a person who was possessed and who required immediate intervention, or as one to be avoided.

There is no doubt that my hairstyle communicated a message that elicited these responses. Of interest to this discussion is to explore what drives the feelings, attitudes and responses that are engendered by certain appearances – nonverbal gestures. How do we see, hear and understand properly according to our community of placement? How did the Yoruba acquire their unique sense of interpreting the dreadlocks hairstyle?

9.4 Basis of the Yoruba Perception of Hairstyles

Just like ornaments, hairstyle is not without social significance, either attributive or representational; it may be a symbol of achievement, religious belief, authority and power or some defined status within a nation. Hair occupies a liminal space (Rosenthal 2004), it represents an intriguing bodily site of upheaval (Tate 2009) and it is vital to the production of social meanings, staging of self and the production of symbolic values (Katz-Rothman 2005). Similar to Carol Delaney (1994), the above data are aimed at untangling the meanings of hairstyle in Yoruba society. To achieve this goal, it is necessary to examine the Yoruba religious worldview against the background of the previously described socio-economic and political configuration. Yoruba peoples' views of a person are encased within the strictures of their cosmology (Idowu 1962; Parrinder 1949; Babayemi 1984). Ori (literally head) is described as the creator (Lawal 2000) and as destiny (Gbadegesin 2003). Against this background a context emerges through which it is possible to understand the motivation for the responses documented in the preceding section.

9.4.1 Cosmology

The Yoruba relationship to hair takes its cue from their creation myth. It is traditionally believed that the creator-deity, Obatala, molds all heads (*ori*), each of which becomes vitalized by the breath of life (*emi*) that comes from Olodumare. An individual who is to be born into the world first goes to the repository of heads of the heavenly potter, Ajalamopin, to pick up a head. The head that this individual chooses at that time is the inner head that contains the power of life, the individual's essence. Within the chosen head is inscribed the course of the person's sojourn on earth, i.e., their destiny. The purpose of earthly existence to Yoruba people is threefold; "*ire owo, ire omo, ire atunbosiaiye*" (wealth, children and longevity). Within an individual's *ori* is the possibility and means of achieving these goals. The achievement of goals by an individual and collectively by the people assures the corporate existence of the Yoruba nation. Without the individual, there is no nation; without the nation, the individual has no existence. This interdependence demands strict adherence to communal ideals and customs that manifest in the form of a cohesive communal lifestyle; furthermore, this collectiveness is structurally reflected in the familial and societal organization, the hierarchical nature of which is parallel to that of the Yoruba gods. Thus, the head leads and directs the individual; as such it sits atop the person. This positioning of the head and its controlling authority over the person is analogous to the hierarchical political set-up of each Yoruba kingdom under the theocratic rule of the gods. So, the physical is a parallel of the spiritual. The spiritual is linked to the physical and can affect and manipulate it.

On earth, the "Yoruba cosmology presents a picture of Man, a solitary individual, picking his way aided by his Ori or Destiny (chosen by himself before coming to earth) between a variety of forces, some benign, some hostile, many ambivalent, seeking to placate them and ally himself with them in an attempt to checkmate his rivals and enemies in human society. Among the hostile powers are the eniyan or witches, and the Ajogun which are personified evils such as death, loss, sickness etc." (Barber 1981: 729). Ever apprehensive of danger, fearful of sudden natural occurrences and evil acts of spirits known as *aiye*, the Yoruba are guarded and watchful, preferring to leave nothing to chance. As noted by Drewal (1990),

> For West African peoples, reality has up to the present included a whole host of spirits, these spirits are considered as the enabling and constraining forces of the past and present that affect, indeed shape, the quality of people's lives. They include the forces of history and tradition, that is our ancestors and deified heroes and heroines; the forces of hardship – infirmity, death, legal disputes, epidemics, disasters of all kinds known collectively as the Ajogun; the spirit of perseverance, *iroju*, as well as the forces of capitalism and neocolonialism which for example, the Mami Wata spirits embody. All of these forces reveal themselves through divination, dreams, masking, and possession trance, all of which are perceived to disclose hidden realities.

Particular attention is given to hair due to its liminal nature, the fact that it mediates within and outside the physical head, among other features previously mentioned. For instance, a newborn's hair is shaved to mark its entrance into the world just as the head of a dead person is shaved to mark their exit. Care is taken to protect the cut hair of the baby from *aiye* who through it could interfere with the child's *ori*. The *aiye*, it is believed, are able to transform themselves into birds at night and to seek out and destroy their victims (Prince 1961). Only the hair of the spiritual child known as *dada* is left unshaved at birth. According to Lawal (2000: 96) "unkempt hair is likened to a jungle and the individual concerned is easily mistaken for a psychopath." Lawal further suggests that Yoruba people "believe that taking good care of one's hair is an indirect way of currying the favor with one's ori Inu (inner head)."

Hair was and remains of spiritual significance within the philosophy of *ori*. This originates with its location on the head, the center of physical existence. A person may continue to live with the removal of many parts of the body; however, if the head is excised, death is definite. Hair is atop the head, thus as the apex of the body it occupies an important position to which several mystical views are attributed. As liminal matter, hair was supposed to mediate communication between the soul and the spirits (Byrd and Tharps 2002). Spiritual entities (called *aiye*) traverse the plane between the physical and the spiritual (also called *aiye*). In essence, they occupy the liminal space as does the hair or a door.

Within the strictures of this cosmology emerges the suspicion of dreadlocks. The person who wears this hairstyle can be perceived as a sorcerer or witch, neither of which is good, as both can scout for and harvest *ori*. One has to be guarded and careful to maintain the necessary balance between the physical and the spiritual, else one's fortune could be turned into misfortune, and one's good head (*orirere*) could become a bad head (*oriburuku*); in which case, one is adjudged as having compromised one's destiny. For a negative transformation to occur in someone whose positive life trajectory was apparent to all is perceived to be a result of the person having fallen prey to *aiye*. Similarly, a person who experiences a sudden radical positive transformation in the form of wealth is believed to have stolen someone else's *ori*. Thus there is no event without cause; consequently, the thought of the possibility of *aiye* interfering with ones' destiny manifests practically as fear and violent reactions.

So we have a sign (e.g., dreadlocks or cornrow – both considered aberrant), that has a referent in the real world as well as in the spiritual world. This referent generates a meaning in the mind of the observer. The generated image or meaning calls up a shared interpretation to which the fight or flight response becomes the only viable option at the moment of perception. Be it an index of evil, a kind of mnemonic device or a signifier, the image/sign as a code elicits responses from the Yoruba person on several levels. On the spiritual level it generates and creates the image of an agent of *aiye* – the physical manifestation of the spiritual world seeking to destroy. On the emotional level, it produces instant fear, revulsion and heightened tension, out of which flows the physical reaction in the form of verbal or physical abuse. The interpretation of dreadlocks thus derives from the sociocultural, political and religious organization of the Yoruba world; and this specific interpretation is necessary for individual and collective survival.

9.4.2 Culture and Perception

> One might say of someone that he was blind to the expression of a face. Would his eyesight on that account be defective? This is, of course, not simply a question for physiology. Here the physiological is a symbol of the logical. (Wittgenstein 1963: 210e)

Hair remains one significant medium for conveying a culturally important message. Once locked in, individuals appear incapable of escaping the prison of their own prisms and as such are not rational observers of events. My encounters show how otherwise rationally thoughtful, educated and cosmopolitan people are driven to irrational behavior under the influence of an underlying guiding spiritual template that had been internalized during the early part of language acquisition and socialization as a functioning member of the Yoruba community. Yoruba culture links dreadlocks with *aiye*. Humans believe what they see, to see dreadlocks is to see *aiye* and to hear instantaneously the prayer of the elders: May we never experience the warfare of *aiye* (*Olorun maa jeki a ri ija aiye*).

As functioning members of society, the verbal and nonverbal behaviors of individuals cannot be understood without knowledge of the community to which they belong. The logic to the approach adopted in this chapter was to find out the proposition to which the users implicitly appeal when a certain phrase is invoked. To have a language, for instance, and to use it appropriately is to participate in the mutual images that words or phrases of the language evoke. We tether meaning to real events and to the picture of our world and reality. The meaning of a deviant hairstyle for the Yoruba is couched in a language of thought that graphically, vividly and consequentially displays the potential threats to their essence, goals and means of achieving the good life.

The source for the sensibilities displayed by native Yoruba to nonconforming hairstyles has been discussed; a question that suggests itself, based on this, is: Why are these Yoruba responses only directed toward their own people? From Yoruba sayings and adages, it can be conjectured that Yoruba people are mainly suspicious of members of their own culture, presuming them to be capable of being complicit in the nefarious works of *aiye*:

Ehinkunle ni ota wa, ile ni aseni n'gbe (The enemy is without, the evildoer that undoes one is within).

Kokoro ti nje efo, inu efo lo wa (The bug that feeds off the leaves resides in the leaves).

Bi iku ile o pani, ti ode o le pa'ni (If the death from within does not kill a person, the one from without will not do so).

Eni to moni ni 'nseni (It is the one that know you that can undo you).

We may presume by the preceding proverbs and sayings that the Yoruba people believe that your own kind is your worst enemy, because they know you; they are the only ones who can undo you. As such, your *ori* is safe with strangers but not with those who know you. In this regard, Yoruba people are ethnocentric, they do not attribute wisdom (*imo*) and knowledge (*oye*) to non-Yoruba people; thus denied, the outsiders are powerless and harmless. (For further discussion of *aiye* see Prince 1961; Drewal 1990 and 1974; and their references)

The responses of Yoruba to dreadlocks reflect the operation of their worldview. The responses have emotional dimensions that lead them to take a distancing stance to a nonverbal gesture they consider threatening. In examining what gesture and sign might reveal about the mind or thought, or the cognitive processing of language and speaking, Kendon (2004: 15) defines gestures as any and all visible bodily actions that are "directly perceived as being under the guidance of the observed person's voluntarily control and being done for the purpose of expression rather than in the service of some practical aim." As an expression of "manifest deliberate expressiveness" the observer is fully responsible and aware of that which they convey: in this case, the Yoruba person sees the wearing of dreadlocks as a brazen show of *aiye*; of an *aiye* that flies in the day time. Since nothing is a sign until it is interpreted as such (Pierce 1931–58: Vol 2, 172), it does not matter to the perceiver if the person actually intends to communicate the meaning which the perceiver has projected onto the sign. Consequently, Kendon (2004: 16) concludes that gesture, nonverbal communication, "cannot be given a definition that is independent of how the participants in any situation are treating each other's flow of actions." Having being socialized to a way of seeing causality, Yoruba people's internalized reactions to objects and appearances that immediately elicit the images of those untoward outcomes of which they have been warned, lead them to then act out their culture. The woven web of significance enslaves the instinct at that moment. The dreadlocks on a male adult excite the imagination of the Yoruba to see an evil spirit seeking someone to destroy. By the use of the term "imagination" is meant bringing to the moment something that is absent in the current surroundings of the participants; this follows Sartre (2004) and Casey (1979) and is also used by Nemirovsky et al. (2012). This usage mainly showcases how interlocutors are sufficiently influenced by the awareness of the latency of a concept to act in certain ways.

9.5 Cross-Cultural Perceptions

Our appearance, through styling, socially categorizes us and affords others readings of us in ways that we may have never intended nor even suggested. Africans and African Americans, in spite of their common roots in Africa, diverge in their response to the same hairstyles. "Conk" was the style of straightened hair that African American men wore most notably after 1945. Unlike African American women for whom it was almost becoming the norm of good appearance to have their hair straightened, African American men, especially those who were upwardly mobile and socially conscious wore their hair shortly trimmed and neatly cut – except for entertainers whose outlandish and eye-catching appearance was indicative of their profession. The conk hairstyle became associated with those rebelling against society and also those of bad reputation. The style lost its popularity with the 1960s Black Power movement, sometimes associated with the increasing wave of political independence sweeping Africa at that time, which ushered in pride in one's own identity beyond that which obtained in the heydays of Marcus Garvey and other apostles of black empowerment. Black power, black beauty, black pride and many other ideas of African consciousness and identity politics elevated the Afro as a popular hairstyle. Angela Davis's striking image comes to mind, so also her thoughts (Davis 1994).

This proliferation of "natural" look, "authentic" African hair was part of the return-to-roots ideology that gained ascendancy in the 1970s. Then there were musicians of worldwide fame such as Peter Tosh, Bunny Wailers and Bob Marley who unquantifiably elevated dreadlocks and promoted Rastafarianism. For African Americans, "hair-styles which avoid artifice and look 'natural,' such as Afro or Dreadlocks, are the more authentically black hair-styles and thus more ideologically 'right-on'" (Mercer 1992). To Yoruba people however, the same look is sinister, diabolical and nefarious. To African Americans, dreadlocks express collective identification with Africa and rejection of cultural and political oppression, but Yoruba see the hairstyle as an agent of menacing spirits. While African American women who were at the forefront of the popularization of the Afro look in the 1950s and early '60s received strange looks from their neighbors upon going "au naturel," (Kelley 1997) Yoruba males with cornrow or dreadlocks draw not just strange looks, but righteous indignation, judgment and even physical punishment.

A 1963 discussion about authenticity between a Yoruba woman living in the United States, Ogunbiyi, and another African American, King, reported in *Negro Digest*, although dated, is still, to a large extent accurate and reflective of extant views. In it, Ogunbiyi painted a picture of the comfort and improvement that would, she felt, be achieved by eradicating the customary, i.e., she recommended that Yoruba people should straighten their hair and do away with local clothes which she called costume. The fact that those who keep their natural hair "don't have to comb the hair everyday, that they can swim, shower and get caught in the rain without worrying about [their hair]" (Benton 1988) – the very epitome of liberation – appeared to have eluded her. These perceptual differences are owing to the workings of different local power relations.

Whatever imagination the presence of dreadlocks calls up in the mind of the looker cannot be divorced from this person's sociocultural experience. If you are Yoruba, then this experience is rooted in the socializing and enculturation process as well as the constant reinforcement from actions in the society. The reinforcing process operates by connecting experience to the things that bear similitude to aspects of this experience. A *were* – that is, a mad person – is often physically assaulted on the street. A young person not only sees this, but also hears the comments that the adults make during the process: *Egba ni oogun were*, "the whip is the cure for madness." Consequently, the dreadlocks hairstyle, one of the physical attributes of a *were*, raises negative responses in the Yoruba imagination. There is no doubt that the perception of hairstyles among Yoruba people reveals the power of community, of culture and of worldview over the mind and over individuals. The different responses, including violence toward the insider with dreadlocks or cornrow, are socially orchestrated rituals that reinforce the dominant ideologies that attribute evil to these hairstyles.

9.6 Conclusion

Interaction, according to Enfield & Levinson (2006: 1), is at the "heart of our uniquely human way of life." Among the Yoruba the forces at work in the response to deviant hairstyles are those necessary for the internal social, political and religious cohesiveness of the people. This chapter has suggested certain historical, economic, political, religious and situational factors that interact to condition the attitude of Yoruba interlocutors to the perception of a person's appearance that is adjudged to violate their sensibilities. A religious underpinning is proffered as being influential in Yoruba perception of deviant hairstyles.

The appeal to the formative nature of culture hinges on the evidence that modernism, education, religion, change of space or any other feature capable of reorienting the core-system of references has been ineffective in influencing interpretations of causality for Yoruba people. The repercussions of any social instability, insecurity, political upheaval and unfortunate personal circumstances have only further entrenched the hegemony of the cultural mode of data organization and processing; the certainty of the traditional theological standpoint seizes the mind comfortingly.

When a community with access to an extensive knowledge base advances refutable propositions as solutions, then one must suspect that certain forces capable of nullifying reason are at work. This is the experience that I have had repeatedly with the Yoruba nation on the continent and in the diaspora. I submit that the roots of Yoruba perception lie in their cosmological philosophy, ritual observances, and apparently insurmountable beliefs carefully packaged and continuously readministered through stories and in contemporary times through the popular media with appropriate images. The way of old, of the elders, remains the highest philosophy of the land, its preeminence and persistence creatively reinforced such that it persists in its ability to coerce subservience across the board.

References

Afonja, S. (1981). Changing mode of production and sexual division of labour among the Yoruba. *Signs (Chicago, Ill.)*, 7(2), 299–313. http://dx.doi.org/10.1086/493883

Agwuele, A. (2009). Popular cultures of Yoruba kinship practices. In: T. Falola & A. Agwuele (eds.), *Africans and the Politics of Popular Culture*. New York: Rochester Press.

Apter, A. (1992). *Black Critics and Kings: The Hermeneutics of Power in Yoruba Society*. Chicago: University of Chicago Press.

Astley, T. (1968 [1745]). *A New General Collection of Voyages and Travel, Vols. 1–IV*. London: Frank Cass and Company.

Babayemi, S.O. (1984). African concept of God, the Cosmos and Man: A Yoruba example, *Institute of African Studies Seminar Series*, Ibadan (February 8).
Barber, K. (1981). How man makes God in West Africa: Yoruba attitude towards the Orisa. *Africa*, 51(3), 724–45. http://dx.doi.org/10.2307/1159606
Benton, A.R. (1988). Hair-Raising. *Feminist Studies*, 14(2), 325–35. http://dx.doi.org/10.2307/3180156
Broomberger, C. (2008). Hair: From the West to the Middle East through the Mediterranean. *Journal of American Folklore*, 121 (Fall).
Byrd, A. & Lori Tharps. (2002). *Hair Story: Untangling the Roots of Black Hair in America*. London: St. Martin's Press/Macmillan.
Casey, E. (1979). *Imagining*. Bloomington, IN: Indiana University Press.
Davis, Angela Y. (1994). Afro images: Politics, fashion and nostalgia. *Critical Inquiry*, 21(1), 37–45.
Delaney, C. (1994). Untangling the meanings of hair in Turkish society. *Anthropological Quarterly*, 67(4), 159–72. http://dx.doi.org/10.2307/3317416
Drewal, H. & John Mason. (1998). *Beads, Body and Soul: Art, Light in the Yoruba Universe*. Los Angeles: UCLA Fowler Museum of Cultural History.
Drewal, H.J. (1974). Gelede masquerade: Imagery and motif. *African Arts*, 7(4), 8. http://dx.doi.org/10.2307/3334883
Drewal, M.T. (1990). Portraiture and the construction of reality in Yorubaland and beyond. *African Arts*, 23(3), 40–9. http://dx.doi.org/10.2307/3336828
Enfield, N.J. & Stephen C. Levinson. (2006). *Roots of Human Sociality*. Oxford: Berg Publishers.
Falola, T. (1987). Power relations and social interactions among Ibadan slaves, 1850–1900. *African Economic History*, 16, 95–114. http://dx.doi.org/10.2307/3601271
Gbadegesin, S. (2003). Èníyàn, The Yoruba concept of a person. In: P.H. Coetzee and A.P.J. Roux (eds.), *The African Philosophy Reader* (2nd ed., pp. 175–91). New York: Peter Lang. Earlier published (1991) in: *African Philosophy: Traditional Yoruba Philosophy and Contemporary African Realities* (pp. 27–59).
Hallpike, C.R. (1969). Social hair. *Man*, New Series, 4(2), 256–64.
Houlberg, M. (1973). Yoruba hairstyles in Southwestwern Nigeria. In: Justine M. Cordwell and Ronald A. Schwarz (eds). *Fabrics of Culture: The Anthropology of Clothing and Adornment*. The Hague: Mouton Publishers.
Idowu, E.B. (1962). *Olodumare: God in Yoruba Belief*. London: Longmans.
Katz-Rothman, B. (2005). *Weaving a Family: Untangling Race and Adoption*. Boston: Beacon Press.
Kelley, R.D.G. (1997). Nap time: Historicizing the Afro. *Fashion Theory*, 1(4), 339–51. http://dx.doi.org/10.2752/136270497779613666
Kendon, A. (1972). Some relationships between body motion and speech: An analysis of an example. In: A. Siegman & B. Pope (eds.), *Studies in Dyadic Communication* (pp. 177–210). Elmsford, New York: Pergamon Press. http://dx.doi.org/10.1016/B978-0-08-015867-9.50013-7
Kendon, A. (2004). *Gesture: Visible Action as Utterance*. Cambridge: Cambridge University Press. http://dx.doi.org/10.1017/CBO9780511807572

King, Helen Hayes & Theresa Ogunbiyi. (1963). Should Negro women straighten their hair? *Negro Digest* (August): 65–71.

Lawal, B. (2000). Orinlonise: The hermeneutics of the head and hairstyles among the Yoruba. In: Roy Sieber & Frank Herreman (eds.), *Hair in African Art and Culture*. New York: The Museum for African Art and Prestel.

Matsumoto, Y. (1988). Reexamination of the universality of face: Politeness phenomena in Japanese. *Journal of Pragmatics*, 12(4), 403–26. http://dx.doi.org/10.1016/0378-2166(88)90003-3

May, D.J. (1860). Journey in the Yoruba and Nupe countries in 1858. *Journal of the Royal Geographical Society of London*, 30, 212–33. http://dx.doi.org/10.2307/1798303

McNeill, D. (1992). *Hand and Mind*. Chicago: Chicago University Press.

Mercer, K. (1992). Black hairstyle politics. In: R. Ferguson, M. Gever, T.T. Minh-ha & C. West (eds.), *Out There: Marginalization and Contemporary Cultures*. New York and Cambridge, MA.: New Museum of Contemporary Art and MIT Press.

Moloney, A. (1890). Notes on Yoruba and the colony and protectorate of Lagos, West Africa. *Proceedings of the Royal Geographical Society and Monthly Record of Geography* (pp. 596–614). http://dx.doi.org/10.2307/1801424.

Nemirovsky, R., M.L. Kelton & B. Rhodehamel (2012). Gesture and imagination: On the constitution and use of phantasm. *Gesture*, 12(2), 130–65. http://dx.doi.org/10.1075/gest.12.2.02nem

Niangi, B. (2000). Hair in African art and cultures. In: Roy Sieber & Frank Herreman (eds.), *Hair in African Art and Culture*. New York: The Museum for African Art and Prestel.

Parrinder, G. (1949). *West African Religion*. London: Epworth Press.

Pierce, C.S. (1931–58). In: C. Hartshorne, P. Weiss, & A.W. Burks (eds.), *Collected Writings* (8 vols.). Cambridge, MA: Harvard University Press.

Prince, R. (1961). The Yoruba image of the witch. *Journal of Mental Science*, 107(449), 795–805.

Rosenthal, A. (2004). Raising hair. *Eighteenth-Century Studies*, 38(1), 1–16. http://dx.doi.org/10.1353/ecs.2004.0064

Sartre, J.P. (2004). *The Imaginary: A Phenomenological Psychology of the Imagination*. New York: Routledge.

Sieber, R. & F. Herreman (eds.). (2000). *Hair in African Art and Culture*. New York: The Museum for African Art and Prestel.

Stone, R.H. (1899). *In Africa's Forest and Jungle, or Six Years Among the Yorubans*. New York: Fleming H. Revell Company.

Tate, S.A. (2009). *Black Beauty: Aesthetics, Stylization, Politics*. Farnham, UK: Ashgate Publishing Limited.

Turner, T.S. (1993 [1980]). The social skin. In: C.B. Burroughs & J.D. Ehrenreich (eds.), *Reading the Social Body* (pp. 15–27, 29–39). Iowa City: University of Iowa Press.

Wittgenstein, L. (1963). *Philosophical Investigations*. Trans. G.E.M. Anscombe. Oxford: Blackwell.

10
Embodying Holiness: Gender, Sex, Bodies and Patriarchal Imaginaries in a Neo-Pentecostal Church in Kenya

Damaris Seleina Parsitau[1]

10.1 Introduction

In recent years, women's dress and fashion have become sites of contestation, scrutiny, public debate and discourse, even being the focus of policy debates about social and moral decay in Africa generally and Kenya in particular. These debates pervade the country's mediascape (particularly radio and television), public and private discussions as well as the church/religious sphere. Institutions of higher learning as well as secondary schools, and government and county officials have also entered into these debates. The result has been calls for intervention and imposition of a dress code for women and girls within Kenya's higher education institutions, faith-based institutions as well as government agencies.

A few illustrations of some of the recent debates and events in respect of female dress codes and bodies in Kenya would suffice here. On July 20, 2012 students of Rwathi Boarding Secondary School in Central Kenya went

---

1   Damaris Seleina Parsitau is a Senior Lecturer in Religion, Gender, Human Rights and Public Life at Egerton University, Njoro, Kenya. She holds a PhD in Religion, Gender and Public/Civic Engagement from Kenyatta University in Kenya. She is also the Director of the Institute of Women, Gender and Development Studies (IWGDS) at Egerton University. Her research interests include African (Kenyan) Pentecostalism, religion, civic engagement and politics, gender, human rights and public life. She has been a Visiting Research Fellow at the University of Cambridge, UK and the University of Edinburgh, Scotland.

on strike protesting the school policy of forcing girls to wear long skirts. Several girls had complained that the skirts were not only too long for their liking but that forcing them to wear such skirts was an insult to their sense of fashion. When the school administration failed to listen to their grievances, the girls took to the streets, demonstrating and rioting, resulting in the closure of the school. But the girls were adamant and when they came back after the strike they still wore short skirts. The incident led the Board of Directors at the Anglican-sponsored school to expel four girls thought to have incited the riots.

This strike spawned huge public and national debates, particularly in the education and religious sectors, on the appropriate length of skirts for secondary school girls. The debate assumed a policy angle when the then Minister for Education, the late Honorable Mutula Kilonzo intervened by directing school heads to desist from forcing young secondary school girls to wear long skirts. "Why are we dressing our girls like nuns? We are living in the present era and teachers and society must conform with it," he argued, and to loud applause from students in another secondary school.[2]

The Minister then went on national television where he displayed a standardized but shorter skirt which he decreed that school girls should be allowed to wear. Needless to say, the Honorable Minister came under harsh criticism from a section of the public, secondary school heads and teachers as well as religious organizations who termed his utterances "reckless and misleading young girls to dress provocatively." The Catholic Church, particularly the nuns, issued a statement to the Minister informing him that nuns actually love their dress and that he should respect the religious orders. The heat generated by this debate was so intense that the Minister retracted his statement saying he had been misquoted by the media.[3]

On January 23, 2013, the Law Society of Kenya (LSK) published guidelines for dress directed mainly at its female members whose function is to certify other members before admission to the role of Advocates of the High Court. In this set of guidelines, female lawyers are forbidden to wear "revealing" clothes including sleeveless shirts or dresses. They are also not to sport fancy hairstyles or clothes or shoes that are deemed too bright or shiny. The guidelines advise women lawyers not just on the acceptable colors for appearance in court but that the colors must coordinate and blend

---

2 http//www.capitalfm.co.ke/news/2012.
3 Faith-based organizations, particularly the mainline churches (Catholic and Protestant), are major stakeholders in Kenya's education sector and the Minister for Education did not want to rattle these major stakeholders and parents.

well. The colors that are considered professional for lawyers include black, gray, navy blue and cream.[4]

Similarly, on July 30, 2013, the Deputy Inspector General of Police in Nairobi issued a directive forbidding policewomen to wear lipstick and other makeup or bangles and other accessories with their official uniforms, ostensibly because this has the potential to distract male offenders, including the notorious public transport drivers and touts who frequently break traffic laws and rules with abandon.[5] Interestingly, female policewomen interviewed by this author explained that they did not find the directive offensive and many said they felt they received more respect when they didn't wear makeup.[6]

Lastly, in November 2013 in Kisumu County in Western Kenya, a female County Representative proposed a motion prohibiting women from straddling a motorbike or bicycle, a popular and cheap though dangerous mode of transport locally known as *bodaboda*, ostensibly because it is "demeaning to their dignity" and "exposes their bodies" as opposed to "covering their bodies." She further argued: "Women who sit with their legs apart are exposing their bodies, while sitting on the side means they can conceal themselves." She described the way women sit while riding these *bodaboda* as "uncultured" and considered it provocative to both passersby and cyclists who can get sexually aroused on the road thereby causing an accident.[7]

These few examples not only serve to show how female dress has become a subject of public and largely sexist debate in Kenya in recent times, but also how the subject has elicited tremendous and sometimes controversial and emotive discourses. Yet such debates are not anything new in Kenya. Women's dress and bodies have elicited heated debate and discourse since the late 1960s and '70s. Kenya for instance narrowly escaped the banning of miniskirts when in 1970 the country's first president, Jomo Kenyatta, flirted with the idea of such a ban. Kenyatta termed the mini-skirt "a catalyst for prostitution."[8] Since then, debates and public discourses on women's dress

4   Law Society of Kenya releases new dress code for female lawyers, *The Star: Kenya*, January 23, 2013. See also allAfrica.com.
5   This is according to circular C/CUS/VOLVIII/16G sent to the press on July 30, 2013.
6   I interviewed a delegation of senior police officers (all females) who paid me a courtesy call in my office at the Institute of Women Gender and Development Studies, Egerton University on August 5, 2013 at 9.30 am.
7   Ochiel Hezron, Kisumu women to sit more decently on bodaboda, *The Standard Newspaper*, November 28, 2013.
8   Waweru Mugo, The day Jomo Kenyatta hinted at partial ban on miniskirts, accessed at www.standardmedia.co.ke.

have become increasingly widespread, although it has not attracted legislative enactments yet.

Attempts to exert control over women's bodies are often made through social and religious pressure as well as public opinion, debates and discourses, which can be used to coerce women to dress in particular ways. Unfortunately such control is also attempted through violence. In the early 1990s, for example, members of the outlawed Mungiki group[9] would strip naked any women wearing trousers and miniskirts in public, especially at bus terminals, on the streets and in market stalls, ostensibly to "teach them manners." Besides, they supported the practice of female genital mutilation as a way to control women's sexuality in the name of protecting African traditions and cultures.

While the attempt to limit women's bodily autonomy and dressing has continued in Kenya since independence, it has not yet attracted serious legislative action. However, debates persist about female dress code and habits, thereby putting tremendous social pressure on Kenyan women, particularly younger women and girls in institutions of higher learning. Yet, the policing and control of women's bodies and dressing is not peculiar to Kenya alone but a common practice prevalent in many African countries, as I discuss below.

10.2 Policing Women's Bodies, Dressing and Sexuality in Africa

The policing of women's bodies and dressing habits is prevalent in many parts of Africa. Moral, cultural and traditional values have historically been cited to justify the control of women's sexuality and dressing choices. This is usually fuelled by religious sentiments or claims to cultural authenticity, and even gender-based violence is often cited to justify such policing. Many governments have argued that they legislate on female dress in order to protect women from violence against them prevalent in many parts of Africa.

Certain items of women's clothing are particularly marked as offensive or at the least unacceptable. The miniskirt particularly is seen as a sign of

---

9 The Mungiki group is an outlawed but dangerous sect composed of mostly Kikuyu youth who have caused tremendous suffering to Kenyans through extortion, killings, rape and many other forms of vicious behavior.

the moral decay of women and by extension the moral decay of society. It is argued that by wearing miniskirts, women are showing that they are sexually available. It is further implied that no respectable, moral African woman would wear such indecent clothing which leads to unwanted male attention and in extreme cases attack from "concerned citizens" to uphold the morality of the nation. Ironically, the miniskirt is used as a sign of protest against gender-based and sexual violence.

For these reasons, in the 1960s and '70s miniskirts were banned in several African countries including Ghana, Tanzania and Uganda (Allman 2004; Tamale 2011; Bakare-Yusuf 2011). Under the 30-year dictatorship of President Hastings Kamuzu Banda, until 1994, women in Malawi were banned from wearing trousers and miniskirts as well as applying lipstick and painting their fingernails. In Malawi and Zambia, skirts had to be at least 3 inches below the knee. In 2008, there were attempts to ban miniskirts once again in Uganda because it was claimed women wearing them distracted drivers and caused accidents.

In April 2013, the Ugandan Parliament passed a bill that would prohibit women wearing miniskirts or other provocative clothing in public.[10] Bakare-Yusuf (2011) reports how in 2008 a Nigerian politician tried to control what women wore through the Indecent Dressing Bill. The Bill, proposed as an Act of Parliament, was to prohibit and punish public nudity, sexual harassment and other related offenses in Nigeria with the goal to reduce sexual violence and alleged immorality caused by women's indecent dress. These types of bills and directives reinforce and perpetuate a culture that blames women for the sexual and gender-based violence prevalent in many parts of Africa.

Though the policing of women's dress is done in the name of protecting them from sexual violence, attempts to control women's bodies have not been limited to legal or policy spheres but are often violent acts carried out by sections of the public in various African cities. Across the continent there is widespread incidence of women being taunted, attacked and publicly stripped and in extreme cases sexually assaulted or abused for wearing "inappropriate items of clothes." In Kenya, women have sometimes been stripped naked, groped, ogled, assaulted and in extreme cases raped for wearing tight trousers or miniskirts.[11] In Lilongwe, Malawi, Bakare-Yusuf (2011) reports that women wearing trousers or short skirts were groped and stripped naked by groups of male street vendors. In Johannesburg,

10　Hezron, Kisumu women to sit more decently on bodaboda (see note 7 above).
11　Mugo, The day Jomo Kenyatta hinted at partial ban on miniskirts (see note 8 above).

South Africa, women were reportedly assaulted at a taxi rank for wearing miniskirts. According to Bakare-Yusuf (2011), women in Nigeria are frequently stripped for "indecent dressing," which has sometimes prompted public campaigns to raise awareness of this "vice." In all these incidents, the push to police the way women dress continues across Africa on the pretext that revealing female clothing causes sexual harassment and violence against women.

But what really underlies this censorship of women's expressions? Women are often considered guardians and transmitters of cultural traditions, so women who wear trousers and miniskirts are seen as embracing new and strange and un-African identity, not only setting a bad example to younger girls but also besmirching the morality of the nation by their indecent choice of clothing. Yet, one common thread that runs in many of these cases involving public stripping, as Chantelle De Nobrega (2014) observed of the South African context, is that it is normally done by men who see disciplining deviant women as a central component of masculine identity.

But as De Nobrega further argues, "this is also a pointer to a particular fixation on sex, sexual identity, gender roles as foundation of morality, and chaos and disorder in nature and society which are often positioned or even framed as being the result of divine retribution. The rationale of many conservatives and spiritual moralists is that restricting women's rights to make choices about their own bodies protects the moral fibre of society, which is essential for maintaining social order." Women's clothing is a means of self-expression, a symbol of empowerment and a right to be. As such, women's right to choose their dress should be protected just like other personal liberties. It is argued here that policing the way women dress is another way of controlling women's bodies and it is oppressive.

All these illustrations may seem inconsequential, but if the rights and freedoms of women are not guarded, such attacks on their liberty may well grow and spread. Even institutions of higher learning, particularly faith-based organizations, limit and control how young female students dress on campus, as I discuss next.

10.3 Sexual Harassment and Moral Imaginaries in Kenya's Universities

Kenya's institutions of higher education have become sites of policing of women's dress and debates about the social and moral decay caused by unacceptable female clothing. Already a number of faith-based universities in Kenya such as the evangelically inclined Kabarak University, the Catholic Sponsored Strathmore University as well as the Catholic University of Eastern Africa (CUEA) and many others forbid their female students to wear trousers, miniskirts, spaghetti tops, tight jeans and any item of clothing that reveals female flesh. Other revealing clothes forbidden by these institutions include short dresses, lace dresses and tops also comically referred as "see me through pieces of clothes," sleeveless shirts and many other styles of clothing.

Male students in these universities are also required to dress smartly in suits and shirts that project a professional image. The universities argue that they seek to shape the lives of these young female and to some extent male students by giving them a holistic worldview that enables them to grow as intelligent but also morally upright students who will fit well into the larger society.

In these institutions, young women's fashion choices are seen not only as a distraction to male students but also provocative for male lecturers. By instituting a dress code for female students, faith-based institutions seek to enforce their own ideas of holiness and moral codes on university students thereby perpetuating the same patriarchal culture prevalent in most African societies. By restricting students' sartorial choices, these institutions of higher learning seek to discipline them and limit their personal rights and liberties, particularly in response to the forces of globalization where Kenyan youth, both males and females, want to dress not just fashionably but also freely like their peers in other parts of the world.

In Kenya's public universities, young women dress fashionably as there are no policy restrictions. Yet emotive debates and discourses about female students' dress codes pervade public universities. Arguments that female students on campus are violated, sexually abused and sometimes even raped because of their wearing skimpy dress are quite pervasive. Sexual and gender-based violence is prevalent not just in Kenyan public universities but also in the larger Kenyan society. The argument usually revolves around the perception that the wearing of revealing clothes by young women in public universities has made sexual violence and harassment a marked feature of university life in Kenya, and therefore imposing and regulating dress code on female students is the only way to stop such crimes.

At the Institute of Women, Gender and Development Studies (IWGDS) where I currently serve as Director, I come across many cases of sexual violence against women which are totally unrelated to the mode of dress. Yet, many of these cases are simply assumed to be caused by inappropriate dressing on the part of the victim. In a security training course for university managers which I attended, a high-ranking military officer told us members of staff that the reason there are many cases of sexual and gender-based violence on campus is because female students are skimpily dressed thereby inviting attack.

When I protested at this simplistic explanation to an obviously complex and emotive question, the audience booed me while the military man asked whether I would allow my daughter to dress as she pleased. I told him to leave my daughter out of it and went on to give my own personal assessment of sexual harassment and violence based on my personal encounters and daily interactions as well as the narratives of abuse of the victims of this at the institute, as reported to me as the director.

Before I could finish explaining my own impressions and assessment of this problem on campus, one elderly female member of the staff angrily exhorted me to become a role model not just to my daughter but also to the girls I mentor at the institute by ensuring that they dress decently. Another added that I must not embrace strange Western cultures but instead advance African culture and heritage. This not so interesting encounter at the security meeting got me thinking about women's bodies, sexual violence and dress in Kenya and this chapter is meant to raise awareness about these emotive issues. The conversations I had at this training that centered on rape and gender-based violence as being brought about by girls' modes of dressing that are presumed to provoke men to rape them as well as induce male lecturers to help them acquire what are referred to as sex-acquired degrees,[12] is sadly echoed in many parts of the country.

Again this is not peculiar to Kenyan universities (Bennet 2002). In 2008, a dress code was introduced at the University of Bea in Cameroon. Here campus security agents have the authority to send "indecently" dressed students, usually female students, home to change their clothes (Bakare-Yusuf 2011). Again and again policy-makers, male citizens, taxi and "matatu" drivers, male street vendors, security agents and heads of institutions of higher learning in countries such as Malawi, Sudan and Kenya police female dress to ensure that it conforms to so-called ideas of decency for African women.

These debates are also perpetuated by religious organizations, particularly Christian and Muslim ones. Religious organizations are locales where women's dress and the length of hemlines are discussed, controlled

---

12 There are pervasive perceptions in most of Kenya's public universities that female students engage in transaction sex with lecturers who then help them pass exams and graduate with sexually acquired degrees. These allegations are not supported by research, but they persist.

and debated. Many members of the clergy have become involved in these debates. For example, Apostle Ng'ang'a of Neno Evangelism Ministries, a Neo-Pentecostal Church based in Nairobi with several branches spread across the country, banned what he considered scantily dressed women from worship services at his church. A notice with graphics at his Neno Evangelism premises in Nairobi cautioned women against wearing miniskirts, tight clothing or any other "provocative" dress when coming to church.[13] Apostle Ng'ang'a's actions and perceptions about provocative clothing are mirrored in many other Christian and non-Christian organizations that argue: "if you are born again or are spiritual and religious, it must show and manifest in your clothes and dressing habits."[14]

Yet the widespread denunciation of women's sartorial choices raises interesting social and religious questions about normative attitudes toward female morality, sex, bodies, sexuality, the state and the economy (Bakare-Yusuf 2011). It further raises questions about the gendered subtexts that make it possible to draw causal links between the previously unrelated issues of sexual intimidation, indecent exposure and women fashions in order to talk about contemporary social tensions and morality. As Bakare-Yusuf (2011) so aptly points out again, what is important to note is that the debate about women's exposed flesh and perceived immorality is less about the personal choices of women but more about how young female bodies are becoming sites onto which many social and existential insecurities are projected.

The arguments that are often advanced to control women's dress appear to suggest that every woman who has been sexually abused or even raped must have provoked the attack and was asking for it. Women are therefore not only responsible for their own personal security but also for the sexual response of men who are visual and easily aroused at the sight of women's flesh. Men therefore are not responsible for their aggression as they are simply provoked by scantily dressed women. In other words, women's dress code must be laid down by patriarchal traditions as well as by the clergy to protect the women from the violating male gaze, as male desire itself must be allowed its untrammeled course. The prescription to avoid gender-based violence is thus merely to dress decently, an argument that is just too simplistic to be acceptable.

This kind of logic fails to place Kenya's women's vulnerability in the context of social and economic inequality, masking the brutal realities of scant

---

13 Miniskirts disturb the peace in East Africa, http://www.speroforum.com.
14 I have heard this statement over and over again in many Pentecostal churches in Kenya.

economic options within a moralistic discourse. Recent trends suggest that there are increasing numbers of Kenyan women who are single mothers due to high rates of divorce. According to a recent report, 30 per cent of women in Kenya are single.[15] This report also revealed an astonishing new face of the Kenyan family, suggesting that more women are drawn into single parenthood as men abandon their traditional role as providers for their families.

An array of factors is blamed for the emerging trend in which three in 10 Kenyan girls become pregnant before the age of 18, including irresponsible fathers, peer pressure and the struggle to cope with modernization. This places many Kenyan women in situations of vulnerability and economic strain. Besides, poverty and unemployment are also in general high, leaving many people in situations of varied vulnerabilities. This trend is worsened by the fact that every year, both public and private universities spawn hundreds of graduates who cannot be absorbed into the job market, leaving many students especially females with fewer options. Some women may even have no alternative than to engage in transactional relationships to survive. It is therefore suggested here that the arguments in respect of gender, sex, dress and bodies must be framed within the larger social, economic and political realities of Kenyan society rather than simply moralizing an obviously very complex issue.

Women's sexuality and agency in urban spaces must be placed within the larger socio-economic anxieties and insecurities including the contesting of modernity, the proliferation of new information technologies, images and semiotics of fashion, increasing economic and social inequalities, and the coexistence of public morality and private vices. Because women's bodies are the trope for the articulation of these anxieties, they also become the site for the attempted resolution of them (Bakare-Yusuf 2011).

10.4 The Ministry of Repentance and Holiness

The Ministry of Repentance and Holiness (MRH) is a unique religious movement that specializes in prayer and fasting, repentance and holiness, prophecy and visions, probity and moral regeneration and the second

---

15 Kenfrey Kiberenge, More women become single mothers as men abandon family roles, *Daily Nation*, August 18, 2013.

coming of Jesus Christ. Since its founding in 2004 by self-proclaimed Prophet David Edward Owour, the MRH has also witnessed a significant demographic spread, especially after the 2007/8 political crisis, to become a sort of mass movement characterized by huge monthly crusades variously dubbed national prayer and repentance rallies or peace rallies.

David Owour was born in Yimbo village in Bondo District of Western Kenya in 1968. According to biographical data on the MRH website and church publications,[16] Owuor studied Science at the Makerere University, Uganda and University of Nairobi, Kenya. It is also claimed that Owour undertook post-graduate studies at the Ben-Gurion University of the Negev and University of Haifa in Israel, and the University of Giessen and Institute for Genetics in Germany where he specialized in molecular genetic engineering, examining DNA cloning and nucleotide sequence analysis for medical drug design and discovery.

Upon completion of his doctorate from Israel, Owour joined the University of Illinois at Chicago (UIC) Medical Centre for Pharmaceutical Biotechnology as a post-doctoral Fellow specializing in signal transduction by cancer chemotherapeutic drugs. He also claims to have lectured to PhD students in pharmaceuticals and pharmaco-dynamics, particularlly drug metabolism by cancer chemotherapeutic drugs. A feature that distinguishes Dr Owour's MRH from other New Religious Movements in Kenya is that its founder's social stature and academic background suggest someone well schooled with a promising and outstanding academic background.

Through elaborate ritual undertakings and alarming prophesies, Owour burst into the public limelight, his Ministry of Repentance and Holiness emerging and evolving into a sort of mass movement that captured the imagination of many Kenyans. His pet subject or message of repentance and holiness was backed by myriads of ritual performances such as prayer and fasting rallies, complete with wailing women wearing sackcloth and riding on donkeys.

10.4.1 A Sinful Nation, Wretched Souls and a Very Wrathful God

The overriding theme and teaching of MRH is "Repentance and Holiness," as its name suggests. This is imaged and framed as the central message of the church as the only remedy for all the problems of this world. At

16 http://www.repentandpreparetheway.org.

the beginning of this Ministry, many of the followers used to wear sackcloth and ride on donkeys along the streets, wailing and repenting for both personal and national sins so that God would spare the country his wrath and destruction. Among the sins are sexual immorality, immoral dressing, abortion, pollution of the houses of worship by false prophets and Pentecostal clergy. These last, according to Prophet Owour, had defiled the altar by preaching the gospel of prosperity and committing sins of sexual immorality with members of the flock and many others. This is what he said in one sermon published in the MRH monthly magazine, *Repentance and Holiness Magazine*:

> Kenya has descended into greater sin and wickedness, with all forms of impunity.
>
> It is as though sin had now become institutionalized in the nation of Kenya. Sexual sin has achieved significant gains, even as far as homosexuality being reported in the priesthood, the preaching of the gospel of the prosperity and the gospel of corruption, now reached a new high, forms of sin became exalted and in the name of Jesus. Corruption is the order of the day.[17]

In another sermon, again published in his monthly magazine, Prophet Owour gives a list of transgressions that, according to him, the Lord had raised against Kenya: rampant sexual sin in the land and within the church, the deceptive gospel of prosperity that was totally bent on enriching pastors through corrupt means, witchcraft, abortion and many others. In an interview, he states:

> Look! God is angry with Kenya because of defiling the altar of the Lord. Abortions had become a norm in Kenya, encompassing high schoolchildren, universities and campuses. The collection of fetuses by the roadside in Nairobi and other parts of the country side is going to attract the wrath of God. The immoral dressing that has now characterized the attire of Kenyan women did not augur well with the holiness requirements of the Lord of Israel, who created Kenya.[18]

In a series of long prophesies concerning the State of Kenya, Prophet Owour lays bare his own impressions about the sins of the nation. He says:

---

17 Sack clothes and ashes and the wailing women, *Repentance and Holiness Magazine*, 6 (November 2009): 2.
18 The man who baptized Raila Nairobi, exclusive interview, *Arise Africa Magazine*, Special Edition, 2009.

On October 19, 2004, the lord spoke to me vividly and clearly about the state of the church in Kenya. In a vision, the lord showed me his altar that had been terribly broken and defiled. Among the things that defiled the house of the lord are sexual sins in the church including among the pastors and bishops, the gospel of prosperity and the love of money by the clergy at the pulpit and hence the congregation, God had built up a case against the clergy because many are false prophets, liars and corrupt individuals who have infiltrated the church.[19]

The Prophet further claims:

... all night prayer vigils (also known as keshas) have not been spared. Keshas have become dens of sexual parties. And many condoms litter the Church compounds in the morning. Because of all these sins, tragedy will befall Kenya. The Lord also showed me the horrific involvement of Bishops and pastors in witchcraft as a means of achieving some illusory powers to attract wealthy people into their congregations and delude them so as to release their wealth such as cars, log books, title deeds for property into the church.

In a sermon about the characteristics of an End time church, this is what Prophet Owour told the congregation:

The End time church is expected to uphold the culture of holy thoughts and communing as a lifestyle. Any nation in which the church followed this path would therefore seek the Lord Jesus, strengthen her mind, elevate her character, and be refined in holiness. This kind of end time church would be Holy Ghost filled, and maturing in stature that she may enter into the wedding of the Lamb of God. Without a doubt the sins of this land must have caught the attention of the Lord Almighty. Kenya needs restoration especially in these days in order to exude forth the mighty last revival.[20]

10.4.2 National Altars and the Construction of Sacred Space

A salient feature of the MRH that distinguishes it from other new religious movements is the construction and creation of spiritual spaces referred to as national altars. These are not churches but any space that is claimed,

---

19 The wedding of the lamb, *Repentance and Holiness Magazine*, 4: 1.
20 Ibid.

cleansed and used for worship, fasting, repentance and prayer meetings. As such the Ministry has created and spawned hundreds of "national altars" all over the country. Besides parks and gardens, large stadiums and show grounds are popular because they can hold thousands of people. Wherever Prophet Owour goes, many people follow and congregate for days, weeks or even months to pray, fast, repent and ask for forgiveness from god for the sins of the nation and the clergy. His followers actually pitch camp days prior to the Prophet's crusades to pray and fast. During the early days of the emergence of national altars, followers of the Prophet used to wear sackcloth and ride donkeys, with scores of wailing women in the group ostensibly repenting for the sins of the nation.

According to Prophet Owour, the wearing of sackcloth was necessitated by the need to repent for the sins of the nation in a bid to cleanse the church in readiness for the rapture and the second coming of Christ. Although the wearing of sackcloth has diminished, this has been replaced by a new and unique mode of dress (described below) that distinguishes the Prophet's female followers from members of other Christian denominations. His followers argue that because Christian churches had ostensibly been defiled by immoral clergy, God sent his "Mighty Prophet," as Owour is commonly referred to by them, to cleanse the church through his unique message of Repentance and Holiness.

Before Owour visits a designated altar many of his adoring followers, especially female members, camp there for many days, praying, fasting and cleansing the altar in preparation for the arrival of "the Mighty Prophet of God" or the "Servant of the Lord" as he is also fondly termed. These groups of women, whether married or single, shun sex before they come to the camp, because sex is considered to pollute the body and the altar of the Lord.

10.4.3 From Sackcloth to Long Dresses

Another important distinguishing feature of the MRH is the distinct way in which women followers dress to embody holiness. Women's bodies and dress not only take center stage in this Ministry but are also linked to the theme of repentance and holiness. Women followers of the MRH have embraced a unique dress code characterized by long flowing and loose dresses, ostensibly to embody holiness as taught by their Prophet. Besides, women are also urged to embrace certain manners and mores and practices that are deemed appropriate and of value to religious life.

The dress code forbids the wearing of sleeveless tops, hemlines at or above the knee, slit skirts that expose the knees and thighs, open shoes, bare legs and uncovered heads. Women are taught to conceal their bodies by dressing in this particularly conservative manner. They are required to cover up not just to embody holiness but also so as not to lead men into sexual temptation. Such control over dressing and sexual needs is in clear conflict with ideas of women's empowerment.

How the Prophet's women followers dress is dictated by his teachings. For example, when he speaks about women's bodies and dressing, he often quotes Hebrews: 12:14, "Make efforts to be holy, for without holiness, no one will see the Lord!" He teaches his female members that their bodies are "Temples of the Holy Spirit" and must therefore be kept clean and covered at all times. Women must cover their bodies also in order that the Holy Spirit may dwell in them. This is what the Prophet told women followers in one prayer rally attended by this writer: "When you cover your body, you are saying: I respect and honor my body which is the temple of the Lord. So make sure you do not defile the house of the Holy Spirit by dressing indecently."[21] In another sermon, Prophet Owour decried the manner in which "current fashions and fads" have rendered most of today's Christian women "virtually nude."[22]

In response to such teachings women in the MRH have evolved a unique dress style that is designed to cover their entire bodies. By covering their bodies, these women not only embody holiness but also protect themselves from men's roving eyes. They are told that in causing men to lust after them, they would sin against God, the Holy Spirit and their own bodies, which would then prevent them from entering the Kingdom of God. Thus women must dress holy before the lord and at all times guard their purity and morals. Portions of the scriptures are often quoted to drive the message home. For instance, Rom 12:1 states: "The Lord is beseeching you to present your bodies as a living sacrifice, holy and acceptable before the Lord."

To further legitimize his teachings on holiness and women's dress, the Prophet likes to portray himself as one who speaks and converses directly with God at all times. This is what he says:

> The Lord also spoke to me very clearly about the abhorrent state of immoral dressing in the church beginning with the pastors, pastors' wives, worship leaders, worship teams, and hence the congregation. The playing of ndombolo dance (a kind of dance from Central Africa) in the

---

21 Sermon preached by Owuor on August 6, 2013 at Afraha Stadium in Nakuru.
22 The man who baptized Raila Nairobi (see note 18): 12.

church as a form of occult worship in Kenyan churches and the dressing of worship dance troupes in T-shirts exposing their navels, playing of rap music, the perming and frying of male worship leaders' hair, including the punching and putting a shiny ring on the nose and at times earrings, these things could not go without catching the negative attention of the Lord. These things defile the altar of the Lord.

The Prophet continues:

Whoever looks at a woman and lusts at her has already fallen into adultery. Pastors have fathered children in church and there are many Sunday school kids fathered by their pastors. You just need to look at these kids' ears to see who they resemble! This is an abomination before the Lord![23]

It is such kinds of teachings that influence how women, and to some extent men, dress in the Ministry of Repentance and Holiness. Holiness is promoted as the only means through which people will enter the kingdom of God. From the foregoing discussion, it seems apparent to me that women's bodies and dress are being used as sites of protest against perceived moral and spiritual decay.

10.4.4 Holy Daughters at the Heart of Religious Life

Women in the MRH must conduct themselves like holy daughters. Holiness is understood in a twin sense: inward and outward. Moral or inward holiness consists of righteous living, thought and speech, guided and powered by the indwelling of the Holy Spirit, which includes abstaining from sex especially in the case of unmarried men and women. Practical or outward holiness, on the other hand, involves maintaining certain standards and dictates among other things modest apparel and maintenance of gender distinctions. Women believers are urged to dress modestly, with restraint and limitations; thus some forms of appearance are considered off limits.

Certain items of clothing are considered immoral, indecent and unacceptable, and by wearing them a woman is said to show dishonor and disrespect to God. Miniskirts, tight pants, trousers or jeans, short dresses, sleeveless tops and so on are strictly forbidden for female followers of the church. In addition, women generally are expected not to wear makeup or jewelry; they must cut their hair short or keep it covered.

---

23 Ibid.: 13.

Women are urged not to dress like men or wear men's clothing because it is clearly started in Gen 22:5 that women should not wear men's clothes. Further, tight pants or trousers are strictly discouraged because they outline the female anatomy which leads men to temptation and lust. In particular while attending church service as well as Bible studies meetings, women are urged to dress holy so as not to cause the terrible sin of sexual immorality. On the other hand, men must be cleanshaven at all times and must not wear tight pants, jeans or shorts. They must always dress officially in suits and always be neat and clean. They are also expected not to watch secular movies or television programs that are not spiritual as this is thought to corrupt their bodies, minds and morals. With the current social trends all over Africa due to globalization, there have been major shifts in how young women and men dress. Yet in this Ministry certain modes and styles of dress are considered immoral. By submitting to the authority of the Prophet and his teachings, women must therefore follow the stringent dress codes established by the MRH so that they may embody holiness.

Women are also taught that they are princesses, daughters of the king, and must carry themselves as such. Many of Prophet Owour's female followers prefer to wear purple because the color signifies royalty. The Prophet himself wears robes of fine white linen and dons a long flowing beard reminiscent of the Jewish patriarchs of the Old Testament. Jessica Meuni, a member of MHR, explains that the way the Prophet dresses is dictated to him by God, through dreams and visions. At times, it is suggested that God personally shows him a picture of the clothes he should wear to a crusade or rally. Even his long beard is a command from God and the reason for it remains a secret between him and God.

Holy Ghost anointing, prayer, testimony, song and all manner of worship and religious life all create definitive markers of what is deemed acceptable Christian holy life in this Ministry. Given that external signifiers of holiness have been codified most rigorously on women's bodies, religious practice provides significant sites for aesthetic analysis. By adopting stringent tenets of comportment and dress, this Ministry actually restricts women's sartorial choices. On the other hand, through empowerment and preaching, the Prophet advances a remarkable theology of inclusion that places women, including those who are single or widowed, at the heart of his Ministry.

The MRH is very popular with women folk who find its message of repentance, holiness and moral probity attractive. Also, the church is good to women, most of all single women: widows, divorcees, single unmarried mothers and others. In fact, women occupy a visible public role in this Ministry. Many are ordained pastors who lead and head a number of altars or churches. Women are also empowered to become spiritual leaders who adjudicate cases of conflict between members. They also sing in church, lead worship services and crusades, as well as provide usher services during large repentance and holiness crusades and rallies.

Church gatherings, crusades, meetings and fellowships become not just sites for the formation of a sort of shared sisterhood and identity making but also, and more importantly, sites of holiness and gendered geographies. Here women are bound together by a common faith and dress code but also by submission to church authority, teachings and rituals. By submitting to the protocols of gendered spaces, women in this church show their conviction and faith in church doctrine which strengthens both their individual religious grounding as well as the Ministry's corporate identity as a holy body. Women's adherence to tenets regarding dress and gendered space strengthens individual and community spiritual identity because the counter binary or agreeable contradiction of revelation is always in play. Their bodies actualize the merging of material, temporal and spatial realms.

This church ferments women with a feeling of belonging to a shared sisterhood of holy daughters. I witnessed ways in which clothing marks and connects these church women in public crusades, prayer groups and camps, in church premises and even in the workplace. These women so to speak *wear* holiness. Looking over the sea of attendees in a huge crusade, their distinctive style (although individualized according to taste and size) are striking and their majority status provides compelling and reinforced evidence of obedience to Owour's messages and teachings. It also speaks of his influence among his thousands of followers. Owour's female followers dress in white, signifying purity and embodying holiness. Their cohesive body of shared sisterhood is bound together by an almost uniform dress code.

In this church, as in many patriarchal Kenyan cultures, women's dress is an indicator of holiness and righteousness and female bodies are seen as locales of sex, sin, immorality and pollution. Holiness and righteousness are rubrics that are markers of self-identity, and a woman's appearance serves as a key indicator of these qualities within her. According to Jessica, women must be holy at all times: they must watch out how they dress and sit even at home, because the Lord can show up anytime. Being decently dressed and covered at all times and places shows respect, honor and the fear of God. This is what one lady said to me in an interview: "If I am a true daughter of God, then my dressing must reflect my holiness and righteousness. My clothes must be truly born again and the words that come out of my mouth must be measured."

Despite women's majority status in the MHR movement and demonstrative worship practices, beneath the veneer of their spiritual empowerment are complexities, tensions and constraints manifested in a subtle control of their bodies, sexuality and relationships, as I discuss next.

10.4.5 Sex, Bodies, Purity and Contested Territories

In the Ministry of Holiness and Repentance, extramarital sex is categorized as one of the worst sins anyone can ever engage in. In fact of all sins such as stealing, gossip, coveting, jealousy and many others, sins of sexual immorality (as it is normally referred to in this church) are considered the most grievous of all. This is the only sin that is committed against the body which is the Temple of the Lord, it is taught. According to Jessica sexual sin must be shunned at all costs because it pollutes the body of Christ.

Sex is only acceptable within the institution of marriage. Unmarried women are strongly discouraged from engaging in sexual activities. If they have decided to be single then they should abstain from men and sex. The Ministry has a welfare fund where vulnerable women (single mothers, widows, unemployed mothers) and orphaned children can find financial and material support. Economically deprived women are thus discouraged from engaging in transactional sex to put food on the table for their families. They are urged to remain single and holy but in the event that they are unable to abstain, they are encouraged to marry and formalize their union.

Married women, while not forbidden from sexual engagement, are often required and encouraged to partake of prolonged "fasting" particularly during repentance days. This fasting not only includes abstaining from food and drink but also shunning sex, especially if they are to approach the "altar of the Lord" the following day or week. It is for this reason that there have been some murmurs that the church is causing strains within the family unit as women traverse the country following the Prophet in his monthly prayer of repentance and holiness meetings, fasting and shunning sex because they have to be holy before the Lord. They are also required to cleanse their conscience before they appear before the altar or pulpit.

On the other hand, men are discouraged from lusting after women and when they are caught, they are expected to repent before the Prophet and their brethren, and seek holiness from God. In this church, the sin of sexual immorality is described as "a very bad sin," "an unforgivable sin" which God hates and which attracts His wrath, a dirty thing that pollutes the body and the Holy Spirit. Prophet Owuor has made this teaching his pet subject and he diagnoses all kinds of social and economic issues as having been caused by sexual sin. He preaches a lot on holiness, purity and the sin of sexual immorality, even offering prophesies about people he has seen in visions engaging in sexual sins and calling them to repentance.

Even thinking about sex, or looking at a man or woman suggestively, is considered capable of polluting the both the body and the mind, a sin against the Holy Spirit, and can result in the excommunication of the culprit. To be one with the spirit, a person must be holy at all times by avoiding sex.

10.5 Observations

In closing, I would like to make a number of observations in respect of gender, sex and bodies as manifested in the MRH. First, women's dress and bodies have become not just sites of contestation, debate and discourse about morality/immorality but also arenas of patriarchal surveillance, control and power, and signifiers of meaning and spirituality. Second, by controlling women's dressing and relating sexual relations to sin, God's wrath and punishment, this church does not portray women's bodies in a healthy way and this may in the long run have a negative impact on women's reproductive health, rights and choices (Mwaura & Parsitau 2012a and b).

Third, women are portrayed as temptresses and seductive witches who prevent men from entering the Kingdom of God. Spiritual moralists like Prophet Owour and patriarchal cultures collude to control women bodies, dress and sexuality. They assume that female sexuality cannot be conceptualized or lived outside its capacity to cause sexual arousal in men (Bakare-Yusuf 2011). Thus when women's sartorial choices have been inundated with sexual meaning in this way, the logical step appears to be regulation and control in order to protect women from inevitable masculine terror that is automatically provoked by the revelation of female flesh. In this simplistic argument that women's dress is directed at men and should therefore be regulated by men, the possibility of women dressing for themselves is totally lost.

This kind of logic places a heavy emotional and psychological burden on women who are made to feel responsible for men's sexual aggression. Following this logic, women who dress contrary to the church's code are considered immoral sinners who lack personal respect and integrity. In seeking to control women's bodies and discipline their sexuality the MHR has entered a contested terrain. However, it is argued by members of the church that the female followers of Prophet Owour embody holiness and choose to conform to societal and church requirements and regulations formulated by modest men.

Finally and importantly, moralizing about sex and portraying it as a dirty sin is highly detrimental to women's reproductive health. Submitting to cultural and religious orders where women and sex are considered polluting is in direct opposition to the building of a positive and strong image of the female body as beautiful and the promotion of women's self-esteem and confidence, all of which are necessary for women's wellbeing and health.

We may conclude from the foregoing discussion that female followers of the MRH embody certain tensions, contradictions and paradoxes. The complexities of women's material and spiritual church work and its articulation with both liberating and constraining doctrines is an interesting dimension of the Ministry of Repentance and Holiness.

References

Allman, J. (2004). "Let your fashion be in line with our Ghanaian costume": Nation, gender, and the politics of clothing in Nkrumah's Ghana. In: J. Allman (ed.), *Fashioning Africa: Power and the Politics of Dress*. Bloomington and Indianapolis: Indiana University Press.

Bakare-Yusuf, Bibi. (2011). Nudity and morality: Legislating women's bodies and dressing in Nigeria. In: S. Tamale (ed.), *African Sexualities: A Reader*. Cape Town, Dakar and Oxford: Pambazuka Press, an imprint of Fahamu.

Bennet, J. (2002). Exploration of a gap: strategizing gender equity in African universities. *Feminist Africa*, 1, African Gender Institute e-journal, http://www.feministafrica.org, accessed January 7, 2009.

De Nobrega, C. (2014). South Africa: Gender equality and morality as citizenship. Accessed at www.opendemocracy.net.

Mwaura, P.N., & Damaris S. Parsitau. (2012a). Perceptions of women's health and rights in Christian new religious movements in Kenya. In: Afe Adogame, Ezra Chitando & Bolaji Bateye (eds.), *African Traditions in the Study of Religion in Africa: Emerging Trends, Indigenous Spirituality and the Interface with Other World Religions*. Farnham, UK: Ashgate Publishing.

Mwaura, P.N., & Damaris S. Parsitau. (2012b). Gendered charisma: Women in mission in Neo-Pentecostal and Charismatic movements in Kenya. In: Christine Lienemann-Perrin, Atola Longkumer & Afrie Songco Joye (eds.), *Putting Names with Faces: Women's Impact in Mission History*. Nashville, TN: Abingdon Press

Tamale, S. (ed.). (2011). *African Sexualities: A Reader*. Cape Town, Dakar and Oxford: Pambazuka Press, an imprint of Fahamu.

Index

access rituals, 115–22
adulthood, 114, 140, 145
aesthetic choice, 26, 51, 90, 153–5, 157, 159, 165, 167
Afrika Shrine, 50, 51, 56
Afrobeat, 7, 37–57
   history, 43
   music, 37–8
   and the Occupy Nigeria Movement, 53–5
   salute, 7, 39, 42, 43, 50–2, 54–6
Afro-Caribbean dance, 17–33
Afro-pop, 98, 101
aiye, 172–5
American gangster clothing, 60, 65
apartheid, 45, 59, 61, 62, 65, 68–70, 72
   ideology, 68
   politics, 45
araferaku, 149
Arie, India, 99
Aso-Ebi, 9, 148, 152, 155–9
   anti-collectivity of, 148
   and collective identity, 158–9
   semiotics of, 155–8
aTonga of Malawi, 6, 8, 111–31

beads 75, 136, 179
binyere, 139–40
Black Power, 43–50, 55, 176
   and Afrobeat, 47–51
   Movement, 43–5, 47, 55, 176
   salute, 39, 44–46, 48, 50, 52, 54, 55
bodaboda, 183
body
   art/decoration and markings, 74–92, 134, 148–55, 158, *see also* facial marking
   language, 7, 41, 42, 67, 71, 94
   posture and gestures, 5, 94–108, 111–31

Brutus, Dennis, 71
Butler, Judith, 96, 97, 106

Carlson, Marvin, 95
ciTonga, 111, 112, 114
Clive Glaser, 61, 64–7
clothing/dress, 7, 9, 28, 58–72, 74–9, 88, 90–2, 94, 104, 105, 114, 134, 136, 138, 140, 148, 155–9, 162, 163, 165, 181–90, 192–8, 200
   codes/restrictions, 8, 181–90, 192–8, 200
   fashion and, 58–60, 62, 64, 66, 69, 159, 181, 182, 187, 189, 190, 195
   and visual language, 59–61
collective identity, 147, 148, 150, 152
communicative *praxis*, 7, 41, 42
cornrow, *see* hairstyles
creoles 19, 25, 30
cultural colonization, 98, 100
cultural/dance continuum, 18, 25–33
culture and perception, 174–6

dada, 167, 173
dance, 2, 9, 10, 17–33
Daniel, Ivonne, 25, 27–29, 33
Davies, Carole Boyce, 97
donza, 134–6
dreadlocks, *see* hairstyles
dress, *see* clothing

eating/dining rituals, 126–30
ecology of language evolution, 9, 18, 30
embodied enactment of memory, 7, 39, 41
ethnic signifier, 163
everyday rituals, 111–30
exchange rituals, 123–6

facial marking, 9, 54, 76, 77, 79–92, 148–55, 157, 158, *see also* body art

family, 86, 88, 91, 102–4, 107, 141, 150–9, 190, 199
  oriki, 75, 80, 167
  royal/ruling, 82, 83, 86, 89
  trees, 30, 31
fashion, 58–60, 62, 64, 66, 69, 82, 86, 90, 114, 159, 181, 182, 187, 189, 190, 195
Fela Anikulapo Kuti, 7, 8, 37–56, 98, 101
Fanon, Frantz, 68, 69, 71
Freeman, Morgan, 162

gender-based violence, 184–9
gender identity, 95–8
gender and power, 104–7
Genet, Jean, 61, 70, 72
George, Olabode, 158–9
gesture, 111, 113, 117, 118, 124, 125, 126
  as craft, 41–42
  and political autonomy, 45
  and transgression, 46, 50
Gesturecraft, 7, 41

hairstyles, 8, 76, 99, 100, 136, 140, 162–78, 182, 196
Hamar of Ethiopia, 7, 133–45
hand slap, 121
handclasp, 119, 120, 121
handedness, 111–31
handholding, 118
handshake, 116, 117, 118
Hebdige, Dick, 58, 64, 72
henna, 81, 82, 91
Hollywood style, 66, 67
hooks, bell, 99, 100
hugging, 120

Ibadan, 87–9, 148, 149, 153, 158, 168–70
Icarus, 102, 108
identity
  group/family/collective markers, 9, 10, 17, 33, 71, 74–7, 81, 82, 86–92, 147–59, 165
  performance of, 94–108
incision, 81, 82, 89, 90
Indecent Dressing Bill, 185

initiation, 134, 135, 136, 143, 145
  ceremonies, 142
  young man's 140
Institute of Women, Gender and Development Studies, 181, 187

Kenya, 8, 181–201
Kenyatta, Jomo, 183, 185
Kerouac, Jack, 63
Kisumu County, Kenya, 183

Law Society of Kenya, 182, 183
lifestyle, 8, 144, 172,193
lip pointing, 3

Magubane, Bernard, 68
Malawi, 8, 111–31, 185, 188
Marley, Bob, 103, 176
Mattera, Don, 58–72
miniskirts, 183–7, 189, 196
Ministry of Repentance and Holiness (MRH), 190–201
  Repentance and Holiness Magazine, 192, 193
modernity, 90, 100, 134, 143, 152, 190
moral values/morality, 10, 102, 107, 148, 157–9, 165, 181, 184–201
Morrison, Toni, 99
motor ability, 142
music, 9, 26, 27, 33, 37–56, 96, 100

national altars, 193–4
Ng'ang'a, Apostle, 189
Nigeria, Southwestern, 73, 77, 148, 151, *see also* Yoruba
nonverbal communication, 1–11, 48, 59, 60, 77, 133, 134, 139, 142, 145, 162, 163, 175

object language, 7, 134
Occupy Nigeria Movement, 7, 39, 53–5
Onwueme, Tess, 94–108
Ori/*ori*, 171–3, 175
oriki, 75, 80, 167
Owour, Prophet David Edward, 191–200

paralinguistic devices, 2
politeness, social, 2, 111, 123–6, 130
Puerto Rico, 9, 10, 17–33

racism, 98
Raitt, Bonnie, 1
Rastafarianism, 176
Rath, Richard Cullen, 30, 33
religion/religious belief, 8, 107, 164–7, 169–71, 181–200
    revivalism, 95

Sampson, Anthony (*Drum* Magazine), 61–5, 67
scarification, 79, 81, 87, *see also* body art
scratching/tickling the palm, 8, 118
sexual harassment in universities, 186–90
Shakara: Dance-hall Queen, 94–108
slavery/slave trade, 18–24, 31–3, 78, 80, 83, 86–9, 149, 153, 154
society, culture and behavior, 1, 2, 5–7, 10, 31, 59, 60, 89, 106, 107, 134–45, 165, 166, 171, 174, 176, 177
    social hegemony, 163, 165
    social/public imagination/imaginaries, 51, 53, 55, 100, 175–7, 181–201

socialization, 113, 143, 174,
    sociocultural paradigm, 142, 143
Sophiatown, 58–72
symbolic interaction, 74, 76, 77, 92

tattooing, 76, 81, 82, 89, 90, 91, 150, 156
Temba, Can, 61
Thompson, E.P., 61
Thompson, Robert Farris, 33
Tosh, Peter, 176
Trinidad, 9, 10, 17–33
Tsotsi, 7, 59–71

uta, 136–9

visual language and perception, 9, 10, 59–61

Wailers, Bunny 176
Widmark, Richard, 66

Yoruba, 8, 9, 20, 26, 31, 32, 74–92, 113, 117
    body art and decoration, 74–92
    collective identity, 147–59
    cosmology, 171–4
    dance, 26, 31
    hairstyles, attitudes to, 162–78

www.ingramcontent.com/pod-product-compliance
Lightning Source LLC
Chambersburg PA
CBHW071843230426
43671CB00012B/2051